Praise for

The Complete Guide to Book Publicity

"Publicity is to books what oxygen is to lungs. Without it, sales suffocate and die. This book is a lifeline for publishing professionals and writers alike."

—Kent Carroll, publisher, Carroll & Graf

"This is not a general publicity book; it is for authors and book publishers. Anyone with a book to promote will be more successful with the detailed advice given here."

—Dan Poynter, author, speaker, and publisher, Para Publishing

"Everyone who is thinking of doing publicity themselves should get this book. Straightforward, easy-to-read with great tips. I've been doing publicity for twenty-five years—I wish my clients read this book before they came to me . . . I recommend this book highly!"

—Rick Frishman, president, Planned TV Arts,
coauthor of *Guerilla Publicity: Hundreds of Sure-Fire Tactics to Get Maximum Sales for Minimum Dollars* and *Guerilla Marketing for Writers: 100 Weapons to Help You Sell Your Work*

"This is a must-have for any serious novelist in today's market, where marketing opportunities must be carefully planned and seized."

—*Writers Write*

"Equally important for eBooks, epublishing, and even online content!"

—Fred Showker, editor, *Designer's Bookshelf*

The
Complete Guide
to
Book Publicity

SECOND EDITION

JODEE BLANCO

ALLWORTH PRESS
NEW YORK

09   08   07   06   05   04   5   4   3   2   1

Published by Allworth Press
An imprint of Allworth Communications
10 East 23rd Street, New York, NY 10010

Cover design by Derek Bacchus, New York, NY
Page composition/typography by SR Desktop Services, Ridge, NY

Library of Congress Cataloging-in-Publication Data
    Blanco, Jodee, 1964–
    The complete guide to book publicity / by Jodee Blanco.—
2nd ed.
          p.   cm.
    Includes bibliographical references and index.
    1. Books—Marketing.   2. Authors and publishers.   3. Publishers
and publishing.   I. Title.

Z283.B48   2004
002'.068'8—dc22   2004005424

Dedication

This book is lovingly dedicated to my parents, Tony and Joy Blanco, who gave me courage, taught me integrity, and empowered my spirit to soar beyond limits imposed by others.

This book is also dedicated to my business partner and soul sister, Lissy Peace. She is my wisdom and my anchor.

And to "Joe" from Cody Jarret . . . Thank you for all the love and homemade pasta. I wouldn't have been able to finish this book without both.

Contents

Preface to the Second Edition

*T*HANK YOU FOR PICKING UP THIS BOOK. IT'S MORE THAN JUST A TOOL to help you learn the ins and outs of book publicity. In these pages are deeply personal stories from the trenches, where I spent twenty years of my life focused on turning books into blockbusters. I was successful, but not without my share of disappointment and frustration. It's the combination of those experiences that I hope you will find make this book even more valuable than the sum of its parts.

There were so many times during the course of my career as a literary publicist that I didn't understand why I had to endure certain challenges along the way. Why was a specific author difficult? Why did some campaigns that even I thought were long shots end up generating enormous results, while others, that I expected to work, threw me a curve in the end? Has the media shifted its priorities or does it just seem like it's so much harder now to obtain media placements for books than it was ten years ago? Why is it that author tours are being done less and less? Does an author appearance on Oprah have the same punch it did in the past? Is self-publishing gaining momentum in the media marketplace? ALL these questions and others are addressed in this new revised edition of *The Complete Guide to Book Publicity*.

I also delve into the evolving landscape of print and broadcast. There's no question that the media is changing its tune when it comes to covering books and authors. That doesn't mean it's impossible to create a successful campaign. It just means more work is required to generate the desired results. That's the bad news. The good news is that there are more *niche* media opportunities for books than ever before. With the growing popularity of digital cable and the Internet, special interest audiences are easier to find and target via these swiftly emerging outlets. You'll also find in this revised edition, updated information about specific television and radio shows, as well as a new chapter on book publicity and the Internet.

On more thing . . . recently, I wrote my memoir entitled *Please Stop Laughing at Me. . . . One Woman's Inspirational Story.* It chronicles my adolescent years, during which I was a victim of severe school bullying, and how I survived. The book, published by Adams Media, an independent press out of Boston, was released the day the United States went to war with Iraq in 2003. Within forty-eight hours of the book's release, with no major media, on word of mouth alone, it shot straight to the *New York Times* extended bestseller list, climbing steadily for six weeks, peaking at number sixteen. The journey of going from publicist to bestselling author was one that gave me exciting new insights into book publicity, which I've shared in this new edition of *The Complete Guide to Book Publicity.*

I wish you, dear reader, a wonderful and rewarding adventure as you set out to master the craft of making books bestsellers. I know you have it in you. My objective is that this guidebook helps to bring those natural talents to the surface and into the marketplace.

Good luck!

Acknowledgments

T HIS BOOK WOULD NOT HAVE BEEN POSSIBLE WITHOUT THE FOLLOW-
ing people, all of whom mean so much to me:

Mary Marino, who brought me to my publisher's doorstep and lovingly let me in.

Diane Glynn, my mentor and big sister, without whom I wouldn't have had a career.

Nicole Potter, my editor, who gives new depth and meaning to the word "patience."

Kent Carroll, my friend, literary hero, and security blanket when the winds of publicity chaos whip mercilessly against my window.

Walter Zacharius and Roberta Grossman, who entrusted me with projects near and dear to their hearts even though I was still wet behind the ears . . . I will be eternally grateful.

Robert Baensch, my dear friend and ally at New York University, whose faith in me was the catalyst for this book.

Peter Mayer, someone I will always look up to, whose respect for me is pure adrenaline to my spirit.

Tod Dell'arringa and Jennifer Crawford at Blanco & Peace, the most loyal soldiers this PR firm has ever known.

Les Garland, the most dynamic and inspiring mentor I've ever known.

My cousin Jeanine, whose support and love keep me sane.

And a profound thanks to all of the producers, editors, and reporters I've worked with throughout the years, and especially Marty Berman, who taught me how to fight with integrity.

Last, and most important, the valued authors I've represented over the years who taught me so much about life. You're the heart of this book, each and every one of you. Thank you.

What Are Publicity, Promotions, and Public Relations, and Why Are They So Important?

*Y*OU'RE HOLDING A MANUSCRIPT IN YOUR HANDS THAT'S ABOUT TO BE published. You're filled with excitement, anticipation, and yes, perhaps a case of the jitters because you're the one responsible for the book's publicity, promotions, and public relations. If you're feeling overwhelmed, take a deep breath and relax. I'm going to hold your hand, and together, we're going to walk through the process, step by step. Let's start with the basics and talk about the differences between publicity, advertising, public relations, and promotions and how each impacts a book's success.

Publicity Defined

Publicity is free, perceived as objective, and defined as any kind of media or news coverage. Every time you see someone interviewed on a television or radio show, in a newspaper or magazine, that's publicity. No one paid the media outlet to do the interview. A persistent and assertive publicist convinced a producer or editor that this particular guest would provide information that would impact lives.

Whether it's an author being interviewed on a talk show or network newscast about her new self-help book; a rock star talking live on the radio with the morning DJ about his newest CD; a plastic surgeon featured in a magazine article about cutting-edge laser procedures he's perfected; a poet included in a large magazine spread on exciting new literary voices; or a mystery writer quoted as an expert source in a newspaper article about unsolved murders; if you see it on television, radio, or in print and it's not a paid commercial or advertisement—it's publicity.

Advertising or Publicity?

Speaking of advertising, many people confuse publicity with advertising and lump the two together, often substituting one term for the other. It's a common mistake, and if you're a publicist like me, it can drive you crazy. So let's nip this in the bud right now.

We'll use bestselling writer Dr. Phil as an example. You're watching *The Today Show* and you see Katie Couric interviewing the author about his book, *Self Matters*. That interview is *publicity*, not advertising. The publisher didn't pay NBC to put Dr. Phil on *The Today Show*. The author's publicist facilitated that opportunity through a lot of hard work, consistent follow-up, aggressive creative thinking, and relentless optimism. She spent time watching *The Today Show*, learning its format and focus, and shrewdly observing topic preferences and patterns. If she didn't have a contact at the show with whom she'd worked in the past, she took the initiative to call the production department and research which producer booked literary guests. She communicated with the appropriate producer through carefully thought-out telephone conversations, e-mails, faxes, and personalized mailings, presenting her client, Dr. Phil, as a *newsmaker* and his book as *newsworthy*.

A publicity placement such as a segment on a major network morning show requires a tremendous amount of effort. When push comes to shove, success (from the media's perspective) is based on ratings and newsstand sales because those are the criteria that define the ad rates they can charge, which, unless it's public television, are their bread and butter. A savvy book publicist understands this reality and knows that the most vital selling point when pitching a media contact is how much the author will affect and engage the audience, because that's the producers' and editors' first priority. If you're publicizing a book and you concentrate your energy on helping your media contacts to do their jobs better by providing topic ideas and authors who are relevant and exciting to their audience, your chances of securing coverage are infinitely increased. Not to mention you create meaningful relationships with members of the media, who come to appreciate your knowledge of their responsibilities as journalists. Later, we'll talk more about the media and how to forge mutually fruitful, lifelong alliances with key editors, producers, and reporters.

Waxing philosophical for a brief moment, think of a publicist as a "salesperson of the intangible," who deftly packages and sells concepts and ideas as *news*. And what I've shared with you above is just the tip of the iceberg. Wait until we dig deep into the trenches of your learning process, immersing you in the minute details of strategy and implementation!

Getting back to our clarification of publicity versus advertising, later that same day, after you've seen Dr. Phil interviewed on *The Today Show,* you're watching CNN, and you see a sixty-second commercial for *Self Matters.* That commercial is *advertising*. The publisher, or perhaps a bookstore chain, created and produced it and *paid* CNN for the airtime. The same applies with newspapers, magazines, and radio. Advertising is paid for. Publicity is free. There are still expenses associated with publicity, but we'll discuss budgetary issues further along in the book.

The Credibility Issue

That's the basic distinction between publicity and advertising. However, there's more to the differences between these two venues than meets the eye. Today's average consumers are sophisticated about the modern marketplace. Though they may not grasp all the subtle nuances, they know on some level that advertising is subjective because whoever places the ad completely controls the content and pays for it to run. Publicity is perceived as objective because it's presented in the form of *news coverage.*

To illustrate the point, let's use you as the example. You want to buy a new car and are torn between purchasing a Toyota Camry or a Ford Taurus, so you start thumbing through the Auto section of your local paper to compare prices. You stumble upon a full-page ad with photo touting the pleasures of owning a Camry. The ad catches your attention, and you take a quick moment to read it. On the next page, you come across a feature interview with the CEO of Ford, who's talking about exciting new features on the Taurus. Curious, you take fifteen minutes to read the article.

Chances are, the interview may have a stronger impact than the advertisement on which car you pick. Why? When information is presented in the form of news, it underscores the credibility of the product or person featured. Please don't misunderstand me. I'm not saying that advertising isn't important or effective. Advertising is a powerful and profound selling tool that ignites both conscious and subliminal awareness and establishes product identity. When publicity and advertising are utilized in tandem, each venue reinforces the other. In some cases, one medium may be more appropriate for a particular campaign than the other. In chapter 6, I'll review with you techniques to help you decide which approach to use for your specific needs.

Public Relations

Now that we've touched upon the differences between publicity and advertising, we need to look at public relations and promotions. Public relations is probably the most difficult to define in concrete terms because it has such an expansive purpose and diverse format. Simply put, public relations is the function of perpetuating an image through a variety of means that connect specific sectors of the public with the product or person that image is attached to.

For example, you've written a book on parenting that is being published in the spring. In May, there's a major parenting convention, during which you participate as a keynote speaker at a luncheon for couples expecting their first child. That's public relations. It's not a media interview or news coverage, which would be publicity, nor a commercial for your book, which would be advertising. You're making a personal appearance, relating to a specific part of the public, hence *public relations:* presenting your image as an author and expert on parenting.

Let's consider another example of public relations. You've written a children's book that's being published at Christmastime. Your publicist arranges for you to visit ten children's hospitals, where you give readings to sick children. Once again, this activity wouldn't be defined as publicity or advertising because you're not being covered by television, newspaper, or radio, or shooting a commercial. However, this public relations gesture could be a *catalyst* for publicity. The publicist could invite local television crews and newspaper photographers and reporters to attend and cover the readings.

In fact, a public relations activity should almost always be strategized with the publicity component in mind. When planning a public relations event, you should ask yourself questions like:

- Who's the target audience?
- What's the message and purpose of the event?
- Can I generate media coverage from this event?

The answers to those key questions will help you to sculpt and refine your idea.

Two Campaigns

One of the greatest examples of public relations in the book business was conceived by *Chicken Soup for the Soul* publisher Health

Communications, Inc. Back in the mid-eighties when the personal growth movement was just beginning to take root in the American consciousness, Health Communications was publishing addiction/recovery books targeting the general consumer who was struggling to get his life back on track. Realizing that getting authors on an occasional television show wasn't enough to propel sales, the publisher held a series of conventions and seminars all across the country, featuring its authors as speakers. It was a brilliant campaign. Not only did it give the authors an opportunity to connect with their core audience in a very real way throughout the country, but it also provided on-site opportunities for book sales and a publicity hook for media.

Public relations can often be utilized as an opportunity to create publicity, as you can see in both examples described above. But we'll get into the interplay between publicity, advertising, public relations, and promotions further along in this chapter.

Sometimes public relations isn't an event or personal appearance, but an outreach effort that casts a positive spotlight on a book or author who could be perceived from a negative perspective. Here's one of my favorite examples.

When I first started out my career, I was working for a terrific woman named Diane Glynn, one of the top PR people in the literary field. She came into my office one day and explained that a publisher had approached her with an "unusual" book that required publicity and asked if we would be interested in handling the campaign. She didn't tell me anything else, except that we had a meeting with the publisher scheduled for that afternoon. I couldn't wait!

The publisher was a sophisticated older woman based in Arizona who had started a small press that did female-driven regional titles—with one stunning exception. One of her dearest friends was a sheriff who built his career chasing drug traffickers working the Arizona/Mexican border. His most challenging case involved the successful pursuit and twenty-year imprisonment of two notorious drug lords and an arms dealer, whom he had hunted for over two decades. While in jail, the three prisoners rehabilitated themselves, with the sheriff's support and guidance. When the sheriff asked to interview them for a book he was writing about their legendary case, they agreed. *Corrido De Cocaine* hit bookstores the day of the author's official retirement from the police force and his prisoners' release from jail. When the publisher came to us to publicize the book, she explained that the sheriff and the two former drug lords and *pistellero* were available for interviews to promote the book.

The correct public relations strategy was key to a successful campaign. I knew that an opportunity to interview rehabilitated ex–drug dealers would be of great interest to the media, but I also realized that we had to create an antidrug outreach effort in conjunction with this title, or we risked the public and media putting a negative, exploitative spin on the book.

Diane and I launched a drug awareness campaign, in which we utilized the author and the ex–drug traffickers as spokespeople against drug abuse. We positioned them as real people who understood the issue from both sides of the law and deep personal experience. From a public relations perspective, it was critical that the public *related* to this book as a vehicle for motivating positive change. Implementing a consumer awareness effort achieved that goal. The author and his cospokespeople were interviewed on dozens of major television shows, featured on drug abuse awareness panels, and described by countless reporters as rehabilitation's most convincing voices. As you can see, on this project, it was the public relations that drove the publicity.

Promotions

Next on the agenda—understanding promotions. Promotions are events or opportunities that target direct and proactive audience response. There are countless categories of promotions, from in-store displays and premium giveaways to contests and call-ins, but for our purposes, we're going to concentrate on promotions developed specifically with publicity in mind. Often, a book publicist will be faced with the challenge of publicizing a book that the media just doesn't consider newsworthy. A good promotion is a cost-effective way to provide the media with the hook they're looking for.

The Evolving Woman

Let's explore some in-depth examples to illustrate what I'm describing. Here's one from my own personal archives. Several years ago, a publisher asked me to publicize a best-selling romance novelist with whom it had just signed a three-book contract. The problem was that this author had been out of the limelight for a few years and needed a media blitz to reignite her popularity. A little insider information about publishing: Romance novels are notoriously difficult to publicize because the media doesn't perceive these books as news. I knew that a promotion was the only way we were going to galvanize print and broadcast excitement. I read all of the author's books, and it dawned on me that her heroines shared a profound characteristic: Each of them starts out at the beginning of the book as self-sacrificing and, by the end of the story, evolves to self-empowering. That was the key—evolve. I created the Evolving Woman contest, which the author and I did city by city over a three-year period.

Here's how the promotion worked: We asked women who had "shaken off the shackles of loving Mr. Wrong" to write the author a letter and, in 500 words or less, share their stories of tragedy, triumph, and renewal. The most inspiring letter in each market would win the internal and external makeover of a lifetime—a free, daylong session with a personal transformation specialist (a psychologist who had written a book I was also publicizing) and a weekend at a famous spa (the spa normally comped the weekend in exchange for the visibility). The promotion was the hook that motivated media to interview the author. When the author came into a town, it wasn't just to talk about her book, but to spread the word about an incredible opportunity for a local woman to be celebrated for her courage.

One of the primary complaints of most book publicists is that securing author interviews in smaller cities is next to impossible these days unless there's a local connection. The contest, which targeted local residents, eliminated that obstacle, as well as provided a compelling human-interest angle. In each city we did the contest, the author was interviewed by dozens of television, radio, newspaper, and magazine outlets, which probably would not have covered her if she was only there to tout her book.

The author who embarked on that adventurous campaign with me was Catherine Lanigan, probably best known for her novels *Romancing the Stone* and *Jewel of the Nile*. Entries poured in from women all across America who bared their souls on paper. In fact, the contest was so successful that, in March 2000, Health Communications, Inc. published a compilation of the letters in a book, coauthored by Catherine and myself, entitled *The Evolving Woman: Intimate Confessions of Surviving Mr. Wrong*. We toured women's shelters across America. The book even received the Celebration of Hope Literary Award!

Putting It All Together

Now that we've explored publicity, advertising, public relations, and promotions, I'd like to walk you through an example that illustrates how all four venues can work together, much like individual parts of one machine.

You're handling the campaign for a book on exciting new party ideas. You decide that you'd like to implement a promotion that would make the book as newsworthy as possible to the media. You choose to launch a contest in five cities. Here's how the contest works: You ask people to try one of the party ideas featured in the book and then write a letter to the author in 500 words or less describing the most unforgettable moment of the party. The most unusual letter wins a free weekend seminar with the author. The contest is the *promotion*.

You pitch newspaper, television, and radio stations to interview the author about the contest and her book. The interviews you arrange are *publicity*. Note how the promotion is contributing to the publicity. You also advertise the contest in the local paper. In fact, the advertisement is so original and innovative that you're able to persuade the business writer at the local paper to interview the graphic artist who designed the ad. That's publicity ingeniously generated through *advertising!* You've been so effective at getting the word out that entries for the contest begin pouring into your office. You pick a winner and hold a luncheon in his/her honor, with the author, the publisher, and individuals in the party-planning industry in attendance. That luncheon is *public relations*. You invite newspaper and television reporters to cover the luncheon and interview the winner. That's *publicity*.

Now you're getting a clearer picture of how it all works. The *promotion* is the contest. The author's interviews with the media about the contest and the business articles about the unique *advertising* campaign are *publicity*, i.e., news coverage. The luncheon to celebrate the winner is *public relations*. The media coverage of the luncheon is *publicity* again.

You should be feeling more confident about your grasp on publicity, advertising, public relations, and promotions and how they impact one another with relation to books. The next area I'd like to review with you is sell-in and sell-through and how those elements fit into the picture.

Sell-In/Sell-Through

Sell-in and sell-through are simple, logical concepts. In order for a person to go to a bookstore and buy a book, the book has to be in the store in the first place. That's *sell-in*—the process of getting the books onto the bookstore shelves. When a publisher talks about its sell-in on a particular title, it means how many books it has *sold in* to the stores. Sell-in is achieved through selling directly to the bookstore buyers, as well as through distributors and wholesalers, which are companies that buy books from the publisher and supply them to the stores. Distributors and wholesalers play an important role in the book business because they help publishers extend and maximize their market reach.

Sell-through is selling books through to the end user, who in publishing is the book reader. Sell-through is when the general consumer purchases the book off the shelf. When you go to the bookstore and buy a book, you participate in the sell-through phase.

Publishers face a daunting challenge with respect to sell-in and sell-through. For one thing, sell-in has become increasingly difficult with the proliferation of the superstores. More and more of the smaller independent stores are closing their doors because they can't keep up with the big chains. Shelf space is being consolidated like never before, and as a result, getting books into the stores is more competitive than ever. Add to that the fact that bookstores buy books on consignment, which means that if a book doesn't sell through within a specifically allotted time frame, the store can return the book to the publisher for refund.

Publicity, public relations, and promotions are the best and most cost-effective weapons for attacking these hurdles head-on. One of the frustrating oversights too many publishers are guilty of is focusing the bulk of their publicity, public relations, and promotions efforts on sell-through and not factoring these elements into sell-in. What they don't realize is that publicity, public relations, and promotions, if timed and executed correctly, can have an unfathomable impact on the number of books the stores commit to buying. For small presses and self-publishers who don't have a lot of leverage with the bookstores, this rings even truer.

Using the Tools to Increase Sell-In

How do you utilize publicity, public relations, and promotions to increase sell-in? The principle is the same as for sell-through. Here's an example: You've written a biography of Russell Crowe scheduled for publication in eight months. Typically, your sell-in would begin about six to seven months prior to pub date, during which time the sales force starts presenting your book at sales conferences. Usually, the sales force's primary sell-in tool is the publisher's catalogue, which features all the books they're scheduled to publish the following season. Most publishers divide their publishing seasons into two calendar periods: Fall/Winter, their biggest season, during which they release the bulk of their A-list titles; and Spring/Summer, the less competitive season, when they release their "make books," lesser-known authors and titles, for which visibility needs to be more aggressively cultivated.

Remember our definition of publicity—*news coverage.* We wouldn't want to get an article in a general consumer publication like *USA Today* six months in advance of the release of Russell Crowe's bio, because readers would flock to the stores, only to discover that they couldn't buy it yet. That certainly wouldn't be good. Where *would* we like to see an article six months prior to pub date? Think about who the most important audience is during this time period and what the sales force is trying to accomplish with them. That's right: bookstore buyers, distributors, and wholesalers—the people who will order the book from the publisher and get it on the shelves. What media outlet specifically addresses the concerns of these three groups?

Publications targeting specific industries are called "industry trades." The biggest publishing trade is *Publisher's Weekly.* An example of an impactful sell-in *publicity* placement for the Russell Crowe bio would be an article in *Publisher's Weekly* that would run approximately five to six months before pub date. Perhaps it would be a quick announcement about the signing of the contract; a short anecdotal piece about the preparation of the manuscript; or any other interesting angle that would ignite retail interest.

Though we'll talk more about ancillary rights later in the book, it would be infinitely beneficial for magazine and newspaper editors, and film and television producers, to be given a heads-up as early as possible on the publication of Russell's bio, too. Magazine and newspaper editors purchase serial or reprint rights; film and television producers purchase dramatic rights. If any of these rights are sold early on, it gives the sales force a mighty edge during sell-in, because it's tangible evidence of the book's imminent popularity.

Once again, it's a matter of logic. If bookstore buyers are thinking of stocking only a few copies of a particular title and they find out that an excerpt of the book will be published in *People* magazine the week the book is released, they'll up their order. They'll know that the excerpt will greatly heighten the demand for the book, and they'll want to ensure an ample supply for their customer base. Imagine if on top of that incredible information, the bookstore buyer also just read an article about the Crowe bio in *Publisher's Weekly!*

A sell-in publicity placement that would reach potential producers who might consider purchasing the film rights to the bio or an editor who may want to excerpt a chapter from the book would be an article in *Variety* and/or *Hollywood Reporter.* These are the two primary trades for the entertainment arena and are also widely read by newspaper and magazine editors. Such a placement would communicate to key players that this bio was going to be the hot literary ticket the following season.

I want to reiterate something important. Sell-in publicity should run four to six months before pub date and primarily include print coverage in trade publications that target industries relevant to the successful marketing of the book. Sometimes, sell-in publicity can also be an article in a general consumer newspaper like *USA Today* or an item on a news broadcast, but you have to exercise *extreme* caution and prudence if you choose to utilize general consumer media for sell-in publicity purposes. If you encourage media, other than industry trades who don't reach the general public, to cover a book before it's on sale, you risk not getting the media you need when the book *is* released.

When we discuss the details and nuances of how the media works, I'll teach you the secret of how to construct powerful sell-in publicity opportunities through selective coverage in big, general consumer media. The operative word is "selective." More on this in chapter 3.

Trends in Author Tours

Earlier in this chapter, we talked about how public relations and promotions impact sell-through. The examples I shared all illustrated successful events that motivated retail sales. Now we're going to look at examples of how public relations and promotions can help *sell-in*. This is an intriguing area because a movement is afoot in publishing that places a whole new creative emphasis on what authors and publishers can do to inspire stores to order their books.

Bold and innovative new strategies are gradually replacing the old formulas. One of the hottest growing trends is the use of author tours tailor-designed for sell-in purposes. For years, publishers utilized the author tour exclusively to generate sell-through. A traditional author tour consists of the author travelling to ten to twenty cities, during which he or she does autographings and as many television, radio, and newspaper interviews in each market as humanly possible. The focus of the author tour is publicity driven.

Sell-in tours are swiftly gaining favor with many publishing houses and authors, because they have finally begun asking themselves, Why not apply some of the principles of the author tour to sell-in, but have the priority be public relations as opposed to publicity? Instead of doing media interviews and book signings, the author would meet with book buyers, distributors, and wholesalers and talk about his or her book and the exciting marketing campaign planned for the book's release.

As mentioned above, the focus of a sell-through tour is book signings and, most important, media interviews (i.e., publicity). The primary purpose of the sell-in tour is public relations, during which an author visits anywhere from five to twenty cities, visiting bookstores, distributors, and wholesalers.

Deciding which type of tour, sell-in or sell-through, is best for your book depends upon several key factors. If you've been published relatively recently and had a strong sell-through on your last title, chances are your sell-in should be healthy this time around, and you'd probably be best served by doing a publicity tour when the book is released.

If you've never been published before, or were published and your last book had a weaker sell-through, you may want to consider a sell-in tour to jump-start bookseller confidence for the release of your new title. Often, the best-case scenario is a shrewd combination of both types of tours. For example, you visit five major markets for sell-in, then revisit those same five markets again for sell-through, during which you do extensive media.

Lots of Imagination—and a Little Tact

Sell-in public relations isn't only relegated to tours. There are countless creative strategies for wooing bookstore buyers, from sending bookmarks or homemade cookies shaped like a book cover, to hosting informal luncheons or doing personalized newsletters. The possibilities are limited only by the boundaries of your imagination. I want to emphasize, however, that if you're an author, it's crucial that you consult with your publisher before implementing any public relations activities targeting bookstores. The bookstore buyer is a client of the publisher, and before you interact with their client, you need to make sure your publisher is comfortable with and supports your idea. Most publishers are cooperative and reasonable, as long as they are kept in the loop and their authors aren't going off half-cocked without their knowledge or approval. Remember, publisher and author are a team and, like any team, need to communicate and collaborate.

Promotions developed to galvanize sell-in are also infinitely helpful. Some of the more common promotions include sweepstakes and contests in which booksellers can win various prizes. One of the more imaginative promotions I participated in was sponsored by Harlequin, the celebrated romance publisher. One of their lead authors, Candy Camp, was known for her steamy love scenes. The publisher thought it would be fun to do a promotional audio tape featuring a reading of one of those sultry passages, which booksellers as well as their own sales force could enjoy while stuck in traffic. Guess who got to go into the studio and record a legendary love scene from one of Candy Camp's books? That's right. Yours truly. The promotion was effective because booksellers are bombarded with sales paraphernalia they have to read. The audio provided a diversion from the norm that was lighthearted, entertaining, and didn't demand much of their valuable time.

The Pay-Off

A final note on sell-in and sell-through and how they're impacted by publicity, public relations, and promotions. Many people have a misconception about publishing. They believe that the marketing budget, particularly the publicity allotment for a book, is based on the advance the author is paid. Not true! The publicity and marketing budget is contingent upon initial print run. The higher the print run, the more money the publisher will spend on publicity, promotions, and public relations for sell-through. How do they pinpoint how many books they should print on the first run? They establish quantity according to sell-in. In other words, the publisher bases the initial print run on the advance orders the sales force secured during sell-in. For example, if the advance orders on a particular title are 30,000, the publisher will print that number of books on its first run.

Pay careful attention here; this is critical information you need to know. How then can someone take proactive steps to ensure that the advance orders (i.e., sell-in) will be as strong as possible? Several ways: sell-in publicity, public relations, and promotions, as illuminated above.

A small side note: Yes, a sell-in tour can be costly. However, there are always methods for significantly reducing costs. More on this when we discuss budgets later in the book. Also, an intelligently and imaginatively constructed, detailed publicity, public relations, and promotional strategy for sell-through should be communicated to the book buyers during sell-in. If the book buyers know that the author is going to do extensive media at the time of the book's release, they will be motivated to up their advance orders.

Here's another secret for galvanizing sell-in that authors and publishers sometimes overlook: Just because authors shouldn't do big media interviews until their book is on the shelves doesn't mean they shouldn't *confirm* as many of those interviews as possible in advance. Why? It's potent ammunition for sell-in. Nothing motivates a book buyer more than a list of confirmed media interviews that the author is scheduled to do the week the book hits the shelves. Setting up these interviews early on is one of the best moves you can make because, just like sharing the marketing plan, it diminishes concerns about returns. Remember, bookstores buy books from publishers on consignment. Nobody wants returns. Sell-in gets books on the shelves, but having a tight rein on sell-through, as early on as I've illuminated above, helps you to stack the deck.

Different Strokes for Different Folks: How the Genre and Format of a Book Affect Publicity, Public Relations, and Promotions

*P*UBLICITY, PUBLIC RELATIONS, AND PROMOTIONS ARE INTRINSIC TO A book's success. However, there isn't one single campaign formula for all book types. Authors and publishers who subscribe to that misconception are doing their books a great disservice. In order to maximize the breadth and scope of your marketing efforts, it's crucial that you understand the different categories and formats of books, and specific strategies for each. In this chapter, we're going to look at fiction versus nonfiction and hardcover versus paperback, with regard to publicity, public relations, and promotions.

Mainstream commercial titles are divided into two principal categories. Fiction includes: literary fiction, horror/sci-fi, women's fiction, romance, erotic fiction, adventures, thrillers, historical fiction, religious/spiritual fiction, and mysteries. Nonfiction comprises: personal growth/self-help, biographies and autobiographies, history, philosophy, textbooks, religious/spiritual, New Age, how-to's, science and technology, business and finance, sports, compilations, and true crime. There are countless other genres under both headings, with new subgroups continually being launched into the marketplace, but the ones I've listed above are the largest and most popular. Think of them as publishing's primary colors.

Capitalize on Credentials

There are two key questions you should ask when planning a campaign for any genre: What's the topic, and what's the author's credibility? Everything else emanates from there. If the topic or story is relevant or compelling and the author boasts a definitive expertise, either through an academic degree, quantifiable personal experience, or a combination of both, chances are the book has significant media potential.

Let's say you're a psychologist who treats teens with eating disorders. You're also the mother of a sixteen-year-old daughter in recovery from bulimia. You've written a how-to book for parents to help guide them through the labyrinth of daily questions and concerns. Your book is media friendly on several levels. Eating disorders are regularly featured in the media, but not covered so frequently to be labeled "old news." Your clinical degree in psychology coupled with your own struggles as a parent caught up in the difficulties of her child's sickness give you tremendous personal and professional credibility as an author. Your book could easily be presented to television, radio, and print outlets as a news story in and of itself. You could also be pitched to producers, editors, and reporters as an overall authority on eating disorders.

If, on the other hand, you had written a book on a more obscure or overexposed topic, or your professional and/or personal link to the subject matter was less tangible, the immediate newsworthiness of your book would be proportionately decreased. Novels tend to fall into this quagmire more frequently than nonfiction.

That doesn't mean that when you're confronted with such a challenge, whether it's fiction or nonfiction, you can't mount an extraordinarily successful campaign that galvanizes sales. What it *does* mean is you may have to stack your publicity deck with clever promotions and public relations to boost media response, like those described in chapter 1.

Choosing the Right Door

When I first started out in the book business, I can't tell you how many times I heard colleagues say, "You can't publicize fiction; only nonfiction is publicizable." On the surface, it would seem to make sense, because fiction isn't real, whereas nonfiction is. Let me state here and now, fiction can be equally as newsworthy as nonfiction. The only limits are the boundaries of the imagination conceiving the campaign.

I teach a course at New York University on book publicity. I often tell my students there are two kinds of publicity pitches—front door and side door. The front door technique is presenting the straightforward, *obvious* media angle, like the example of the book on eating disorders. The theme was bulimia, and the author's life and career defined her authority. "Front dooring" is the direct approach and is only effective when the premise of the book itself can be positioned as news and the author's credibility is explicit.

When these criteria are not as easy to define or don't meet newsworthy standards, as is often the case with fiction, the side-door method is a useful creative solution. "Side-dooring" is providing alternative angles to the press that framework the book and author from a perspective not inherently apparent. For example, you're publicizing an espionage thriller set in modern-day China. The author lived and worked in China for three months while researching the book. If you take the front door route and pitch the feature writer at a newspaper to do a conventional author interview, it's likely the editor won't bite, because the book is fiction and the author isn't an academic expert on China. However, if you seek a side door, you open up a whole new spectrum of possibilities. For instance, you could pitch the travel writer on doing an article about China as seen through the eyes of a celebrated novelist. Or you could pitch the reporter who covers the Far East for the newspaper's international section on interviewing your author for an article about the experiences of American writers who've lived in China. Opportunities abound!

Make no mistake about it: Side-dooring is a powerful weapon in a publicist's arsenal of persuasive techniques. The majority of books published today are not big news stories waiting to happen. On top of that, producers and reporters are inundated with calls from literary publicists every waking moment. One of my dearest friends, Marty Spanninger, a senior producer at NBC, says that, on average, she receives 200 or more books a week from publishers. "When I sift through my pile, I search for fresh, original story ideas and unexpected angles," she says. "The obvious pitch often has the dullest edge."

Actions speak louder than words. Let's look at some examples of campaigns for fiction titles that illustrate Marty's point. As we're going through these actual histories, remember what we talked about before: *subject and author credibility.*

Side Doors for Fiction

In the early seventies, *The Soul,* a controversial thriller about televangelists, was published. The author, Ron Gorton, was an entrepreneur who had enjoyed a plethora of diverse careers—from truck driving, farming, and construction, to writing books, directing B-films, and teaching high school. Fiery and gregarious, he was the quintessential Renaissance man. Gorton's novel, which reflected his passionate sentiments about evangelism, shot straight to the *New York Times* bestseller list. Shortly thereafter, he took a hiatus from writing, resurfacing two decades later with *The Hucksters of Holiness,* the sequel to his first blockbuster, which I was assigned to publicize.

This project presented a hornet's nest of challenges. Due to the author's eclectic professional past, he would be perceived by the press as a jack of all trades and a master of none. The fact that twenty years earlier he wrote a book that became a short-lived bestseller made him the literary equivalent of a "one-hit wonder." On top of that, his only link to televangelism was his personal conviction that most of its practitioners were unethical and manipulative. Feelings and opinions don't constitute author credibility. In addition, his publisher was a small press with limited resources and distribution. Author and publisher were in dire need of publicity coverage, because without it, they couldn't get books on or off the shelves.

My associates and I knew that to circumvent the hurdles, we had to probe *beyond the obvious* and aggressively *explore* every option from as many vistas as possible. How could we turn the author's emotions about evangelism into *legitimate* expertise? Was there a way to create a news story out of the theme of the book?

We interviewed Ron in depth, inquiring about everything under the sun, from his childhood memories, hobbies, education, proudest achievements, worst failures, and pet peeves, to his marriage, political convictions, religion, future goals, and motivation for writing *The Hucksters of Holiness,* among countless other areas. We left no stone unturned. Our central objective was to extrapolate fragments of information that could be used as the building blocks for a campaign premise. It didn't take long before we had our blueprint. During the course of our Q&A with Ron Gorton, he explained that he wrote both books to ignite healthy debate about the role and responsibility of televangelists in America.

We engineered a public awareness crusade, positioned Ron Gorton as its leading spokesperson, and presented him to the press as the "Exorcist of Evangelism." We contacted all the major media outlets in the country, encouraging them to host a panel of televangelists, whom Ron would spar with verbally on air. Even we couldn't have predicted the colossal response from journalists. Our phone rang off the hook. Ron was interviewed on the nation's top-rated television and radio shows and featured in dozens of gripping newspaper and magazine articles.

Remember, there's no such thing as a book that's impossible to publicize. A good publicist engages her investigative instincts until she unearths the most enticing angle. Then, she molds and sculpts that angle to conform to the needs of each target media outlet. In the case of *The Hucksters of Holiness,* if we had taken the front-door approach and pitched the media on interviewing author Ron Gorton about his novel, we would have secured little or no coverage. By employing the side-door technique, we were able to shape the message of the book into a consumer advocacy campaign and establish author credibility on the consistency of Ron Gorton's commitment to focusing public scrutiny on televangelism.

Sometimes, especially with certain types of fiction, it isn't the message of a book that offers the best media angle, but the provocative questions *raised* in the book that can be packaged as news. In *The Deep End of the Ocean* by Jacquelyn Mitchard, a couple struggle to save their marriage after the mysterious disappearance of their youngest son, who shows up on their doorstep nearly thirteen years later, completely unaware of the truth about his past. A bitter custody battle ensues between the boy's biological parents and the family who raised him, who never knew he was a stolen baby. Though the story was fictional, the book struck a chord with the media because it prompted real questions about the rights of children caught in nontraditional custody battles. Additionally, it explored the subject of missing children from the intriguing perspective of the parents' psychological and spiritual struggle. The publicist who handled the campaign for *The Deep End of the Ocean* did a wonderful job ferreting out and focusing the media on the newsworthiness of the book.

Another approach when publicizing fiction is to examine the "what if" angle. One of my favorite examples is Michael Crichton's *Jurassic Park.* The plot was based on the scientific hypothesis that a dinosaur could be cloned by extracting its DNA from mosquitoes fossilized in amber. When the film version was released, hundreds of newspaper articles featured interviews with renowned scientists from around the world, who speculated on the plausibility of such an experiment. Though *Jurassic Park* was fiction, the "what if it could really happen" pitch provided a non-fiction angle that could be massaged into substantial coverage.

Make It Newsworthy

The bottom line is that in order to execute an effective campaign, you have to look at fiction in a whole new way. See novels as news stories made of clay. The substance is there, but you have to sculpt the clay into the proper shape and dimension. When you're devising your campaign strategy, ask yourself the following questions:

- What are the main themes of the story?
- Does the book address these issues from an uncommon, controversial, or provocative perspective that's newsworthy?
- Are there parallels between the author's life and the novel that could be used as media hooks or to reinforce credibility?
- Can the author share entertaining anecdotes surrounding the research and writing of the book that could be publicized as news?
- Does the book focus attention on an issue of specific concern to any professional organizations, foundations, or other special-interest groups who would benefit from a copromotion?
- Can the premise of the book be tied into any stories currently being covered in the news?

For example, say you're publicizing a romance novel about a May-December relationship. Your first job is to analyze which theme or themes featured in the book could be packaged as media angles. Sometimes it's the main premise of the book, or it could be an element of a subplot. In this particular example, the

May-December angle is powerful because it's controversial and relevant. You may even be able to piggyback current events. For instance, if you were mounting your campaign during the Monica Lewinsky scandal, it would give you the perfect tie-in pitch. There might also be another news angle lurking in the story line. Perhaps the heroine gets impregnated out of wedlock by her older paramour. That's an interesting theme. You could develop an intriguing human interest angle out of the idea of older men fathering children and its impact on the family. Using this angle would also open up opportunities for copromotions with special-interest groups, such as foundations for unwed mothers, support groups, and other similar entities. We'll get more into copromotions in later chapters.

Your second task after scouring the book for media angles would be to interview the author, asking as many details about his life, career, and experiences as possible. Your goal would be to unearth information that could contribute to author credibility or even comprise a possible news story in and of itself. Perhaps the author had been involved in a May-December relationship when he was younger, and it was one of the primary motivations for writing this book. Such a personal connection to the subject matter is good fodder for a human interest article. Or maybe the author was a couples counselor, and the novel was inspired by real case histories. Again, the key is to discover through the author interview process something with an interesting edge that you could use to establish author credibility and engineer a campaign.

Remember:

STEP 1: Read the book as if you were an investigative journalist searching for a story idea.

STEP 2: Interview the author thoroughly to uncover elements of his life that could either establish his credibility as an expert or be used as a news story by itself.

STEP 3: Sift through the subplots of the story for possible peripheral media angles. Every time a media contact says "no" to a pitch, you want a bucket full of other ideas that you can pull out in a flash.

Side-Dooring Nonfiction

We mentioned nonfiction briefly in the beginning of this chapter, and I'd like to get back to that category for a moment. As we already discussed, nonfiction is traditionally a more straightforward pitch and requires less intensive digging for angles. As in the example of the author who penned a nonfiction book about bulimia, the main theme of the book is the angle, and the author's academic background and personal experience comprise the credibility factor. Let's explore some exceptions to that rule and how to handle them.

The most common obstacle in difficult-to-publicize nonfiction harkens back to the credibility issue. If an author pens a book and her expertise on the subject matter is weak or too far removed, a campaign is required that shifts media focus away from the discrepancy. For example, a journalist writes a book about rebuilding your life after divorce. The author herself has never been divorced, nor does she have a clinical or academic background in divorce. Her only link to the topic is that she interviewed twenty divorced couples about their own experiences. If you were to take the "front door" approach with the media and pitch them on interviewing the author about postdivorce survival, chances are you'd get little response. Most producers and reporters would say the topic was fascinating, but that the author wasn't a definitive authority. In this kind of situation, you could construct the campaign around the couples themselves. You could ask the author if any of the couples would be willing to be interviewed by the media, then pitch the author along with them. The couples would be what the media call "personal stories." We'll go into detail later about how personal stories can be used in media pitching.

Another direction to take when faced with a nonfiction title with limited author credibility is the "story behind the story" angle. Here's one of my favorite examples: Several years ago, I was hired to publicize one of the most unusual personal growth books I'd ever come across in my career. It was called *Brain Tricks*. The author, David Weiner, was a brilliant and successful entrepreneur who had built one of the largest industrial advertising agencies in the Midwest. All his life, he had been fascinated with the mechanisms of the brain, how it worked, the neurological explanations for human behavior. He began vigorously researching and studying the subject in his mid-thirties, consuming complicated medical books, articles, and anything he could get his hands on for twenty years. *Brain Tricks* was his personal perspective on how the cerebrum functions, featuring his own step-by-step guidelines for how to reprogram your mind to improve your life.

Publicizing the book was one of the most formidable challenges I'd ever encountered; I honestly thought I would pull out every single strand of hair on my head. I knew we could never take the "front door" approach on this book, because the first thing the media would ask would be, "Is the author a neurologist or psychiatrist?" Though Dave Weiner was well-read on the subject, he didn't have the necessary credibility. Dave and I had many animated exchanges about the best campaign strategy. I finally convinced him that we should go with the human interest angle of a wealthy businessman who was so enthralled with the human mind that he spent over two decades immersing himself in a jungle of scientific data, hunting for knowledge. This angle worked on several levels. It positioned Dave as a man with an unusual hobby, as opposed to someone who could answer complicated questions about brain function. Additionally, it lightened the tone of his interviews, allowing him to share humorous anecdotes about his research. We were able to secure him front-page stories in major newspapers, as well as numerous magazine articles and broadcast spots.

As a side note, Dave has just finished writing another book called *Battling the Inner Dummy: The Craziness of App-*

arently Normal People, which he coauthored with a leading Ph.D. from Northwestern University. This time around, Dave has the added credibility factor of an academic coauthor, which should give his new book tremendous wings.

In a nutshell, if you're confronted with a challenging nonfiction book, apply the same investigative techniques you would for fiction. Interview the author thoroughly about every conceivable aspect of her life. Look at all the themes in the book, and analyze which ones would make the best news stories. If the author features any real-life case histories in the book, ask the author if those "personal stories" would be available for interview. Keep an eye on the news to see if you could piggyback your campaign onto any unfolding current events. Think about whether or not there are any issues dealt with in the book that would be important to a special interest group with whom you could implement a copromotion. In other words, if you have to publicize a book that makes you shudder with insecurity because, on the surface, it seems like such a tough sell to the media, don't panic and shut down creatively. Look at how it *can* be done, and not why it *can't* be done.

Trade versus Mass Market

We've reviewed fiction versus nonfiction. Now, let's take a look at the different formats of books. The book market is divided into two prongs—trade and mass market. *Trade* refers to the publishing trade and is primarily defined as bookstores. Though the arena is changing rapidly with the proliferation of online book buying and Web sites such as Amazon.com, trade is still widely considered to mean bookstores.

Mass market is defined as any retail outlet that isn't a book or entertainment superstore. This includes, for example, pharmacies, airport newsstands, grocery stores, wholesale chain stores such as K-Mart, Walmart, etc., among other retail outlets that carry a diverse product array not specific to books or entertainment.

An *original trade hardcover* is a book released in hardcover that's being published for the first time. Think about your last trip to a bookstore. The vast majority of all those hardcover books you saw were original hardcover trades. The predominant retail outlets for original hardcover trade titles are independent and chain bookstores and entertainment superstores.

An *original trade paperback* is the same size and shape as a hardcover and is also sold in bookstores. The only difference is that it's a paperback format and the retail price is lower than a hardcover trade. Most hardcover trade books have retail prices between $19 and $35, whereas trade paperbacks are between $12 and $22. To give you an idea of what a trade paperback looks like, the *Chicken Soup for the Soul* books are all trade paperbacks. Trade paperbacks are more affordable to produce, and that savings is passed on to the consumer. Sometimes publishers will opt to do a book in trade paperback because they want to reach a larger audience. There are myriad reasons why publishers choose one format over another. The basic factors involved are usually a combination of economics and demographics.

There are also *trade paperback reprints*. A trade paperback reprint is just like a trade paperback original in size and look, except that it's a reprint of a book that was published in hardcover first.

Next on our agenda is understanding *mass market* titles. There are mass market paperback reprints and mass market paperback originals. All mass market books are rack size. Rack size are the smaller, fatter paperback books that you typically see on racks in drug stores, grocery stores, etc. Think about the last time you saw someone on the beach reading a paperback of a Stephen King book. What you saw being read was a rack size paperback.

Now that you understand what mass market paperback titles look like, let's explore the formats themselves. A mass paperback *reprint* is a rack size paperback version of a book that was *already published* in hardcover trade. Major hardcover books are usually released in mass market paperback eight to twelve months after their hardcover publication. A mass market paperback *original* is a rack size paperback that has *never been published* before. Many romance, sci-fi, horror, and fantasy novels are released straight into mass market paperback and not published in hardcover first.

The process for devising a publicity strategy for paperbacks is the same as for hardcovers. A book is a book. The degree of news coverage you generate is contingent upon your imagination and persistence and the willingness of the author to support your creative efforts as much as possible.

Publicizing Reprints

One small caveat—paperback reprints. Whether it's a reprint in trade or mass market paperback, it presents a slightly larger challenge to publicize because many reprints have already been promoted in the past. Here's the secret to overcoming this hurdle: All it really involves is adding one step to the campaign strategy process. If you've got to publicize a paperback reprint, thoroughly research the campaign, if any, that was done on the book when it was released in hardcover. Look at all the press materials, the news clippings, video of author interviews, anything you can get ahold of. Once you know what the first campaign entailed and if it was successful, you can then begin building fresh campaign ideas, based on new angles that you engineer.

After you've reviewed all the old campaign components, do what you would normally do. Read the book from the perspective of a journalist seeking story ideas. Interview the author. Design your front- and side-door pitches. Don't let reprint publicity intimidate you. It just requires the extra research step to ascertain what was achieved before, so that you have a clear landscape to cultivate new opportunities.

Novelty Books

There are two other types of books that we need to talk about before we close this chapter: novelty/gift books and coffee-table books. Novelty/gift books are unusually sized books normally sold in special market outlets such as greeting card stores, novelty shops, gift shops, etc. Coffee-table books are those large, gorgeous photography and art books you often see adorning people's coffee tables or in the waiting rooms of offices.

I emphasize once again: These books, too, are publicizable. The same steps you take to publicize other types and formats of books apply here. The only real difference is that sometimes novelty/gift and coffee-table books don't have one author per se, but a series of authors or editors. If you're facing that situation, the best solution is to work with the publisher on choosing one of the editors or authors as the primary spokesperson for the book. Once you have that spokesperson, you follow the normal campaign strategy process that we've been discussing.

Pushing the Envelope

Let me share a trade secret with you about publicity, public relations, and promotions that you're unlikely to hear on the job or glean from a manual. Whether you're publicizing a celebrity autobiography or a novel, a paperback reprint, a hardcover original, or a novelty joke book, if you consistently rely on formulaic approaches and conventional theories, or listen to the inhibiting gibberish of others not willing to take creative leaps, you will surely encounter roadblocks on your path. If, on the other hand, you're willing and eager to look *outside of the box,* engineer your *own* news-making opportunities, and set *new* precedents in literary marketing, there's almost nothing you can't do. The bottom line is, if you're serious about putting books on the map, you'll need to take risks and be daring. Meek marketing campaigns garner weak results.

Close your ears to those who tell you that publicizing fiction, reprints, or novelty and coffee-table books is almost impossible, and open your mind to the limitless bounty of your own imagination. Keep in mind what my friend and media colleague Marty Spanninger from NBC said earlier: "I'm always looking for that fresh pitch, the angle that I would never think of myself."

Onward to our next chapter, which is a detailed overview of the media!

What Is the Media, and How Does It Work: Focus on Print

*T*HE MEDIA'S IMPACT AND INFLUENCE ON CONTEMPORARY CULTURE IS immeasurable. Think about it. Most people, when they're watching the news or reading an article in the paper, don't question whether or not what's being reported is objective, accurate, or true. If the information escapes from the lips of their favorite anchorperson or pours forth from the pen of a prominent local journalist, chances are that whatever is communicated is taken at complete face value. Consider for a moment the indelible imprint that reviewers leave on the American psyche. When's the last time you were thinking about buying a CD or catching a certain movie, but then you read a negative review and decided to pass? Conversely, how often have you heard yourself tell someone, "Oh, I'm dying to read that book; the reviews have been incredible"?

Public opinion is cultivated out of the soil of media coverage. Our knowledge of current events and our perspective on how we as individuals fit into the whole of society is largely shaped by the media. The average person doesn't reflect on the slant of a particular network news story or read between the lines of every front-page article. People don't chew on the news and digest it slowly; they swallow it whole, smacking their lips for more. The media in America has the daunting task of satisfying our ever-increasing appetite for information. It's up to us to distinguish between the junk food and the balanced meals.

Do you ever wonder how the media works? Who controls it? Why some stories get news coverage and others don't? In the next two chapters, we're going to explore these questions and more. Please keep in mind, however, that this subject is a book in and of itself. My goal here is to provide a comprehensive breakdown of the media that equips you with the specific knowledge necessary to make sound judgments and decisions about publicity, public relations, and promotions strategies. For a more inclusive understanding of the media, I've provided a list of resources at the end of this book.

Let's start with the basics. The media is divided into two primary categories: print and broadcast. Under both of these headings are two subcategories: national and local. National media reaches the entire country. Local media targets regional audiences. The Internet is its own medium, which we'll examine in a separate chapter later on in the book.

Newspapers, supplements, magazines, wire services, syndicates, and newsletters are print media outlets. Television and radio shows, which we'll explore in chapter 4, are broadcast media outlets. A combination of both types of media coverage is crucial to a powerful campaign. Let's look at the print media outlets listed above in detail.

All the News That's Fit to Print

Do you ever read *USA Today,* the *Wall Street Journal,* or the *New York Times?* Those are daily national newspapers. They're circulated and sold every morning to millions of readers coast to coast and cover prominent national stories. Other major national dailies include the *Christian Science Monitor,* the *Financial Times,* and the *International Herald.* A diverse plethora of national newspapers are also published in the United States that appeal to narrower demographic groups delineated by religion, career, lifestyle, and ethnic background, among other criteria. In chapter 9, when we talk about media research, I'll explain where and how to find more information about these newspapers.

There are also weekly national newspapers, such as *Barron's* and *National Employment,* which are almost a hybrid cross between a newspaper and a magazine. National newspapers are formidable print media outlets. A *USA Today* article, for example, is read by over thirty million pairs of eyes. *That's* influence.

Local newspapers fall into three categories: dailies, weeklies, and "multiple publishers." Make no mistake: Regional newspapers can be influential in their respective districts. Too many publicists overlook the impact of grassroots press. I want to share a story from the trenches that illustrates the large effect small newspapers can have on a literary campaign. I mentioned in the preface of this book how my memoir *Please Stop Laughing at Me. . . .* made the *New York Times* bestseller list and climbed for six weeks. What I didn't mention was the enormous part a tiny neighborhood newspaper played in making this happen. The third week that my book was on the list, it dropped down to number twenty-six, nearly falling off. My publicist, business partner, and best friend Lissy Peace was determined to put my book back up on top. She contacted a small town paper in the suburb where I grew up and convinced them to do a story on me. Remember the newspaper in Mayberry that Andy Griffith read? This newspaper was about the same size. Because I was a big fish in a small pond, the paper not only committed to a feature, but also put it on the front page. The story of my book actually bumped war coverage from Iraq. That is what I mean about small town papers. Their coverage priority is always local news. Working with these papers can alter the course of a campaign.

After I did the interview, Lissy called the local bookstore and arranged a book signing for the day my story was scheduled to run. That front-page feature packed the bookstore. In fact, there were so many people at the signing, they had to park in the lot for the competing bookstore across the street! That week, my book leaped from number twenty-six on the *New York Times* List to number sixteen, because of one article in a tiny regional paper in a town few people who live outside of it have ever heard of.

The moral of the story? Don't underestimate the power of little papers and tiny towns. Grassroots buzz is often more valuable than national exposure because it has longer legs. National exposure is like a brilliant flame that burns out quickly. Grassroots attention is a slow burning ember that stays lit long after the fire is out. That's not to say national media isn't important. Of course it is. But local communities are loyal longer.

The Hometown News

Local daily newspapers are a staple of American culture. I remember as a kid, seeing my dad clad in his red terry cloth robe and PF Flyer gym shoes, running out to the end of our driveway every morning to get the *Chicago Tribune,* which he'd peruse over breakfast. He read the front and business sections, my mom took the lifestyle pages, and I opted for the comics and TV and movie listings. It was a cherished family ritual that, to this day, I look back upon with warmth and nostalgia. Ponder for a moment your own childhood. What local paper did you grow up reading? I've worked with authors and celebrities the better part of twenty years. Nine times out of ten, when I ask my clients where they'd like to see themselves featured, their first response is always "my hometown paper."

Most larger markets have two major daily papers. One is usually a foldout like the *Chicago Tribune,* and the other is a tabloid format like the *Chicago Sun Times.* Foldout papers tend to be more conservative and understated in their coverage, whereas the local tabloids lean towards a more aggressive and colorful presentation of the news. From a publicist's perspective, each town is different in terms of the dominant paper. If you read several issues of both, analyze the tone of their reporting, and research the circulation numbers, it will help you decide which paper would be your first choice for a placement.

Community papers, or weeklies, as they're referred to in PR circles, are great vehicles for generating visibility. They represent the voice of local neighborhoods all across America. Unlike the dailies that cover bigger stories over a larger landscape, community papers focus on the day-to-day activities and achievements of the person next door. Articles that might normally never appear in the daily paper often make headlines in the community paper. It isn't unusual for a weekly to do a front-page spread on the local high school football hero, the retirement party of the district fire chief, the new playground near Town Hall, or a search-and-rescue mission to find a lost pet. Community papers are free and circulated all over, from grocery stores and office lobbies to coffee shops and beauty salons. Many are also available via subscription.

Multiple Publishers

Multiple publishers are companies that publish clusters of weekly community papers. Liberally scattered throughout the United States, multiple publishers vary in size, some churning out as many as two to three dozen neighborhood weeklies. One of my best kept secrets, until now, has been how to use multiple publishers to jump-start public relations campaigns. More on that later in this chapter! But first, let's delve into some details about these wonderful media outlets.

Most multiple publishers cover a specific geographic area. For example, one might have the suburbs on the southwest side of a city, another the northwest suburbs. Typically, a multiple publisher will print a separate, regionalized edition of the same weekly paper for each individual suburb in its territory. Sometimes, parts of the advertising sections, one or two of the features, or the actual names of the editions may vary, but they all share the same core editorial content. In fact, it's usually one central writing staff that does all the reporting.

Multiple publishers are a delightful publicity tool, and nailing a placement with one can be a real coup. Why? Let's say you secure an author interview with a multiple publisher. That article is likely to appear in every edition they issue. I can't tell you the mounds of clippings you can generate from multiple publishers. Several weeks ago, a multiple publisher in Chicago interviewed one of my touring authors. The piece ran as a front-page spread in all thirty of its editions. It was amazing.

I've seen countless examples of the impact of multiple publishers on author campaigns. One sticks out in my memory in particular. John Bradshaw, early on in his career, was touring to promote his first commercial title, *Bradshaw on the Family*. Though he was enjoying a growing fan base, the big daily newspapers in his tour markets were resistant about interviewing him, because he still hadn't achieved mainstream recognition. Some of the dailies did smaller pieces on him, but snagging a feature article was proving to be a challenge.

I was working for his publicist then, and she and I decided that since the front door seemed jammed, we'd start trying side doors. We pitched a large multiple publisher in Cleveland to cover one of John's book signings and to interview him afterwards. Not only did that article run as a huge feature in every one of this publisher's twenty-two suburban editions, but it got picked up by a wire service and ran in 500 other small papers across the United States. We received so many clippings from this single interview that we were able to send them out to national print and broadcast media, who booked John on the spot because of his obvious "grassroots" appeal.

Always remember what we keep talking about in this book: front-door and side-door approaches. Multiple publishers are a side-door entrance to a ballroom of visibility opportunities. Too many talented publicists overlook multiple publishers when they're touring authors. Yes, multiple publishers require a local angle, but a persistent and ingenious publicist who looks *outside* of the box can always create a regional sell idea.

For example, if your author is touring to promote a children's book, set up a reading at a local hospital and invite the multiple publisher from that area to cover the reading. Every community has a local weekly paper. Believe me, where there's a will and a creative willingness, there's a way. Multiple publishers are worth the extra energy. They can pay off greatly in the end.

One other type of newspaper published in some of the larger urban areas is the alternative weekly. Similar to a community paper in that it covers many stories the mainstream dailies don't, the alternative paper targets a youth-driven demographic. A tabloid format, it's an effective media outlet if you have a book or author considered on the fringe. Alternative papers prefer edgy, controversial cultural angles.

Lifestyle, Metro, or Travel?

Now that we've described national and local dailies, weekly community papers, multiple publishers, and alternative papers, let's examine the general format, substance, and editorial structure of newspapers. Newspapers are divided into four primary sections: news, business, lifestyle/features, and sports. Though some papers may adhere to a slightly different structural model, they all share the same fundamental format. Here's what you need to know.

The news or front section of a paper is comprised of the major stories of the day. Journalists who work the hard news beat file their copy right up to the last minute to ensure coverage of the most recent developments. Editors frequently engage in animated exchanges over which articles should headline the front page and how much space should be devoted to each item, among many other nail-biting details. Some newspapers print one front section that includes the international, national, and regional stories. Other papers divide hard news into two sections. One features the international and national stories; the other, often referred to as the Metro section, offers news items of local significance.

The business section is a window into financial, economic, and corporate dramas as they unfold. It boasts a diverse spectrum of articles, interviews, features, and columns on everything from

personal finance, economic trends, corporate leaders, and entrepreneurs to key company profiles, mergers and acquisitions,
research and development, and corporate deals.

The lifestyle/feature section covers a broad range of topics from entertainment, gossip, health, leisure, parenting, celebrity
and author profiles, and food to advice columns, culture, education, fashion, and human interest. Daily newspapers dedicate special sections each weekend that expand on some of the categories
covered regularly in the lifestyle/feature section of their daily editions. The most typical weekend pullout sections are Entertainment and/or Arts & Leisure, Travel, Real Estate/Home, Health,
and Book Review. Most dailies also publish a weekly magazine
insert available on Sunday.

The lifestyle/feature element is where newspapers vary
the most in terms of structure. For example, some papers publish
only one weekly entertainment pullout section, while others do
one on Friday and Sunday. Some papers don't have a separate
weekly book review and include literary critiques in their entertainment section. The best way to research how each individual
newspaper compiles its various components is to obtain a week's
worth of the paper itself. Nothing informs like good old firsthand
knowledge.

If you're publicizing a book, don't buy into conventional
wisdom that author interview opportunities are relegated to
lifestyle or book review. In chapter 10, when we talk about the
art of pitching, I'll show you there are *many* more ways to skin a
media cat than *that*. I'll give you a hint—side door versus front
door. More on this soon!

. . . And Don't Forget Sports

Ah, sports . . . The sports section of the newspaper is straightforward. It features national and local sports stories, game scores,
profiles, and trends. Most book publicists, unless they are promoting a sports title, don't consider the sports section as a placement

alternative. You want to know something? Many of my colleagues and I have gotten sports sections to do book features that weren't directly related to athletics. It wasn't because we were any smarter than anyone else. We simply took an *unanticipated* approach. In fact, I have a great story about this. I should probably hold off telling it until chapter 10 when we discuss pitching techniques, but it so proves my point here, I just have to let it out of the bag now.

Several years ago, my company, Blanco & Peace, signed a contract to publicize a novel about the drug trade. The author was a former DEA agent who was now penning fiction full time. If you recall what we talked about in chapter 2, fiction publicity tends to demand more side-door approaches than nonfiction. It requires a creatively aggressive stance. My account executive started with the front-door route. She pitched the book reviewer, along with the lifestyle and feature sections. She pitched the crime writer; the police beat reporter; the business section, on the financial details of drug dealing; and even the education writer, on how drugs— once they're smuggled into the country—physically reach the school yards. All great pitches, but still no dice. When I got to the office later that same day, she was deep in thought, trying to locate a side door she might have missed earlier.

"The only section I haven't pitched is sports," she quipped. "You're right, that's a terrific idea," I enthused. She looked at me as if I were bananas. "There's absolutely no sports angle whatsoever with this book," she continued. "What *are* you thinking?" Suddenly, it dawned on her.

She had already pitched the education writer about drugs in schools; this was just the next step. Every newspaper has a high school sportswriter. These reporters have a vested interest in the youth culture in their local communities, because it correlates to attitudes about sports and overall athletic performance. If a publicist pitches a high school sportswriter about a story distinctly different from what they normally cover, but still within the boundaries of his beat, it can be fruitful for everyone. In our situation, my account executive called up the high school sportswriter and pitched him on interviewing the author about steroid and other drug use among adolescent athletes. She positioned the story as a how-to angle, telling the reporter that her author would share with the readership the "Ten Warning Signs" that a teen athlete may be on steroids.

The reporter loved the story idea and interviewed the author later that week. The interview ran with photos as a full-page feature. That same high school sportswriter still does numerous stories with us to this day. We make his job fun, and he offers us a warm, receptive side-door entrance.

The People Component

Speaking of reporters, let's examine the people component of newspapers. Every newspaper has graded levels of editors and reporters. The bigger the paper, the more they have of each. No publicist can or should memorize every editor and reporter at every newspaper. It would be impossible. All you need to understand is the basic premise of how editors and reporters work so you can collaborate effectively. We'll review these details during our discussion of the pitching process in chapter 10.

For our purposes now, we'll examine the general internal structure of newspapers. Each section of the newspaper has its own department or "desk." The city desk handles the hard and breaking news stories that appear in the front section. The other three desks are eponymous with their sections: feature desk, business desk, and sports desk. Each department has several editors and numerous reporters. Freelance writers are also assigned to stories on an as-needed basis.

Sunday Reading

Next on our list of print media outlets is the Sunday supplement. The two dominant, competing supplements in America are *Parade* and *USA Weekender.* You've probably seen one of these supplements. They're tabloid formatted and resemble a daily newspaper's Sunday magazine insert. Virtually every daily in America includes one of the two supplements in their Sunday edition. Thus, supplements carry a tremendous amount of weight, especially in the publishing and entertainment industries. A Sunday supplement cover story is considered one of the biggest media bookings you can get, as Sunday supplements reach tens of millions of readers every week.

Magazines: Long Lead versus Short Lead

Moving on to magazines, or periodicals, as they're sometimes called. In the interest of space and expediency, I won't overwhelm you with unnecessary details. I'll give you the knowledge you need from a publicity and promotional perspective. Let's get started.

Magazines fall into two broad categories: long lead and short lead. In fact, all media outlets are grouped under one or the other; however, the terms long and short lead are most commonly associated with magazines. Later in the book, when we explore publicity, promotional, and public relations terminology, we'll address how the labels long and short lead apply to other media situations. For now, let's stay focused on magazines.

Long lead means a magazine that plans its articles four to six months in advance of street date. Most monthly magazines are long lead. *Vogue, Elle, Cosmopolitan, Life, GQ, Playboy, Woman's Day,* and *Redbook* are all examples of long leads. Say you're publicizing a book about plastic surgery that's being released in March and you want *Redbook* to run an author interview in the March issue. You would have to pitch them somewhere between September and early November to meet your time frame. The earlier you contact long leads, the better. Other long lead magazines include bimonthlies (two issues per month), quarterlies (four issues per year), and annuals (one issue per year—sometimes their lead is even longer than six months).

Short lead means a magazine that plans its articles less than three months in advance of street date. Weekly magazines are short lead. News magazines like *Time, Newsweek, U.S. News & World Report,* and entertainment publications such as *People* and *Entertainment Weekly* are examples of short lead publications. Their lead time can be anywhere from three months to three days, depending upon the story. If it's breaking or hard news, or a story on a timely topic, you could pitch them a few weeks or even days before you'd want the piece to run and be well within their deadlines. Bigger features and profiles that aren't tied to a hot current event or trend tend to need a slightly longer lead.

If you're trying to decide which magazines to pitch for your literary campaign, your first consideration should be timing. Divide your wish list into long leads and short leads. Your next criteria should be national versus local. The big national magazines are delineated by genre. Here's a breakdown of the basic ones:

- news
- women's interest
- politics and culture
- business and finance
- sports
- entertainment
- the arts
- men's interest
- health and medicine
- education

There are numerous other groups, but chances are that whatever type of magazine you seek will fall under one of the above headings.

Local magazines abound throughout the country as well. Almost every major city has one big regional magazine that features art, entertainment, food, events, people, and culture in that market. Many cities also have a local business journal. Both are usually independently published monthlies.

Special-Interest Periodicals

Today, there are hundreds of categories of magazines covering an infinite range of topics. It's positively mind-boggling. There are national and local magazines on everything from movie stars, politics, puppies, music, automobiles, and surfing to candle making, banking, carpentry, medicine, knitting, and nail care. I guarantee that whatever book you're publicizing, no matter how obscure you may think the content, there are at least fifteen to twenty magazines of varying sizes and formats that cover the subject of your book. The trick is knowing how to find them. Hang on, because that lesson's coming in chapter 9.

Since we're on the subject of magazine categories, don't forget what we talked about in chapter 1 about sell-in and sell-through, and trade versus general consumer. The magazines I've alluded to above are general consumer and cover stories of interest to different demographic groups within the general public. Trade magazines cover specific industries and target professionals in those respective fields. If you're publicizing a book, you want coverage to run in publishing and entertainment trades six to eight months prior to pub date to inspire stores to stock the book (i.e., sell-in). You want coverage in the general consumer magazines to run when the book comes out in order to motivate retail sales (i.e., sell-through).

An interesting fact about magazines that every publicist needs to know—the bulk of their money isn't made from subscriptions or newsstand sales. The real profit maker for a magazine is ad sales. The bigger the circulation, the higher the ad prices they can charge. Magazines, just like all other media outlets, must keep their readership engaged and continually coming back for more. That's why editors and reporters have such an awesome responsibility. They must provide an ethical and balanced treatment of a story, while simultaneously providing the audience with content that maintains their rapt attention. As we mentioned in chapter 1 when we talked about how important it is for PR representatives to understand how to make producers' and editors' jobs easier, a good publicist is the media contacts' best ally. We're the idea vendors who can help keep their shelves stacked with potential news stories.

Placing Your Story

All magazines share a similar editorial structure. The publisher and editor-in-chief work in tandem. The publisher's primary focus is advertising, and the editor-in-chief's main responsibility is the magazine's content. Underneath them are several levels of editors, reporters, writers, columnists, and freelancers who generate the stories. As a publicist, I work with the editors and reporters. If it's a smaller magazine, I generally pitch the managing editors. At the bigger magazines, I tend to approach the senior writers and/or editors.

The bottom line when researching magazines for possible placement opportunities is that you need to ask yourself four key questions:

1. Is this magazine long lead or short lead?
2. Is it national or local?
3. Who reads this magazine?
4. Is it trade or general consumer?

Once you analyze the answers, you'll know which magazines should be part and parcel of your campaign strategy.

How Wire Services Work

Arguably the most pervasive of all the written forms of media are wire services. They provide a continuous stream of national, international, and local news twenty-four hours a day to virtually every media outlet in the world, who then disperse and disseminate it through their own venues. The next time you're reading the paper or thumbing through a news magazine, notice the bylines of the articles. A byline is the name of the reporter who wrote the article. It's usually printed at the beginning or end of the item. Count the number of times you come across an article or interview bylined by Associated Press, Reuters, or Bloomberg. These are huge wire services, and they're priceless in terms of the coverage that can be facilitated through publicity placements.

There are many wire services of varying sizes and reach throughout the country, but for our purposes, we're going to use Associated Press as our model. It's the largest and most established, and if you learn how it works, you'll have an intrinsic understanding of wire services overall.

Associated Press has two main bureaus, one in New York and another in Washington, D.C., as well as dozens of smaller bureaus in other cities throughout the United States. Most of the beat reporters, i.e., writers assigned to one topic area, are based out of New York or Washington, D.C. The regional bureaus are manned by stringers, who cover national news or big local stories emanating from their respective markets. Wire services like Associated Press are an expedient means to generate coast-to-coast awareness of a book or author. In chapter 10, I'll teach you how to secure placements on the wire.

The Syndicates

Syndicates are agencies that offer news stories, columns, and features to print media outlets, who then run them as bylined items in their own publications. Think of these mighty and dynamic entities as high-end information wholesalers. Book publicists are keenly familiar with their importance. If you generate a placement with a syndicated writer, it will run in hundreds of newspapers coast to coast. Some of the more well-known syndicates are Knight-Ridder, Scripps-Howard, Gannett, and Tribune, among others. Most major newspapers have their own syndication services. For example, Tribune is the syndication entity for the *Chicago Tribune*. Gannett is connected to *USA Today*.

Coverage in a national column is the neon sign version of publicity. It's visibility that "pings." There are hundreds of nationally syndicated columnists, specializing in everything from celebrity gossip, relationships, health, psychology, sports, and crafts to business, personal finance, parenting, entertainment, and cyberspace, among many other subjects. Many of these syndicated columnists are staff writers at local daily papers and make themselves easily accessible to publicists. Some syndicates also have feature writers in-house, who are usually more than happy to listen to a pitch.

What About Newsletters?

When you think about media outlets, newsletters may not come to the forefront of your mind. Don't kid yourself. Though newsletters may be perceived as infinitesimal in the grand scheme of big-time print, these quiet communications speak loudly to a captive audience all their own. Newsletters are chatty and personal. They take the sting out of information dissemination and, as a result, can genuinely affect the opinions of their readers.

You can work with newsletters on a multitude of levels. Newsletters are written and compiled by individuals or small editorial teams and distributed via subscription to special-interest audiences. Many of them are sponsored by associations, foundations, companies, and other organizations. They can range from an extravagant corporate newsletter issued by a Fortune 500 company to its staff and clients, a newsy brochure-type format mass mailed to an alumni association, a mom-and-pop neighborhood newsletter for parents who coach Little League, or a health-and-wellness newsletter offered by a clinic or medical facility to its patients. Whatever the audience or size, newsletters can be a terrific booster shot to any campaign.

On the publicity side, editors of newsletters are open to doing author interviews, as long as the author can comment on a subject pertinent to their readership. They're also wonderful sources for events and other visibility-generating opportunities. Most newsletters are affiliated with a specific group or groups, and the editors always know about upcoming activities that authors could be incorporated into. You can explore ideas with them for innovative author events targeting their subscription base. I've always preached the value of newsletters. But it was during the promotion of my own memoir that I learned just how wonderful they can be in terms of boosting a campaign, especially now when mainstream media is becoming harder and harder to secure for authors. I was feeling mighty frustrated with the national press. Our country was in the middle of war, and the media wasn't covering any other types of stories. My memoir was getting lost. I was booked on *Good Morning America* five times and cancelled five times because events in Iraq kept bumping me off the producer's storyboard. Only one outlet my publicist pitched yielded a result at the time—a national newsletter for educators. They reviewed *Please Stop Laughing at Me. . . .* and did a boxed piece on my availability as a speaker. The day that newsletter started hitting people's desks, my manager was flooded with phone calls from schools wanting to book me as a speaker. In fact, it was the beginning of a whole new career for me in the professional circuit. It also led to a cover story in *Teen Newsweek,* a boxed feature in *Parade* magazine, a one-on-one interview on NBC TV, and an endorsement from the School Board Association, and the National Crime Prevention Council. Let no one ever say that I don't practice what I preach when it comes to newsletters.

Now that we've examined print, let's turn our attention in the next chapter to broadcast.

What Is the Media, and How Does It Work: Focus on Broadcast

*I*F YOU'VE EVER BEEN AN AUTHOR OR WORKED WITH ONE, YOU'VE probably said or heard these words at least once: "My book is perfect for Oprah!" *Oprah* is one of the most successful and powerful talk shows in television history. In fact, it is so influential that one appearance on her show can skyrocket a book to the *New York Times* bestseller list or ignite a cultural trend. Though not every broadcast venue has such an impact on the masses, there's no denying that broadcast media triggers people's impulses. This is especially true in the book business.

Broadcast media is divided into two primary categories: television and radio. Under each of these headings are three subgroups: national, local, and regional. Understanding the dynamics of broadcast will enable you to master the publicity, public relations, and promotions game on a whole new level. We'll start with the basics of television. For our purposes, we're going to focus on informational programming, rather than dramatic, as the latter presents a more limited scope of coverage opportunities. We'll briefly discuss the few exceptions to that rule during chapter 10.

National Television

National television means shows that air across the entire country. In terms of author visibility, national television is key. There are several forms: network, syndicated, cable, superstations, and satellite. Let's review each of these in depth.

Networks

There are four leading commercial broadcast networks in this country: ABC, NBC, CBS, and Fox. PBS is the public television network. All five produce and/or air a variety of live, taped, and live-to-tape news and talk shows that do author interviews. Before we move forward, I want to define live, taped, and live-to-tape, as they're expressions we'll use often. *Live* coverage means that you're seeing or hearing it *as it's happening*. For example, the Oscars are live. *Taped* means taped in advance, edited or post-produced, then aired. The majority of television shows in today's market are taped. From *Sesame Street* and *Inside Edition* to *Wheel of Fortune* and *Charlie Rose,* taping is often the preferred production choice, as it allows for greater artistic control. *Live-to-tape* means taped in front of a live audience. Most talk shows and sitcoms are live-to-tape. Unlike many straight taped pieces, live-to-tape shows are not edited extensively.

Back to our central discussion on networks. The networks carry a lot of weight in the broadcast community. Patriarchal in stature, they command a trust level from their audiences that affords them a formidable place in the hearts and minds of the public. The networks also have an edge over other national television outlets, because, unlike cable or satellite, audiences can access their programming for free as long as they have a television set.

Each network has affiliates in every major market in the country. Those affiliates carry the network's programming, select syndicated shows, as well as some of their own locally produced shows. We'll talk about syndicated and local programming later on in this chapter. The networks own some of their affiliate stations, which are called O&O's (owned and operated). If you want to know which are the network affiliate stations in your market, you can look it up in your television guide.

The Ratings Game

The networks are extremely competitive with one another for ratings. Remember what we've said about ratings. Television networks turn a profit from the revenues they charge for commercial airtime. The only exception to this is public television, which is privately funded through government grants, corporate sponsorships, and individual pledges. Public television doesn't sell ad time. The other networks make their bread and butter that way. The bigger their ratings, or market share, the more money it costs advertisers to buy a spot.

The ratings battle is a relentless tug-of-war for viewership. Publicists who understand the rules of the ratings game can use this knowledge to their advantage. May, November, and February are "sweeps" periods. During these three months, Nielsen, the entity that measures ratings, monitors the audience numbers for every show that's aired. It's these numbers that define ad rates until the next sweeps period. Network executives go all out during sweeps with explosive materials to tantalize viewers. If you're writing or publishing a book, be aware of sweeps. Controversial books or celebrity tell-alls published during sweeps benefit the most, because their content fits well into producers' sweeps agendas. Any author interviews aired during sweeps will get significantly more on-air promotion from the shows, which can translate into bigger audience numbers and more sales. If you've got a book on a serious or obscure topic, it will be more difficult to secure television coverage during the sweeps months. Sometimes pub schedules can't be adjusted just based on sweeps period, but it's a good thing to keep in the back of your mind if you have an option on pub date.

Please stay aware of how competitive the networks are. It's not just during sweeps either. That very competition is part of what propels their newscasts and talk shows to such market dominance. They have to pack a real wallop with their topic and interview choices, because another one of the networks is always waiting in the wings, ready to seduce their viewers away. If you keep this in mind whenever you pitch network producers, it will give you an edge. With that said, here are the different kinds of network shows that do author interviews and/or coverage.

Morning Shows

Network morning shows boast the largest and most consistent audience base. *The Today Show, The Early Show,* and *Good Morning America* are all examples of top daily network morning shows. Though the names, anchors, and ratings may change over time, the format and structure of these shows remain ostensibly the same. They are broadcast live from New York in-studio, air from 7:00 to 9:00 AM, and are hosted by two or three regular anchors. They do a combination of hard news, lifestyle and entertainment, and weather, and feature one or two author interview segments per show. If you're publicizing a book, securing an author interview on a network morning show is a real coup. The typical author segment on one of these shows lasts anywhere from three to five minutes. ABC, NBC, and CBS also have weekend editions of their morning shows. The longest running of the three is *CBS Sunday Morning.* Author segments on *CBS Sunday Morning* are usually ten to fifteen minutes in length and are taped on location.

Prime-Time Magazines

Another type of popular network news show is the one-hour prime-time newsmagazine. Examples include *20/20, Dateline, 60 Minutes,* and *48 Hours.* Taped on location, these news-driven shows are hosted by teams of well-known, on-air journalists. Unlike morning shows, which feature short interview segments done live in-studio or via satellite, prime-time newsmagazines dedicate at least twelve to fifteen minutes per story, shoot a lot of background video footage or "B-roll," and present only a few stories per show. It isn't unusual for a two-hour taping to be edited down to a twelve-minute piece.

Until recently, prime-time newsmagazines were weekly. However, viewership has risen so much over the past five years that some of them have increased their air schedule to two or three broadcasts per week, as well as frequent specials. Network prime-time newsmagazines give equal time to both sides of an issue. If you're pitching one of these shows on a specific topic, remember—they will always present both sides. Make sure that whomever you're trying to book on one of these shows understands this completely before you pitch any of the producers.

Prime-time newsmagazines also do extensive one-on-one, in-studio and on-site interviews with major newsmakers, such as Monica Lewinsky's interview on *20/20,* Bill and Hillary Clinton's interview on *60 Minutes,* and Michael Jackson's interview on *Prime Time Live.* Prime-time newsmagazines reach tens of millions of viewers. Their producers enjoy working with publishers because authors are excellent expert sources who round out coverage.

Prime time is 8:00–11:00 PM Eastern and Pacific Standard Time. All shows after the 11:00 PM news are considered part of the late-night lineup.

Talk, Talk, Talk!

The late-night talk arena is arguably the most volatile of all the network timeslots. Late-night shows come and go in the blink of an eye, so it's important, if you're targeting author interviews on any of these outlets, that you do continual research on which shows are hot and which are being replaced. They air Monday through Friday, range in running time from a thirty-, sixty-, or ninety-minute format, and are live-to-tape. Some examples of late-night talk shows are *The Late Show with David Letterman, The Tonight Show with Jay Leno, The Late Late Show with Craig Kilborn,* and *Late Night with Conan O'Brien,* among many others. Some of these shows are taped in the afternoon or early evening and aired that same night; others are aired live and take viewer call-ins.

There are three standard variations on interview formats for late-night talk. Letterman and Leno, for example, do one-on-one interviews, giving each guest one or two short segments, but allowing them to remain on-set during the entire show. When the guest completes her interview, she relinquishes the "hot spot" or guest chair to the next person and moves quietly to the other end of the interview couch. This format allows for a comfortable and entertaining banter between guests. When the *Tom Snyder Show* was in production, it offered a more formalized one-on-one environment, in which each guest was interviewed on-set alone over several longer segments. Snyder was shot live, and his guests took viewer call-ins. *Bill Maher* is a stellar example of the third variation, the panel. It's shot live-to-tape in the afternoon, then aired in the evening.

Though late-night producers tend to shy away from straight author interviews, they will occasionally invite celebrities who are touting a book to make an appearance. Panel shows such as *Bill Maher* on HBO offer the most opportunities for literary guests, as they use experts in addition to mainstream celebrities. A spot on a late-night talk show can dramatically increase book sales. A word to the wise: Don't pitch a late-night producer on a book unless there's an obvious celebrity angle, a quirky, comedic hook, or the show is a panel format and you have a strong expert. If you pitch to producers promiscuously, it's like crying wolf. You lose credibility. Be conscious of their busy schedules and selective about what you present to them, and they will respond to you with more enthusiasm and respect.

More Network Ops

In addition to morning shows, prime-time newsmagazines, and late-night talk, network newscasts present a provocative array of coverage options for authors. Some examples include: *World News Tonight with Peter Jennings, The Evening News with Dan*

Rather, NBC Nightly News, and *Nightline,* which combines elements of both a network newscast and a one-on-one talk show. The network news shows are the most watched of any national newscasts in the country for myriad reasons. As mentioned earlier, if you have a television, you can access network programming, whereas cable and satellite are subscription driven. The broadcast networks have been in existence for over half a century. Though cable is starting to give the networks a real run for their money in terms of ratings, cable has only been widely embraced by the mainstream for a little over a decade. When it comes to viewer loyalty, the networks are still on top. I'm fascinated by the evolving competition between network and cable news and wonder how long the broadcast networks will maintain their dominance.

Every so often, network news shows do author interviews. The circumstances are specific, however. Major breaking stories require a steady stream of camera-savvy experts to comment on events as they develop. A resourceful and proactive publicist knows how to seize the reins in these situations. Once a hot story is unleashed on the public, all the news shows scramble for exclusive interviews, video footage, or any angle their competitors don't have. Consider for a moment big stories that have hit and how the networks, as well as other news organizations, handled them: John F. Kennedy, Jr.'s plane crash; the O. J. Simpson chase and subsequent murder trial; the Monica Lewinsky scandal; 9/11 and the war in Iraq; among countless others. In each instance, virtually every television news outlet dedicated hour upon hour of coverage. Producers must fill that airtime with compelling content. Authors are an ideal resource.

Expertise Sells

Remember when the gang riots in Los Angeles exploded onto the news front several years ago? At the time, I was representing football Hall-of-Famer and activist Jim Brown, whose autobiography I had helped to put on the *New York Times* bestseller list about a year earlier. Jim was now in the process of building a successful prison rehabilitation program that utilized former gang members as project facilitators. He understood the hearts and minds of these young men from a rare and intimate vantage point not shared by conventional academic experts. Jim and I both knew that his perspective on the gang wars was newsworthy in and of itself because of his close and unusual proximity to so many of its members. I contacted all the producers at the major news and talk shows, offering Jim as an authority from the inside. The response was overwhelming. Jim did dozens of national interviews, each one more moving than the next. In fact, his presentation touched so many viewers that, to this day, letters are still coming in. As you can see, network news is a great place for an author, but there has to be a hard news connection the author can be tied to.

Special Programming

Broadcast networks are always adding new information-based shows to their lineup and experimenting with different formats. *The View,* on ABC, is a midmorning talk show, featuring a panel of female coanchors led by Barbara Walters. Another example of programming that falls under this umbrella are prime-time specials. Prime-time specials are typically produced in one of two ways. The first is in-house, in which the production team works for the network. The second is an outside production, in which an independent production entity produces the special and the network airs it. These specials can be terrific platforms for author visibility and shouldn't be overlooked. You won't find information about them in media guides, however. You have to call the programming departments at the networks, inquire what specials they have in production both in-house and outside, and obtain the contact names and numbers. More on this when we discuss media databasing.

Syndicated TV

Now that we've examined network talk, I want to introduce you to the world of syndication. The vast majority of national television talk shows aired on local broadcast stations are syndicated.

One-hour, live-to-tape, female-oriented shows like *Oprah, Sharon Osbourne, Montel,* and *Ricki Lake;* entertainment newsmagazines such as *Entertainment Tonight, Access Hollywood,* and *Extra;* late-night formatted afternoon shows such as *Caroline Rhea* and *Live with Regis & Kelly;* and tabloids like *Inside Edition* are all syndicated. Other types of syndicated programming include game shows like *The New Hollywood Squares* and *Wheel of Fortune,* dramatic series such as *Buffy the Vampire Slayer* and children's shows like *The Mighty Morphin' Power Rangers,* among many others.

Nationally syndicated television is a complex topic. From a book publicity standpoint, here are the basics you need to know: A syndicated television show is owned and produced by one company—the production company; sold to local broadcast stations all across the country by another company—the syndicator; and bought by programmers at local stations—the affiliates. The affiliates can be independent stations or network affiliate stations.

Let's use *Oprah* as our model. *Oprah* is owned and produced by Harpo Productions; the show is syndicated by King World; and the stations who broadcast it are the show's affiliates. In Chicago, for example, *Oprah* is broadcast on WLS channel 7, the local network affiliate for ABC. If you book an author on a new, nationally syndicated show, you need to inquire about the show's "clearances," meaning how many markets have bought the show. This is critical information, because it will tell you exactly what percentage of the country will see the interview.

Syndicated Talk

Let's explore in more detail the formats of the most common types of syndicated talk shows. Though each show will occasionally vary its approach to boost ratings, if you understand the fundamental structure, you can always adjust your pitch depending upon the author and subject.

One-hour, live-to-tape talk shows, such as *Crossing Over with John Edwards, Montel,* and *Oprah,* air daily, Monday through Friday. They tape on average two shows per day, four to five days a week, and air them anywhere from a few days to several weeks after they're taped. They feature one topic per show, with four to five personal stories and an expert. "Personal stories" are individuals whose lives or experiences illustrate the topic of the show. For example, if *The John Walsh Show* is doing "children from divorced homes who become violent," the producers would want four violent children who were raised in broken homes, their parents or stepparents, and an expert on youth violence. Or say, for example, *Montel* was focusing a show on rape. The producers would want four or five rape victims and their assailants or family members, and a psychologist. The bottom line on personal stories is that they are the meat and potatoes of every show. No matter how good an expert or topic, if the personal stories aren't dramatic and compelling, the show's ratings can suffer.

The one-hour syndicated talk show has changed enormously over the past five years. More and more, these shows are driven by entertainment rather than information. As a result, authors who are booked as experts are getting far less airtime. One of the ways book publicists are responding to this problem is by pitching authors, whenever possible, for their personal stories rather than their expertise. Consider for a moment our example in chapter 1 of the psychologist who wrote a book about bulimia, who also had a daughter with the disease. That author would be an ideal personal story candidate because of her own experiences. Not every author fits the mold of a personal story or wants his private life used as a publicity hook. Those who do have a decided media advantage.

Let Me Entertain You

Entertainment newsmagazines such as *Entertainment Tonight* are widely watched and among the best outlets for author coverage. They air daily in the early evening (most of them five, some six nights a week), are taped on location, and run one half-hour. The format of these shows is straightforward. They spotlight one or two five-to-seven-minute cover stories per episode, and several shorter pieces typically ranging from one to three minutes. Though some stories vary greatly, typically, they combine two elements—an interview and B-roll. The interview is conducted at a relevant location, perhaps a film set, soundstage, bookstore, celebrity's home, or on-site at a major event. Often these shows will shoot their own B-roll footage, or they will ask the publicist if the interviewee has any video footage available in his personal archives.

Let me give you an example of a typical entertainment newsmagazine piece to help clarify your understanding. You've written a cookbook of movie star cake recipes. *Entertainment Tonight* wants to do a cover story on your book. Here's how they'd probably construct the piece: The show would send a correspondent and camera crew to your home for a one-on-one interview. Then, you would be asked if you had any video footage of celebrities who are featured in your cookbook actually baking a cake. If you had such footage, the show would edit in parts of it as B-roll. If not, the producers would assign their own production crew to shoot it with your approval.

Entertainment newsmagazines, like all syndicated programs, are competitive with one another. If an author does one of these shows, the others usually won't take him. When we delve into the art of pitching, I'll teach you my secret for how to negotiate around this hurdle.

What's B-Roll?

I want to take a moment to explain exactly what "B-roll" means. The best way is by example. Say Nicole Kidman is interviewed by David Letterman, and during her interview, a short clip from her newest movie is shown. That clip is B-roll. Here's another example: You're an author, and you've written a book on country line dancing. *Extra* is scheduled to interview you at home. The crew is also going to your favorite club to shoot footage of you teaching people these line dances. When the piece airs, it features your one-on-one interview, with video from the club edited in. That video is B-roll.

Live-to-Tape

Shows such as *Sharon Osbourne* are live-to-tape, run one hour, and feature several one-on-one interviews per show. Their format mimics late-night talk, but their content is female-driven. These shows spotlight personalities and experts, as opposed to personal stories representing one topic. The producers of these shows look for celebrity authors, as well as books on parenting, personal growth, health and fitness, and fashion, among other subjects of interest to women. Of all the syndicated shows, these offer the most on-air opportunities for authors who don't have extensive media experience.

Sometimes, syndicated talk shows are live. For example, *Live with Regis & Kelly,* hosted by Regis Philbin and Kelly Ripa, is produced live in front of a studio audience. More and more, however, syndicated talk is going with live-to-tape as opposed to live format. *Live with Regis & Kelly* is a terrific show and an exception to the new norm.

Fundamentals of Cable Programming

National cable television presents a colorful bounty of author coverage possibilities. There are countless cable networks, the vast majority of which air many news and talk shows. It would be impossible to review every cable station in the country and the formats of all the different shows, but if you know the fundamentals of how cable programming functions, you'll be able to pitch any show on any cable network.

CNN, CNBC, Fox News Network, and MSNBC are among the leading cable news networks in the world. CNBC and MSNBC are part of the NBC family. Fox News Network is owned by Fox. There are so many opportunities for author coverage on these networks, it boggles the mind. Though they produce a broad range of programming, all their shows fall into one of two categories: live and taped. The live shows tend to focus more on hard news, hot topics, and opinions of prominent personalities and experts; the taped shows offer up a more expansive array of feature stories that may or may not be hard or breaking news. Most of the shows on these networks are produced in-house. However, if you're researching author interview options, it's always a good idea to call the programming department of each cable network and ask if they have new shows in production that may not be listed in current media guides or specials that are being produced by outside production companies. Remember, all you need are the names and numbers of production contacts for whatever show you're interested in pitching.

In addition to news outlets, there are dozens upon dozens of special-interest national cable networks covering a range of topics from sports, health, home and garden, entertainment, government, music, biographies, history, and medicine to education, travel, science and discovery, adventure, animals, books, cooking, shopping, weather, and nostalgia. These networks are chock full of shows that do interviews. The secret is knowing how to research their programming.

The Rewards of Good Research

A quick side note: Some of the dramatic cable networks, such as USA, Lifetime, the Sci-Fi Channel, American Movie Classics, and premium channels like HBO, Showtime, and Cinemax also air shows that do interviews. Though we'll get into details about research later in this book, there's one thing I'd like to point out again here, as it's so important. The shows on these networks are either produced in-house or by outside production companies. Often, the media guides will only tell you about the shows produced in-house. You must physically telephone the programming departments at the cable networks and inquire about every show that does interviews and how and where they're produced. Once you have a handle on who produces what for which networks, getting your author on cable becomes infinitely easier.

Let me share an example with you. One of the authors my company represents was touring New Orleans, the largest city near her hometown. We wanted to land her a major national television interview, but there weren't any viable national network or cable possibilities out of New Orleans. One of my account executives was watching the Romance Channel one evening and saw a travel special on romantic escapes for couples. The next day, she called the programming department at the Romance Channel and asked if that show was still in production. They informed her that yes, another thirteen episodes were being shot, but it was an outside production. They gave her the name of the production company and executive producer, whom she called immediately. She pitched the producer on interviewing our author about romantic vacation ideas in New Orleans and other out-of-the-way places in Louisiana. The producer loved the idea and booked a one-on-one, on-location interview with our author that ran over thirty minutes, during which her book was promoted vigorously.

Bear in mind, this travel show was not listed in any of the media guides, because it was a special series produced by an independent production company. Had my account executive not called the programming department and asked aggressive questions, we would never have known about this fabulous opportunity. Remember what we talked about with front- and side-door approaches? Cable is a palace of side doors just waiting to be opened.

Before we exit cable, let me leave you with one more thought that underscores this point. A&E, Lifetime, and The History Channel, among other national cable networks, do biographies and documentaries that require on-air experts. These shows aren't listed in most media guides. If you call the programming departments of these cable networks and ask them which production companies they work with most frequently, they're usually quite happy to provide you with contact information. Then you can call the production companies directly and discuss with them what they're working on and how your author (or authors) might be worked in as expert interviews. Remember, look beyond the obvious. The media guides will tell you what's obvious. It's up to you to take it to the next level.

Superstations

Returning to our discussion of national television, superstations are another superb national outlet for author interviews. There are two primary superstations: WOR out of Secaucus, New Jersey, and WGN out of Chicago, Illinois. Both of these stations air in hundreds of markets across the country. They aren't cable, syndicated, or network. They're broadcast outlets that air nationally. If you get an author interviewed on either one of their newscasts or on one of their talk shows, it will reach tens of millions of viewers, just like a network.

Satellite Networks

The popularity of satellite television, such as DIRECTTV, is slowly gaining momentum. There are many satellite television networks that do author interviews. The problem with satellite networks is that unless they have some cable clearance, their audiences are not as large as other national television outlets. When we talk about how to research media, I'll explain where and how to find information about satellite networks.

Television to Fly By

An interesting digression, before we conclude our discussion on national television outlets—many of the broadcast and cable networks, such as NBC and CNN, among others, have started producing special news and informational programming for airport gates and in-flight entertainment. If you're struggling to secure author coverage on mainstream programming, these specialized productions present an exciting and viable option.

Local Programming

Let's move on to local television. There are three types of local television channels: independent, network affiliate, and regional cable. All three outlets produce and air a variety of local shows that welcome author interviews. Some cities have more local programming than others. On average, local network affiliate shows pull in bigger audience numbers than their independent counterparts, but there are exceptions to that rule in certain markets.

There are three basic types of locally produced shows that do author interviews: morning or afternoon shows, newscasts, and public affairs shows. The local morning shows are a critical part of a successful author tour. Local morning shows air live with a studio audience somewhere during the 6:00–11:00 AM time slot. Depending upon the market and show, they are typically sixty or ninety minutes in length, though some are two hours, and feature news and lifestyle stories. Though all local morning shows vary in terms of format, length of interview segments, and number of on-air hosts, they are consistent in their focus—events, people, and news of local interest.

In some markets, instead of a big local morning show, they have a midafternoon broadcast. Similar in format and substance to the morning show, it airs near lunchtime or in the 2:00–3:00 PM range. Larger cities can have two competing local morning shows, or a competing morning and afternoon show. Whenever you pitch one of these shows, always ask if it's directly competitive with another local production. Otherwise, you could end up booking two competitive shows and harming your relationship with both producers.

Local newscasts, like their network counterparts, cover hard and breaking news, with an occasional intriguing or warm, fuzzy feature piece. Local news producers usually only book author interviews if there's a local angle such as a tie-in to a local event, or if the author is a major celebrity or newsmaker. When I walk you through the pitching process, we'll talk about publicity techniques for circumventing the local angle obstacle and securing author interviews on regional newscasts.

The third type of local television program is the public affairs show. The PBS affiliate often has the most popular public affairs programming. Public affairs shows focus on issues specific to their municipality, such as city government, the school board, local law enforcement, etc. Most of them are taped, run thirty to sixty minutes, and air early on Saturday or Sunday mornings.

Another type of local television show peppered throughout the country is the one-on-one interview show hosted by a local personality or celebrity. Unfortunately, these shows are slowly being erased from the broadcast landscape and are being replaced by nationally syndicated programming that pulls in higher ratings.

Regional cable is one of the swiftest growing mediums in the country. It offers book publicists an ocean of new author coverage opportunities. Almost every major market has at least one regional cable station; many have several. Most regional cable stations are twenty-four-hour local networks. They're like mini-CNNs for local areas. Some examples and their territories include: NY1—the five boroughs of New York; Chicagoland Cable—the Windy City and all outlying suburbs; New 12 Connecticut—the southeastern part of the state; and Bay TV—San Francisco and the entire Bay area. Many of these regional cable networks have their own live morning and afternoon shows, one-on-one talk, and special interest programming, among other productions ideal for author interviews.

On the Radio

The other major broadcast medium is radio. There's an old saying in publishing: "Radio sells books." To this day, even with the proliferation of cable and satellite television and the Internet, radio has the most ongoing impact on book sales. There are so many nuances and details to the radio business. In the interest of time and space, I'm going to concentrate on the basics you need to know to facilitate book publicity.

There are three types of radio talk shows: national, regional, and local. Under the national umbrella are network and syndicated. Radio networks are similar to television networks.

They have affiliate stations throughout the country that broadcast their news and talk programming. Examples of major radio networks include CBS, ABC, NBC, Bloomberg, Associated Press Radio, and Talk America Network, among many others. Most of the central bureaus are on the East Coast, although some shows are produced in other parts of the country. NPR (National Public Radio) is to the sound waves kind of what PBS is to television. It's the public radio network. A quick note on NPR—its programming, like that of PBS, is upscale and educational and presents terrific interview opportunities for literary writers. NPR's main bureau is in Washington, D.C.; however, it can facilitate interviews through its affiliate stations.

Syndicated radio shows, like syndicated television shows, are sold to local stations to be aired. *The Howard Stern Show, The Jim Bohannon Show, Entertainment Tonight with Leeza Gibbons,* and *Imus in the Morning* are all examples of top syndicated radio shows. Regional radio shows reach several local markets in one geographic vicinity. Sometimes these shows are syndicated by a small syndicator, who sells them to specific regions as opposed to nationwide, or they're broadcast on a local station that has such a powerful signal that the show reaches markets outside the station's primary demographic. Take, for instance, WGN Radio in Chicago. Though the station's main audience is the Chicago metropolitan area, WGN is so powerful that its shows can be heard in Wisconsin, Indiana, and parts of Michigan.

Local radio is the most intimate and persuasive broadcast venue today. Local radio stations carry a mix of their own live and taped programming, as well as syndicated and network shows. Local radio is divided into two frequencies: AM and FM. AM stations are talk- and news-intensive, ranging from general interest and sports to urban, Christian, nostalgia, and public affairs. FM stations are music-oriented and include a vast spectrum of formats. The rock and roll and alternative music stations on FM have what's called "Morning Zoo" shows, which are edgy, controversial, live early morning talk shows with listener call-ins that target a younger, hip demographic. Morning Zoo shows frequently do in-studio author interviews, but the author has to be on his toes and have a good sense of humor. Some FM stations are completely dedicated to talk. Those that are traditionally target a younger, less conservative audience. Other FM interview options include early morning guest spots on soft rock, adult contemporary, and smooth jazz stations, which mix in select interviews with their morning news, traffic, and weather.

Words to Drive By

Radio time periods are categorized as dayparts and include morning, afternoon, evening, and nighttime drive, plus late-night. The most desirable daypart for author interviews, in terms of selling books, is morning or evening drive. The top-rated, locally-produced shows on AM are live with call-ins during drive times. When people are in their cars listening to the radio, they're a captive audience. The best radio coverage you can obtain for an author is a live-drive show with call-ins. Authors get anywhere from fifteen to sixty minutes on air, depending upon the news of the day and the overall format of the show. Sometimes if it's a slow news day and the host and author are really hitting it off, they'll keep the author on for two or even three hours. Though this is rare, if an author knows how to give good radio interviews, it can and does happen.

Geography for Radio Interviewees

Whether you're doing a live or taped interview on network, syndicated, regional, or local radio, you have three logistical options: in-studio—you are interviewed at the radio station; phoner—the interview is done over the telephone; and on-site remote—you are interviewed in person at an event or location outside of the studio. The best option is always live in-studio, because you'll get maximum airtime, the sound quality is far superior, and the rapport between you and the host is much richer. Phoners should only be done when an in-studio isn't possible.

Radio phoners are most effective when they are booked in clusters over a specific period of time. In publicity, we call those clusters "Radio Telephone Tours." What that means is an author does twenty or thirty radio telephone interviews, one after another over several days, in order to create a broadcast blitz effect. However, I again emphasize, radio phoners should only be done in conjunction with a Radio Telephone Tour, or if an in-studio is not viable. In-studio is always the better alternative. Radio can also be done via a satellite tour, which I'll explain in further detail when we examine publicity tours. Stay tuned.

In addition to radio shows, radio newscasts will some-times feature author interviews. These are usually done one of two ways: Either the author will be interviewed live for five or ten minutes, or they will be taped for fifteen or twenty minutes, then the piece will be edited down into vignettes and aired on news-casts throughout the day.

The Subtle Giant

There's something about radio I want you to take to heart. If you're publicizing a book, radio is a powerful medium for inspir-ing sell-through. Yes, of course television and print are important, as they ignite the big bang of awareness necessary to get the sales ball rolling. But it's radio that keeps books consistently moving off the shelves long after the frenzy of pub date marketing has passed. Think of radio as the subtle giant with the longest reach.

The Role of the Book Publicist

*N*OW THAT WE'VE JUST REVIEWED ALL THE DIFFERENT TYPES OF PRINT and broadcast media, I want to let you in on something that the average person isn't aware of. Eighty-five percent of the feature stories you see on television or read about in the newspapers are publicist generated. In this country, publicists play a key role in the dissemination of information. We're in a position to be the media's greatest asset or worst nightmare. It all depends upon our own individual sense of professionalism.

Producers, editors, and reporters are challenged with the formidable task of providing a steady flow of news that informs, entertains, and enlightens. Not an easy job, even for the most seasoned veterans. Publicists who know how to play their cards right can develop lifelong, mutually fruitful relationships with powerful print and broadcast journalists and gain entrance into their inner sanctum.

A good publicist is acutely aware of exactly how the media works. She recognizes the day-to-day responsibilities of her contacts, ranging from the creative aspects of the job, deadlines, and lead times to policies, procedures, and the rules of the game.

A media contact can spot a greenhorn publicist immediately. Why? It's more about attitude than aptitude. A confident, elegant voice speaks volumes. Many novices are either too tentative or overly cocky on the phone. For experienced media people, either scenario is a dead giveaway that they're dealing with an amateur who doesn't yet fully comprehend her role. In this chapter, we're going to talk about the role of the book publicist, the terminology we use, and the subtle nuances of public relations rarely discussed in a classroom or on the job. You'll find yourself referring back to this chapter throughout the course of reading this book. Let's start with the basics.

A Delicate Balance

The book publicist is the middle-person between the source of news (i.e., the author or book) and the media. As a publicist, you're always doing a precarious balancing act between garnering coverage for your author that motivates sales and giving the media what it wants. Sometimes it's tough to engineer opportunities that achieve both ends simultaneously. For example, say you've got an author who's written a provocative book on women's issues, with a chapter on abortion. Though it's only one small part of the book, the media chooses to make abortion their primary focus, because it's controversial and will likely goose ratings. It's up to you as the publicist to get things back on track. The trick to being successful in this type of situation is knowing how to pitch alternative angles that are equally interesting, but that don't misrepresent or exploit the book.

Remember what we explored earlier about developing myriad angles for every campaign, which you can grab like rabbits out of a hat? This is one of the reasons why that's so important. As a publicist, you never want to get caught off guard, without at least ten or fifteen fresh story ideas that you can pitch right on the spot. It will be your saving grace time after time. If you're a novice in publicity, before you even pick up the telephone to pitch a producer or reporter, you should be prepared with ten solid and diverse story ideas, so no matter what initial response you get from someone, you can counterpoint with impressive ideas. As you become a more seasoned practitioner of the craft, you'll find that your response mechanism is honed automatically. After nearly twenty years of publicizing books, if I'm on the phone with a producer and he tells me, "No, I'm not interested in that," I go into automatic gear, generating angle after angle as naturally as breathing. The same can happen to you if you cultivate your creative instincts. It's so critical because the media, as mentioned before, will often go for the ratings, the tabloid perspective. It's the publicist's job to temper media demands and provide angles that meet their needs, while still showcasing the book and author in a dignified, intriguing light.

Sometimes you have to exercise the excruciatingly painful privilege of saying "no." That's often easier said than done. Imagine that you've been pitching a specific national television show for months to interview an author. Finally, after endless conversations, faxes, and mailings, you're rewarded for your persistence, and the booking comes through. The only caveat is that the producer wants to sensationalize the topic of the book. You try to convince her otherwise, spewing forth a barrage of additional angles. Alas, no dice. It's the controversy that's got her hooked. What do you do? You don't want to cancel the booking because it's good national exposure for your author, nor do you wish to alienate the producer with whom you're likely to book many shows over the years.

Nobody ever said being a publicist was easy. Here's the rule of thumb: Stick to your guns, but communicate with the author your dilemma and make the final decision as a team. In the end, it's the author who will be in the hot spot. Share with her your perspective. If the author still insists she wants to do the interview, despite the risks, coach her on how to control as much of the interview environment as possible. Later in this book, we'll talk about the interview process in depth, so whether you are the author or the media coach, you'll command a firm grasp on interview techniques, which will be helpful in these and other types of circumstances. The balancing act is never simple, but it's one of the publicist's most important responsibilities. In many ways, as a publicist you serve two masters—your client, who is the author or publisher, and the media. Without a solid relationship with the latter, you're restricted in what you can accomplish for the former.

Keeping Current

Literary publicists must also have a keen eye for current events. Let me put it to you this way: How can you pitch an author to a major television show that you've never seen or a magazine that you've never even skimmed? Too many publicists don't do their homework before they start pitching an author to the media. It's the pet peeve of producers, reporters, and editors: A publicist calls them up and pitches a story that's completely inappropriate for their format or audience. For example, you wouldn't pitch *Nightline* to interview a psychic about predictions for Hollywood romances, because *Nightline* is a serious news show, and that wouldn't fit its format or be appropriate for its viewers. Conversely, the psychic could be a great interview for an entertainment news magazine like *Entertainment Tonight* or a one-hour talk show like *Montel* or *John Walsh*. The bottom line here is that, if you're publicizing a book, it's really up to you to monitor the media you pitch. That doesn't mean sitting in front of the boob tube all day long. What it does mean is recording the big national shows once a week and spending a few hours watching the tape, perusing the major national newspapers and magazines once or twice a month, and following regular bylines. You can also stay on top of what the national television shows are doing through the newspapers. *USA Today,* for example, does a daily boxed feature in the Life section, listing the talk show topics for that day. Local newspapers do the same thing for radio. I can't emphasize how vital it is to watch, read, and listen. Journalists *know* when a publicist hasn't ever read their paper or seen their television show. It makes them angry because they feel as if everyone's time is being wasted.

Care and Feeding of Authors

Another role of literary publicists is hand-holding, and its impact and influence on a campaign should never be underestimated. Authors need reassurance. They need to feel protected by their publicists and secure in their role as experts and spokespeople. If you're an author and you're publicizing your own book, this may sound odd, but you need to hold your own hand. In other words, you need to make a conscious effort to maintain an emotional and psychological balance throughout the course of your campaign.

Publicity can be a frustrating and overwhelming endeavor, especially if it's new terrain for you. The only way to conquer the challenges publicity presents is to keep yourself anchored and grounded. The same is true if you're a publicist and you're representing an author. Authors often have fragile egos. Think about it. Imagine if you put all your time and energy into writing a book, spilling your mind and soul on parchment for all the world to see. It can make people vulnerable. It's up to the publicist to imbue the author with a sense of strength, enthusiasm, and most importantly, perspective. The publicist needs to communicate with authors regularly, helping them to develop realistic expectations about what their campaign can achieve. Additionally, you need to be honest with authors and tell them if they're making any mistakes.

One of the most valuable insights I can impart to you concerns detail. It comes down to basic human nature. When you communicate with an author, whether it be in writing or verbally, share with her pertinent details. For example, if you just confirmed an interview for an author, tell the author how the producer responded, if he was excited about setting up the interview, and what it was you said that finally clinched the booking. If, on the other hand, it was a tough sell and you had to cajole the producer into committing to an interview, tell the author that, too. Why? The more information you give an author before she does an interview, the more prepared she will be, and thus more confident and secure.

If you're the author and booking your own interviews, do the same for yourself. When you confirm an interview, ask the producer or reporter questions like: How long do you anticipate the piece will be when it runs? Is there any information you didn't see in my book that you'd like me to have handy? Is this interview live or taped? Will you be interviewing any other author or experts about this subject? Is there anything in particular you'd like me to focus on? Whether you're a publicist for someone else or yourself, details are critical. Information is not only power, it's security and will give you a profound sense of confidence going into the interview.

A good publicist knows how to calm down an angry or hysterical author. The natural human instinct when an upset author calls, complaining about publicity issues, is to react defensively. Don't do it. Simply sit back and encourage the author to vent. When he's finished, thank him for his honesty, and explain how wonderful it is that he feels comfortable enough to share his feelings and not make you guess what he's thinking. This caring, calm response will disarm the author and defuse his wrath. Then, quickly and efficiently extricate yourself from the conversation, explaining to him that you've taken notes on all his comments and will get back to him tomorrow with a response and plan of action. That way, you have time yourself to cool down, collect your thoughts, and seek advice from a colleague if you need to.

The Fine Art of Positioning

The book publicist's most critical function is the art of positioning. Positioning is the subtle element that creates the single largest impact on a campaign. If you want to know the ins and outs of publicity, public relations, and promotions, positioning is the key that unlocks all the mysteries. It's like painting. Pros do it with a brush; novices do it with their thumbs. The best way to explain positioning is through example.

Positioning isn't something that's only done in the public relations business. We use positioning every day in our lives without even being aware of it. Let's say you're a teenager and you need to borrow your father's car for the evening, because you want to study with your boyfriend at the library. When you ask your father for the keys, you say, "Dad, I've got to study tonight for finals. Brad's even getting out of football practice to help me. Do you mind if I take your car to the library?" When you confirm with your boyfriend that you'll see him later, the way you present it to him is, "Brad, I can't wait to see you tonight. Yeah, we can get some studying done, but the best part is going to be holding your hand."

You were truthful to both your dad and boyfriend about what you wanted to do and where you wanted to go, but your *presentation* to each was different. That's what positioning is. *Positioning is presenting a specific perspective to a specific audience for a specific response.* We'll apply this definition to our example. You had two audiences to whom you had to deliver a message: your father and your boyfriend. You altered how you presented your perspective, based on your understanding of their needs, point of view, and predisposition.

Let's look at a hypothetical publicity example. A major movie star has written a tell-all autobiography in which he reveals intimate details of his life, from his early religious upbringing, Ivy League education, and hungry years as a struggling actor to his five marriages, deeply felt political convictions, and experiences raising children. The book, fueled by a mammoth marketing budget, is already igniting controversy because of its deeply irreverent undertones. As the publicist, you're responsible for sorting out the positioning of the book.

Your positioning to the publishing industry is that this book promises to be one of the hottest titles of the year, due to the enormous sales push behind it. Your overall positioning to the mainstream public is that this book is refreshing in its unprecedented honesty. You decide to position the candor, which could, for some, be turning a negative into a positive.

Your next step is how to position it to *specific* audiences within the general populace. For example, a large Christian literary group wants your author as a keynote speaker at one of its luncheons. You want the author to participate because it's great for book sales; however, you also recognize that you need to present a *specific perspective* about the book to this *specific audience.* You emphasize to the Christian literary group the parts of the book in which the author reflects on his spirituality and early childhood memories about religion. You engage their interest by describing how the author will share warm, wonderful anecdotes about this element of his life.

That same day, you receive a tip from someone that the Screen Actors Guild, the union for film actors, is hosting a huge special event for up-and-coming actors, and they're looking for celebrities to speak. You immediately pick up the phone and call the director of SAG to pitch your author as a candidate. When you talk with SAG, you're not going to use the same positioning that you did with the Christian literary group. Your positioning to SAG is that your author knows better than anyone what young actors endure trying to get their big break, and he will dazzle the audience with anecdotes from his own career that are featured in his book.

Here is one of my favorite positioning stories: Several years ago, I was doing publicity for a book on incest coauthored by a psychologist and one of her patients who was a victim. I pitched *Geraldo* on a one-hour special on recovery from sexual abuse. The producer was quite ho-hum and indicated that they'd covered that issue ad nauseam and didn't want to revisit it yet again. I waited a couple of weeks, then repitched the same producer with the following tag line: "Daddy Raped Me—A Daughter's Story of Pain and Forgiveness." The producer flipped and immediately booked an interview with the authors. In fact, when it aired, the broadcast was so moving that it generated thousands of letters from other victims all across America who were inspired to seek help. What happened here? Positioning. When I first spoke to the producer, I positioned the book as more clinical and informative than emotional. In my second conversation with the producer, I positioned the dramatic, human interest side as the focus.

The Three Tiers of Positioning

Positioning is everything. It defines an audience's perspective. The secret to effective positioning is knowing what questions to ask yourself to help you determine what that perspective should be. Positioning a book is three-tiered. Tier one is industry positioning—how should the book be positioned to the publishing trade. Tier two is general positioning—how should the book be positioned to the overall public. Tier three is special-interest positioning—how should the book be positioned to particular sectors of the general populace, such as special-interest groups. Following are the questions I always ask myself before I make positioning decisions.

Questions for Tier One—Industry Positioning

- Does this book set any industry precedents or break any new literary ground?
- How is this book different from any other titles recently published that may be considered similar?
- Is there a large marketing campaign planned or an unusually high publicity budget?
- Are there any marketing, promotional, or publicity plans for this book that could be considered unusual or above and beyond the ordinary?
- Is this book part of a large multibook deal?
- What are the early dramatic rights and ancillary interests, if any?
- Are advance orders higher than anticipated?

Once you answer these questions, you'll have a strong sense of how to present the book to the publishing industry in a way that will intrigue and excite them about its forthcoming release. Tier one positioning is for *sell-in* purposes and should be decided six to eight months before the pub date. If you want to review the timing on sell-in, flip back to the end of chapter 1.

Questions for Tier Two—Mainstream Consumer Positioning

- How will this book affect people's lives?
- What are three words that you feel best describe the message of this book?
- Who will be most interested in this book and why?
- Who will buy this book?
- What will make them buy it?
- Why are the author and book important?
- What's the most fascinating component of this book?
- Is there anything in this book that could make people uncomfortable? If so, what is it and how would it make them uncomfortable?
- Is there anything about the book or author that's unprecedented, trailblazing, or surprising?
- Is this book controversial?
- Does the author reveal any secrets?

Tier two positioning is for sell-through. In essence, this tier establishes the book's image and identity to the public at large.

Questions for Tier Three—Special Interest

- Are there any parts of the book that would appeal to or offend any special-interest groups or individual sectors of the population? Who and why?
- Does this book communicate a message of special significance to any one demographic? If so, how might it impact that audience?
- Is there anything in this book that should be de-emphasized to some people and highlighted to others? If so, which groups and why?

Tier three is also for sell-through, but targets smaller audiences within the general public.

If You're Handed a Lemon . . .

Sometimes positioning is the answer to a crisis. It's so important that you grasp this concept. When you were growing up, did your parents ever tell you to "look on the bright side," "don't be negative," or "it's all in how you look at things?" If they did, consider them your first teachers in the art of positioning. Let me share one more example with you to clarify positioning.

I was doing a twenty-five-city tour for a well-known relationship expert, who was pushing a terrific marriage manual, chock full of great insights and advice for struggling couples. This author was also a wonderful interview, savvy and professional, the kind of person to whom the media gravitate. We were rolling like thunder on her tour. I had all the top national television shows booked, as well as the leading media in all the local tour markets. Suddenly, it started to happen—phone call after phone call from producers, wanting to cancel interviews. I couldn't believe it! After I pulled my shocked self together, I asked them why they were canceling at the last minute like this. It made no sense. One of the producers faxed me a copy of an article announcing that the author just sued her third husband for divorce. "How could someone who's in the process of their third divorce give our audience advice on saving their marriages?" everyone asked.

There had to be a way to reverse the problem and reposition the author to the producers. What did the author and I do? We issued a memo to all of the producers who were trying to cancel, saying, "Who better to relate to couples who are facing marital trouble than a kindred spirit who understands both the joy of healthy love and the pain of disappointment?" The next day, we rebooked nearly all of the interviews that had been cancelled, and the book hit the *New York Times* bestseller list shortly thereafter. Positioning was the key. Although the author's divorce may have momentarily undermined her authority as an expert, we were able to position it as an experience that enabled her to identify and communicate with audiences on a richer level.

Talking the Talk

Next on our agenda for this chapter—publicity lingo! Here are several common terms and phrases book publicists use that I'd like you to familiarize yourself with. I've divided them into two categories: media and publishing.

Media

Hard news stories are divided into three primary time categories: An event that is still unfolding is *breaking;* something that just happened, literally moments ago, is a *spot item;* and a story that has a long shelf life in terms of its relevance and newsworthiness is an *evergreen.*

    B-roll, which we talked about in chapter 3, is video footage edited into an interview to supplement the visual element of the piece. If you've written a golf book and you're interviewed on ESPN, they may ask you to provide *B-roll* of people golfing.

    When a producer promises to *edit-in a still of the book,* that means a close-up shot of the book cover edited into a television interview. For example, when Stephen King was interviewed on *60 Minutes,* they did a close-up shot of his latest book. That's editing-in a still.

    Post-tape and *pre-tape* are phrases publicists use with television producers. Say, for example, you've booked an author to do a live interview on a local network affiliate morning show, and the producer wants to cancel because another celebrity is coming into town on the same day as your author and has no other availability. The best way to handle this frustrating situation would be to encourage a post- or pre-tape. A pre-tape is a taped interview done in studio on the actual set of the television show immediately before a live broadcast. A post-tape is done immediately after a live broadcast. The reason post- and pre-tapes are such a fabulous alternative is that they're easier on a producer's budget, because they're done when the television show is still "up" (i.e., camera crew, host, set, etc.).

If a producer wants to book an author on a television show, but logistics prohibit an in-studio interview, you can always suggest *satellite*. National shows rely on this option all the time. The author goes to a studio near her home, sits in front of a camera, has a small microphone placed in her ear so she can hear the interviewer's questions, and responds directly into a camera. Most satellite sessions are live, although some are taped. The advantage of satellite is that you don't have to lose last-minute interview opportunities because you can't get to a television show on time. Satellite interviews are most frequently used for big breaking stories, when experts are needed right away. Many celebrities are also interviewed by satellite. Satellite is a more expensive option for a television show, usually costing anywhere from $3,000 to $5,000 an interview. Usually, if a show wants a particular guest badly enough, it will gladly absorb the expenditure into its production budget. Sometimes, if a producer is on the fence about booking a satellite interview because of the added cost, it can help if the author and/or publisher are willing to pitch in.

The Skinny on Exclusives

Exclusive and *first* are critical terms to know. I can't tell you how many huge disagreements have ensued between book publicists and producers because of misunderstandings over the misuse of these words. Pay close attention here. There are several kinds of exclusives.

If you give a television show a *full exclusive,* that means you will allow *no other media outlet,* print or broadcast, to interview the author. A *television exclusive* means *no other television show* will be granted an interview with the author, but radio and print are fine. If you offer a television show a *broadcast exclusive,* that means the *author can't do any other television or radio interviews,* but *could do newspaper or magazine interviews.* Most television shows prefer broadcast exclusives, because the print coverage permitted under this arrangement generates tune-in for them.

Genre or format exclusive is the type most frequently requested by television producers, as it's a way for them to win individual battles in the ratings wars. When you promise genre or format exclusive to a show, it means the *author won't do any other interviews on similarly formatted, directly competitive shows.* For example, if you give genre or format exclusivity to *Entertainment Tonight,* your author can't interview on other entertainment newsmagazine shows, such as *Access Hollywood* or *Extra.* The same thing with prime-time newsmagazines. If you give *Dateline* genre/format exclusivity, you will betray the producers' trust if you turn around and book *20/20, 60 Minutes,* or *48 Hours.* Interestingly enough, once you grant any kind of exclusive to a show, other shows are unlikely to book the author anyhow, because they don't want to do a big story that their competitors got first.

Print exclusives are less straightforward. If you offer a magazine or newspaper *a full exclusive,* that means *no other media outlet* will interview your author. *Print exclusive* means *no other print outlet* will interview the author. *Newspaper exclusive* means no other newspaper, and *magazine exclusive* means no other magazine. Wire services and syndicates rarely request exclusives. Genre/format exclusive doesn't apply to print as much as it does to television, because sometimes editors are concerned about competing outlets that may not necessarily be the same genre or format. Instead of genre/format exclusive, editors will often request a *national print exclusive,* which means no other national print. For example, even though *USA Today* is a daily newspaper and *People* is a weekly magazine, they sometimes take a competitive position on interviews.

Radio exclusives are simpler. It's done by genre. For example, Don Imus and Howard Stern have competing shows. Usually, if an author does one, she can't do the other. In terms of local radio, the rule of thumb is that an author can't do radio interviews with two competitive shows and must choose one or the other. Radio is by far the least demanding in terms of exclusives.

A general note on exclusives: *Always ask producers and editors* exactly *what they mean when they say to you, "Do I have an exclusive?" Conversely, be sure you are crystal clear about* exactly *what you are offering when you tell a producer or editor, "I can get you an exclusive."* When negotiating an exclusive with a media contact, make sure you are absolutely clear concerning the following issues:

- What kind of exclusive, specifically, are we talking about?
- Do you mean my author can't do any other interviews at all, or just with outlets that compete with you directly?
- Now that we've clarified what type of "exclusive," I'm going to review with you a list of interview opportunities I'd like to arrange for my author. Please let me know which of these you consider in violation of the exclusive, so that I don't inadvertently make a misstep.

Never lie to the media. *Always* play it straight. This is part of the balancing act we talked about earlier in this chapter. Even though you're fighting for as much coverage for the author as you can get, you must also protect your relationship with the media. Besides, if you try and pull the wool over the media's eyes, the author ends up paying for it in the end, because she gets caught in the crossfire. If a producer or reporter asks you what other interviews the author has done or is scheduled for, tell the truth. It will be discovered one way or another, and you do irreparable damage to your reputation if you try to pull one over on media people.

Granting exclusives, no matter what type, has its pros and cons. On the positive side, when a media outlet is given any kind of exclusive, it promotes the interview much more heavily, which increases author exposure enormously. The negative component, however, is that it limits an author's number of interviews, and can therefore decrease visibility potential.

There is a way to have your cake and eat it, too. Though this won't always work for every book, you can grant different exclusives to different outlets. Say, for example, you're publicizing a celebrity autobiography, full of juicy revelations, and you want to secure all three competing entertainment newsmagazine shows. You could offer one show an exclusive on the author's love life and provide them with a rare, never-before-seen B-roll of the author's first marriage when she was still in high school. The B-roll would be for this show only, and no other outlet would get it. You could give the second show an exclusive sneak peek behind the scenes of the author's newest movie and provide early film footage that has yet to be released to the public. You could pitch the third show on a straight book feature. The secret to this approach is being honest with the producers. Tell each of them up front what they have an exclusive on. Don't try and be cute with them. They'll appreciate your candor, and it will only heighten their respect for both your commitment to do the best for your client and your determination to honor their needs.

First, But Not Only

Exclusives are often contingent upon something called "first." In fact, publicists, producers, editors, and reporters sometimes mix these two words up, saying "exclusive" when what they really mean is "first," and vice versa. That's why I can't recommend enough how important it is to communicate openly with the media contact, to ensure you're both on the same page about what you're promising each other. These two terms can get confusing. Let me try and clear it up for you now.

In television, there are two types of firsts: *first broadcast* and *first genre*. When you grant a television show first broadcast, it means they have the very first author interview out of the gate, and that no other show will air before them. If you give a show first in their genre, it means they have first author interview among their direct competitors, i.e., first entertainment newsmagazine show, first network morning show, etc. Print firsts are slightly more complicated. If you're negotiating first with a newspaper or magazine, the best course of action is to inquire specifically which media outlets they need to precede. That way there's little room for misunderstanding.

A word to the wise: Being honest doesn't mean being a wimp. If a producer tries to strong-arm you, stand up and be heard. Bear in mind what we talked about before. The ratings game is serious business, and a producer's job is to land the most sought-after interviews. In a perfect world, their preference would always be that their show is the only show that gets the story. Obviously, producers understand this isn't realistic from a publicity perspective, but sometimes, just like publicists, they can get a little too aggressive.

For example, you've negotiated a first genre with the entertainment newsmagazine *Entertainment Tonight,* which means your author may do other newsmagazines, but *Entertainment Tonight* has first in its format. You've also promised an exclusive genre with the morning show *Today,* which means *Today* is the only network morning show who gets your author. When you tell each show about the other, they both demand first and threaten to cancel if you don't choose.

In this case, neither one of them has the right to make this request, because neither of them asked for first broadcast. *Entertainment Tonight* wanted first in its genre, and *Today* agreed upon exclusive for morning show only. This is one of the times, as a publicist, that you would have to point out exactly what was negotiated and take a position. Ninety-nine percent of the time, if you're faced with this kind of dilemma and you confidently but respectfully talk it out with the producers, they'll be reasonable and accommodating.

Publishing Terms

Publishing terminology is vast and complex. For our purposes, we're going to focus on words and phrases specific to publicity and public relations. Though all publishers' working calendars vary slightly, outlined below is the average sequence of events.

Galleys are bound, uncorrected page proofs of a book. They are printed three to five months before pub date for publicity, review, and sub rights purposes. They are much more expensive to produce than books, and as such are sent to a very select mailing list. *Pub date* is the official publication date of a book. *Bound book date,* which usually precedes pub date by four to six weeks, is when the actual book is off press. *Ship date,* usually two to four weeks before pub date, is when books are shipped from the warehouse to the distributors and retail outlets.

Blurbs, or *endorsements* as they're sometimes called, are quotes about the book from noteworthy people, generally printed on the back cover or inside jacket. As noted in chapter 1, *sell-in* is selling books into the retail outlets. *Sell-through* is when the general consumer buys the book. A *regional bestseller* is a book that has made the bestseller list of a local daily newspaper, such as the *Los Angeles Times,* the *Chicago Tribune,* and so on. A *national bestseller* is a book that appears on several regional lists or in a major national newspaper, such as *USA Today* or the *Wall Street Journal.* A *New York Times* bestseller is a book that appears specifically on their list. Later on, we'll talk about how a book achieves bestseller status.

Our next chapter covers the publicity process from nuts to bolts. Stay tuned!

The Publicity Process from Nuts to Bolts

*O*NE OF THE FIRST QUESTIONS I ALWAYS ASK NEW CANDIDATES-FOR-hire is if they know the publicity process. If they give me a quizzical look, they've already answered my question. The publicity process is a fundamental element of public relations. No matter how creative you are or how many contacts you have, if you don't know the publicity process itself, it's the equivalent of owning a gas station on an island where there are no cars.

The publicity process is methodical and precise, and must be followed with respect and attention to detail. Rather than simply describe the steps, I'm going to walk you through a mock campaign. Generally speaking, though each campaign is different, the *process* for generating media coverage is the same. Please bear in mind that the purpose of this chapter is to give you a comprehensive overview of the publicity process. We'll cover each step in depth later in the book.

The publicity process is an adventure! The book we're publicizing is entitled *Love 'Em and Leave 'Em* by first-time author Dr. Taylor Lawson. A controversial personal growth title on how to walk away from unfulfilling relationships, it's pub-dated for March, which is eight months from now. The publisher is an independent midsize house, and this book is its lead title for the spring. *We've* just been hired to implement the publicity campaign.

Bear in mind what you've learned about sell-in. Because we're lucky enough to have been brought on board early in the game, we have time to consider how we might contribute to this part of the equation. The publicity process can begin at either sell-in or sell-through, depending upon how much lead time you have before pub date.

Step 1: The Inquisitive Phase

The first thing we need to do is ask the publisher a series of vital questions to help us pinpoint our campaign strategy exactly:

- Could you please confirm pub date?
- When will galleys and bound books be available?
- When are books shipping?
- What are the advance orders so far?
- What's your best guess on initial print run?
- Can you give us a ballpark figure on estimated publicity budget?
- Is there any advance serial rights interest?
- From your perspective, is the author media savvy, or does she need coaching?
- Have you found this author to be easy or more challenging to work with?
- Would your publicity department work in tandem with us, or would we be the primary implementational arm for this campaign?
- When can we get a copy of the manuscript?
- What in-store promotional efforts are your marketing department planning?

Next, we'll need to ask the author some pivotal questions:

- Is this your very first book?
- What are your credentials as an authority on this topic?

- Is your expertise academic, clinical, personal experience, or a combination of all three?
- Have you ever done media interviews before? If so, what interviews did you do? Do you have them on video, and how did you feel about your performance(s)? If not, do you think you would be strong in this area, or will you need media coaching?
- How much time and energy are you willing to spend promoting and publicizing your book?
- Would you be able to help procure personal stories for national television talk shows?
- Do you have any of your own media contacts whom you'd prefer we pitch first?
- Can you send us a detailed bio and résumé?
- Is there anything from your past that might come up during the publicity campaign that we should know about?
- Where are you based?

Once we complete our question-and-answer sessions with both the publisher and author, we can begin step 2 of the publicity process.

Step 2: Devising the Campaign Strategy

Let's summarize the key facts we've learned about Dr. Lawson and *Love 'Em and Leave 'Em.* This is Dr. Lawson's first book, though she's been interviewed extensively on television and radio about abusive relationships. A licensed therapist who was a victim herself of severe emotional abuse at the hands of a longtime lover, she knows this subject inside out and isn't shy about discussing it. Yes, she will do anything and everything to sell books, from finding personal stories, going on tour, and doing radio phoners at the crack of dawn to making personal appearances at women's shelters, giving seminars, and addressing special interest groups. (For all of you reading this book who are authors yourselves, you're probably saying, "That's me! I'll do anything for my book, too." If you're not saying that, you need to readjust your mindset right this minute, because *it takes that kind of commitment to sell books.*) She lives in Philadelphia.

Her publisher is equally as supportive of the book's success, and though they haven't received all their advance orders yet, the staff anticipate a 25,000-copy initial print run. Galleys will be off press in three months, which is five months prior to pub date. Bound books will be available and begin shipping in early February. The publisher doesn't want to spend an exorbitant amount of money on publicity, but will allocate a realistic budget that will enable us to generate the necessary visibility. (In chapter 13, on how to budget PR campaigns, we'll review specific figures and the formulas for arriving at them.)

It's time for us to devise our campaign strategy. Let's look at what we've got to work with. Since we have some lead time, we can pursue sell-in publicity placements in industry trade publications, as well as coverage in long-lead magazines for sell-through. It's always a good idea to do publicity in the author's hometown, so we'll include Philadelphia and northeastern Pennsylvania as key local target markets. We should also create a newsworthy promotional or personal appearance opportunity in Philadelphia to maximize coverage potential. I wouldn't recommend touring Dr. Lawson nationally, as the print run is only 25,000. The rule of thumb on author media tours is that unless the initial print run exceeds 35,000 copies, or you're planning a special grassroots strategy, it's more effective to streamline the approach. (We'll examine tours in depth in chapter 12.)

In lieu of a tour, I'd suggest pursuing national print and broadcast interviews out of New York and Los Angeles, the country's talk show hubs, with the possibility of doing national interviews in other cities, contingent upon individual media interest. I'd also encourage a radio telephone blitz, in which we arrange twenty to thirty radio interviews for Dr. Lawson that she can do by telephone. The radio interviews would be done in clusters, one part of the country at a time.

Now that we've defined our plan of action, communicated it to the publisher and author, and obtained their approval, we can move on to the next step of the publicity process.

Step 3: Writing the Press Kit

Before we even push the power button on our computers, we need to interview Dr. Lawson thoroughly. Remember back in chapter 2, we talked about the importance of the publicist interviewing the author in depth. If we're going to present the most powerful news angles possible to the media, we must know everything we can about Dr. Lawson. What's her personal connection to the subject matter in her book? Why did she write *Love 'Em and Leave 'Em?* What's the primary message of the book? What other issues surrounding the book could be massaged into news stories? What were some of her experiences researching the book? For more thoughts on what kind of questions to ask, flip back to chapter 2. Once we've gently but thoroughly extrapolated every nugget of information we can from the author, it's time to brainstorm *positioning, angles, story ideas,* among other components that will comprise the press kit content. In chapter 8, we'll examine press kits in detail, exploring their function and content and the secret to writing top-notch kits. For our purposes now, we'll touch upon it briefly.

The press kit is a package of materials written specifically for the media, outlining:

- What the book is about
- Why it's newsworthy
- How and why the author is a newsmaker
- Angles and concepts for news stories spotlighting the book

The purpose of the press kit is threefold: to illuminate the newsworthiness of the book and author, persuade the media to interview the author, and provide an enlightening, yet succinct, overview of the book for media who don't have time to read it.

I've always been a firm believer in the impact of press kits. Chock full of valuable data, they can make or break a campaign. Our press kit for Dr. Lawson should include:

- A press release announcing the publication of the book and outlining its newsworthiness
- A bio of the author, skewed to reinforce her credibility as an expert on the subject of her book
- Suggested interview questions
- A topic suggestions sheet for talk producers, listing possible ideas for shows featuring the author for her expert advice or for her personal story
- A pitch letter personalized to each media contact, encouraging him or her to book the author

The press kit is the anchor of a campaign. As soon as we've finished writing the first draft of the press kit pieces, we need to send it to Dr. Lawson and her publisher for their comments and approval. Once we've received their input and edited in their changes, if any, and printed and stuffed the press kit materials into folders (more on press kit folders later), we're ready for the next step in the publicity process.

Step 4: Researching and Databasing Target Media

We're ready to roll with our press kit. Our task now is to assemble our target media list. Remember, we want to hit publishing trades (because we have enough lead time to generate sell-in coverage); national long-lead magazines; local Philadelphia and northeastern Pennsylvania print and broadcast; the top thirty radio stations in the country, in three clusters of ten according to region (i.e., Midwest, etc.); and national print and broadcast outlets.

Quality media research requires an enormous amount of tenacity and creativity. You've got to look under every stone. It's one of the areas where too many PR people get sloppy. The better your research, the more successful your campaign will be.

There are a myriad of annual reference guides and CD-ROMs available that list media outlets. Over the years I've used them all, and I recommend *Bacon's* media directories. Divided into four primary volumes, including Television, Radio, Newspapers, and Magazines, *Bacon's* are easy to work with, thorough, and the most accurate on the market. Let's review each media category in our strategy, and briefly address the nuts and bolts of assembling our target pitch lists.

We can find the publishing trades and long-lead magazines in *Bacon's Magazine Directory*. We'll need to decide what types of magazines would be most appropriate for Dr. Lawson and research specific publications under those headings. For example, I'd suggest we look up women's interest, news, health, and psychology magazines. For local Philadelphia and northeastern Pennsylvania media, the first thing we must do is consult a map to see which markets comprise Philadelphia's outlying areas, as well as the northeastern part of the state. Too often, publicists don't use maps. They hit the well-known cities and don't consider smaller, grassroots markets right near them. This is a mistake. The smaller the pond, the bigger the coverage you can obtain for your author. *You've got to maximize every opportunity.*

Once we have the names of the towns and cities, then we need to look up, by state, all the local and regional television, radio, magazine, newspaper, wire, and syndicated outlets. In this particular case, we'll be researching New Jersey, too, because some of the Philadelphia suburbs are on the New Jersey border. See why maps are so important?

Our next category is national print and broadcast. That means we need to pull from: *Bacon's Newspaper Directory,* which has all the national print outlets listed in the back; the magazine guide, because we're also checking for short-lead publications such as *Newsweek,* etc; the television reference guide, which lists national programming in the front section, delineated by network, syndicated, and network cable; and finally, the radio guide, which lists national radio in the front section and local radio by state and city.

Updating Your Info

Before we start entering all the outlets we've uncovered into a computer database, we have to do verbal updates. Media guides, whether you use *Bacon's* or another source, are compiled annually. There's a tremendous amount of turnover in the media arena, which means that the contact names and other information listed for each outlet may be inaccurate. To ensure we have the most updated media lists as humanly possible, we need to get on the horn and call each and every outlet, verifying if the contact names are correct. For example, let's say the lifestyle reporter for the *Philadelphia Inquirer* is listed as Joe Smith. We would telephone the lifestyle desk and ask, "Is Joe Smith the contact for lifestyle or feature stories?" Though this extensive telephone follow-up may seem tedious, it saves enormous time and money in the long term. Additionally, one of the most unprofessional moves a publicist can make is sending a book and press kit to the wrong person.

When we've verbally confirmed every outlet and contact, we can enter all the information into a media database. Most computer databases are straightforward. Each PR person has her own system, but I'd recommend separate databases as follows: national television, national radio, national print (including magazines), local media, and top thirty radio stations. Each database entry should have: the name of the outlet (*Time* magazine or ABC-TV); title of the show if it's radio or television, or desk if it's print (*The Oprah Show, Howard Stern Show,* or Feature Desk); contact name; telephone number; e-mail; fax number; and contact comments, such as contact's deadlines, production schedules, etc. Each of the databases should also be capable of printing out labels.

With confirmed media lists in hand, we're ready for our next step.

Step 5: Pre-Pitching and Media Mailings

Many publicists do their media mailings immediately upon assembly of their target media lists. I strongly recommend pre-pitching first. Pre-pitching means calling all the media contacts you've compiled, briefly letting them know what you're sending and who the author is. This accomplishes several crucial objectives: It excites the media person and motivates him to keep an eye out for the press kit and book; it establishes an early rapport between you and the media contact, which makes him more receptive when he receives your press materials; it allows you to monitor his initial response, which indicates what interests him the most or least about your book and author, enabling you to tailor your written pitch accordingly; and it gives you an opportunity to ask him to suggest other reporters and producers who should also be on your media list. For example, if you pre-pitch the producer of a local television morning show, he may direct you to a radio show that the morning show works with, or vice versa.

Personalize Your Pitch

Once we've pre-pitched all the contacts on our list, we need to write personalized pitch letters to each. One of my pet peeves is when I see publicists sending out generic pitch letters that say "Dear Editor" or "Dear Producer." Would you like it if you got a letter that was asking you to consider something important, and it didn't even address you by name? It's *absolutely terrible* to do generic mailings. It offends the media and will cause you to lose valuable interview opportunities. I realize that when publicists do generic pitch letters, it's because their backs are against the wall with deadlines and they simply don't have the time to personalize each and every pitch letter. There's a simple solution to that. Instead of formatting the pitch as a formal letter, write it up as a memo, without the "To" in the heading. The heading of the memo would say "Topic" and "From." After Topic, you would write a short, newsy sentence about the book and author. After From, you would have your name and phone number. You'd print out these letters in bulk, and at the corner of each letter, you'd quickly handwrite the contact's name with a quick note and sign it. For example, you might write: "Dear Patty, let's talk soon! Best, . . ." This is the best compromise. You're still printing out a generic pitch. And it takes mere seconds to scribble a five-word note in the corner of each memo. Believe me, when producers and reporters see you took that little extra effort to acknowledge them personally, *it will make all the difference in the world.* Let's take a look at a sample pitch letter.

September 2, 2004

TO:
FROM: Jodee Blanco 312/573-2070

RE: THE NEW YOGA FOR PEOPLE OVER FIFTY

Picture this – a seventy-eight year old man, balding and gray at the temples, with a slight paunch, doing a head-stand, legs reaching out towards the heavens, for thirty minutes; a sixty-seven year old woman plagued with arthritis for years, sitting in a lotus position, arms outstretched, her pain a distant memory; a fifty-five year old attorney, who for decades couldn't touch his toes if his life depended on it, seemingly defying the laws of gravity in a posture that makes his limbs seem made of rubber; a sweet little old grandmother who while waiting for her cookies to finish baking, lays on the kitchen floor, throws her legs clear over her head, and stays like that for twenty minutes, feeling the energy and life-force fill her body; a fifty-year old executive, whose days are riddled with stress, turning her desk chair into a wondrous exercise tool that enables her to reduce the emotional, psychological and physical symptoms of chronic tension.

For years, Yoga was considered a benchmark of the "New Age," and something that conservative, mainstream Americans would be unlikely to adopt as a part of their daily lives. Those days are long gone! Now, Yoga is one of the fastest growing and most talked-about personal health practices in the country. As more and more research emerges about the life-enriching, and indeed sometimes even life-saving benefits of this ancient form of exercise, people from all walks of life are exploring how it can help them.

Suza Francina, author of THE NEW YOGA FOR PEOPLE OVER FIFTY, is one of the most respected and cutting-edge Yoga experts in the world. Her specialty is teaching people how to apply Yoga to help de-accelerate the aging process. With a background in hospice care, she has a profound understanding of what can happen when a person succumbs to aging. "We all have the power to stay younger, longer," Suza emphasizes. "The secret is making a conscious choice to do it, and then following up with consistent action."

Energetic, ebullient, and articulate, Suza Francina is not an interview. She's an experience. She can share with your audience compelling information about:

- Yoga's special benefits for women during the menopausal years
- Yoga's role in preventing and reversing heart disease and other common problems intrinsic to middle and upper age
- Yoga's role in preventing osteoporosis and arthritis
- How Yoga can relieve and reverse the debilitating symptoms of stress
- How Yoga can contribute to a healthier, more vibrant complexion
- Yoga and plastic surgery – the surprising connection
- The surprising facts about Yoga and how it can help combat depression, and other chemical imbalances typical in middle age and older men and women
- Yoga and change of life pregnancies
- Among numerous other subjects

In addition, Suza can create compelling and illuminating visuals on-camera, including a live on-air Yoga session, featuring Suza along with some of her most remarkable students (they range in age from fifty to nearly ninety—we could send you photos and video on each student and you could choose who you'd be most comfortable with); a Yoga session for your audience, in which she could teach them how to transform an ordinary folding chair into one of the most effective and sophisticated exercise tools available; among others.

If you'd like to pre-interview Suza to brainstorm ideas, I'd be happy to set something up. I'll be in touch soon. Thanks for your kindness.

###

The Complete Mailing Package

An impressive and professional PR media mailing should include:

- Personalized pitch letter
- The press kit
- A copy of the book (or galley)
- Your business card

I recommend using strong white envelopes or Jiffy bags. It's best to send mailings first class or priority mail (guaranteed to arrive within three to four days). It's a little more expensive, but your package will get there sooner. That's important. Why? You're trying to impart to the media contact a sense of urgency, that this book is news. If you don't get it there quickly, it diminishes that impression. If first class or priority mail isn't in your budget, make sure when you pre-pitch the media, you let contacts know realistically when they'll receive the book. You can say something like, "As a courtesy, I wanted to get to you in advance. The book should be arriving within the next couple of weeks."

It's also a good idea to have stamps or stickers made that say, "Deadline materials enclosed," which you put on the outside front flap of every envelope. Media contacts receive so many books in a week that often these packages sit on their desks for months, unopened. If you've emphasized on the package itself that you have deadline information inside, it will motivate the media to review your materials immediately. Just a little trick I learned, but it's profoundly effective.

Now that we've done our media mailing, it's time to start pitching!

Step 6: Pitching/Booking and Confirming Media Interviews

I've dedicated a whole chapter to pitching because it's the heart and soul of good publicity, public relations, and promotions. Right now, however, I'm going to walk you through it in synopsized version, so you see how it fits into the publicity process.

About a week after our mailing goes out, we should begin booking. Pitching media is an art form like no other. You need a response mechanism that works faster than the most expensive modem on the market. We're going to pull out our media lists and begin calling people. If you're lucky enough to get a contact on the phone on your first try, terrific. Introduce yourself, explain you have a story she may be interested in, and then, with enthusiasm, authority, and confidence, start pitching. A word to the wise: It's always better to preface the conversation with, "I've got a great story idea," as opposed to, "I've got a book and author I want to talk to you about." Producers, reporters, and editors are so deluged with literary pitches that if you position the sell as a book up front, it can decrease the enthusiasm of their response. Tell them you have something that will excite *their* readership or audience, that *you* want to help *them* educate or entertain their audience, then weave the book and author into the sell from that perspective. Again, we'll review pitching from stem to stern a little bit later, but this gives you an idea.

As you continue through the pitching stage, you'll find that you get people's voice mail ad nauseam. It can be profoundly frustrating, but there are a few secrets I can share with you that will make it easier. First, don't leave more than three voice mail messages. You appear pesky and inexperienced if you leave countless messages. It irritates the media to no end. If the producer or reporter you're trying to contact simply doesn't return your calls, or you can never catch her, fax or e-mail her. Sometimes, I'll write a funny, friendly note, briefly outlining the pitch and asking the person to please return my calls, then I Federal Express or messenger the note with a flower or piece of chocolate. A touch of human kindness works wonders. Please realize that producers and editors aren't avoiding you. They're swamped with deadlines and sometimes just can't return all the phone calls from publicists, as they receive so many. Be creatively aggressive. Those humble gestures will impress media, and they will call you back.

Stay organized when you pitch. Have all your media lists in front of you, and note each contact's responses. If someone tells you he's on deadline and to call him back Thursday, write it down on your booking sheets and your calendar. Keep copious records of your conversations and follow up. I always keep coming back to contacts with as many different angles as possible and don't stop pitching someone until I get a confirmed interview booking for my author or a definite "no, we just can't do it."

When you do book an interview, you need to write up a confirmation sheet. The confirmation sheet should outline: the author's name and the title of his/her book; day, date, and time of the interview; location (if it's by telephone, be sure to indicate both the author's time zone and that of the media outlet); media outlet; media contact name, phone number, and address; and your name, phone number, and address. Confirmation sheets are critical. Interviews that aren't confirmed don't count.

We're on to our next step! But first, let's look at a few sample confirmation sheets.

MEDIA BOOKING CONFIRMATION

Book Title:	THE COMPLETE GUIDE TO BOOK PUBLICITY
Publicist:	Kelly Doral 312/573-1075
Guest Name:	Jodee Blanco
Guest Phone Number:	610/807-4444
Media Outlet:	Leeza on Books/WNBC TV
Contact:	John Sebastian
Contact Phone Number:	212/956-5555

Interview Date	Monday, December 15th, 2004
Interview Time:	12:00 noon
Interview Location:	30 Rockefeller Plaza, New York, NY
Length of Interview:	Thirty minutes
Nature of Interview:	One-on-one
Interview Logistics:	Live-to-tape in studio
Comments:	John, thank you so much! Jodee is so looking forward to this interview. If you need any additional information, please don't hesitate to contact me.

MEDIA BOOKING CONFIRMATION

Book Title: THE COMPLETE GUIDE TO BOOK PUBLICITY

Publicist: Kelly Doral 312/573-1075

Guest Name: Jodee Blanco

Guest Phone Number: 610/807-4444

Media Outlet: Publisher's Weekly

Contact: John Sebastian

Contact Phone Number: 212/956-5555

Interview Date   Monday, December 15th, 2004
Interview Time: 12:00 noon
Interview Location: 30 Rockefeller Plaza, New York, NY
Length of Interview: One hour
Nature of Interview: One-on-one
Interview Logistics: In-person interview
Comments: John, thank you so much! Jodee is so
                                  looking forward to this interview. If you
                                  need any additional information, please
                                  don't hesitate to contact me.

MEDIA BOOKING CONFIRMATION

Book Title:	THE COMPLETE GUIDE TO BOOK PUBLICITY
Publicist:	Kelly Doral 312/573-1075
Guest Name:	Jodee Blanco
Guest Phone Number:	610/807-4444
Media Outlet:	WMVX AM/Boston, MA
Contact:	John Sebastian
Contact Phone Number:	212/956-5555
Interview Date	Monday, December 15th, 2004
Interview Time:	12:00 noon central/1:00 pm Eastern
Interview Location:	BY TELEPHONE
Length of Interview:	One hour
Nature of Interview:	Live one-on-one with call-ins
Interview Logistics:	WMVX AM will call author Jodee Blanco at the above time.
Comments:	John, thank you so much! Jodee is so looking forward to this interview. If you need any additional information, please don't hesitate to contact me.

Step 7: Media Schedules and Author Prep Sessions

We've been pitching away and have confirmed ten interviews for Dr. Lawson. We need to put together an author interview schedule. I'm a firm believer in doing extremely detailed schedules. The more information you give authors, the more in control they'll feel. Much of the tension that crops up between authors and publicists is caused by a lack of communication about details. An author interview schedule should have a flow to it. If you want to flip quickly to the end of the book, I've provided several samples of actual schedules.

The schedule should include:

- Day, date, and time of each interview
- Location
- Contact name and phone number
- Studio phone number if it's radio or television
- Estimated interview length
- Interview format, i.e., live, taped, live-to-tape, etc.
- Name of the interviewer
- Audience size and demographic
- The angle upon which the interview was booked
- *Any* other pertinent information

Before the author begins the interview gauntlet, you need to do an author prep session. In Dr. Lawson's case, it'll be a little bit easier, because she has extensive media experience. We'll still need to prepare her. We need to review the schedule with her and answer any questions she may have. We should also coach her on verbiage and presentation, to ensure that her positioning of the book and subject matter is consistent with that of the press kit. Additionally, we need to review visual details, such as wardrobe, hair, and makeup, among other elements that comprise the external image. It's *very* important that the author knows as much as possible about each interview situation before going in. This knowledge will empower the author, giving her self-confidence a lift and eliminating the stress that unfamiliar situations can cause, and this is sure to impact positively upon her on-air focus.

Our work doesn't end here. Now it's time for post-interview follow-up!

Step 8: Post-Interview Follow-up

This is one of the important stages of the publicity process. If you don't pay attention to it, all your hard work getting the interviews in the first place could very well be for naught. The purpose of post-interview follow-up is twofold: to ensure that taped television and radio interviews air, and that the shows have all the elements they need prior to air date, such as B-roll, photos, and specific author information; and to thank the media contact. Remember, courtesy and kindness make lasting impressions.

After Dr. Lawson completes each interview, it's up to us to call the media contact and ask the following questions (these questions apply to taped broadcast interviews and print—for live broadcast interviews, most of these issues must be handled *before* the interview):

- How did the interview go?
- Do you need B-roll or still photos?
- Can you confirm that you'll be editing in a still of the book?
- How is the author identified in terms of credentials?
- Are you interviewing anyone else for this piece?
- When will it air/run?

I can't emphasize enough the importance of follow-up. It's especially crucial if you've negotiated a series of firsts or exclusives, as you have to make sure all the media outlets air and run their pieces in accordance with what's been agreed upon.

Step 9: Parlaying Placements into New Coverage Opportunities

Now that the author's done her first round of interviews, we need to generate the next level of visibility. We must obtain clippings and video of each interview Dr. Lawson has completed. There are several methods. For print, we'll call all reporters who interviewed Dr. Lawson and ask when their pieces will run. We can also request they send us clippings. As a backup, we can always call back issues after a piece has appeared and ask to be sent a copy.

I also recommend subscribing to a weekly clipping service like Burrelle's or Luce.

All clippings should be mocked up. That means cutting the article out and pasting it onto blank white stock. When you mock up an article, you should cut out the main masthead of the newspaper or magazine from front page or cover (the masthead is the name of the publication, e.g., *Cosmopolitan* or the *New York Times*), the masthead from the section of the paper or magazine where the article appears (e.g., Health and Beauty or Lifestyle), and the article itself. Paste the main masthead at the top, the masthead identifying the section directly underneath, and then the article so that it reads from left to right or top to bottom. If an article is long, use one full page for the mastheads. At the end of this book, I've provided several examples of mock-ups.

We also have to obtain video clips of Dr. Lawson's television interviews. Sometimes if an author brings a VHS tape with her to the interview, the producer will make a clip reel on-site. You can also call the producer several days after the interview and ask if he would be kind enough to send a video clip, or you can order it from a video monitoring service. Monitoring services are affordable and abundant, and listed in the telephone book. As videos come in, we need to review and choose the best footage, then have a service compile a clip reel.

Our next task at hand will be to utilize the print clippings and author interview footage to garner additional coverage. The trick is positioning the news coverage as a story in and of itself. For example, we take the press clippings and compilation reel and package it with a pitch letter describing how Dr. Lawson's book is making news all across the country. Media generates media.

Step 10: The Campaign Recap

At the conclusion of the campaign, a comprehensive, detailed recap of media coverage needs to be submitted to both the publisher and author, outlining:

- Confirmed interviews that have been completed
- Audience reach
- Demographics
- Air dates and print runs
- Media coverage that's still pending and why
- Media outlets who weren't interested in interviewing the author and why

The recap is valuable on numerous levels. It provides a record of successes, challenges, patterns of media interest, and author strengths and weaknesses with regard to interviews, among other data that can prove profoundly helpful for the paperback campaign, as well as the author's next book launch.

Recapping the Steps

Let's briefly review the publicity process:

Step 1: The Inquisitive Phase

Step 2: Devising The Campaign Strategy

Step 3: Writing The Press Kit

Step 4: Researching and Databasing Target Media

Step 5: Pre-Pitching and Media Mailings

Step 6: Pitching/Booking and Confirming Media Interviews

Step 7: Media Schedules and Author Prep Sessions

Step 8: Post-Interview Follow-up

Step 9: Parlaying Placements into New Coverage Opportunities

Step 10: The Campaign Recap

Our next chapter addresses different types of campaigns and how to choose what's best for you. Onward!

The Different Types of Campaigns and How to Choose the One That's Best for You

*E*VERY BOOK LAUNCH IS DIFFERENT. EACH HAS A PARTICULAR SET OF circumstances that need to be considered before finalizing a blueprint of action for publicity. In this chapter, we're going to explore different types of publicity campaigns and how to choose what's best for you. Keep in mind that there are infinite variations of campaigns. My objective here is to provide a basic understanding that you can expand upon with experience.

Did you ever play with blocks when you were a kid? You always used the same set, but you mixed and matched the pieces differently every time you built something. Constructing a publicity campaign is similar. One quick note: In this chapter, I'm focusing on general consumer campaigns as opposed to trade, which we already touched upon in the first two chapters.

There are four major types of general consumer publicity campaigns: national, regional, local, and grassroots. Let's take a look at the core building blocks comprising each one. Bear in mind that the building blocks for each campaign type can be mixed and matched differently. Before we delve into the secret for knowing which combination of blocks to use, we need to define the building blocks themselves.

Campaign Building Blocks

A national campaign means publicity that reaches the entire country. It can consist of three building blocks:

1. Print coverage, such as national newspapers, magazines, syndicated columnists, and wire services
2. Broadcast coverage, such as network, syndicated, and national cable television talk shows, and network and syndicated radio outlets
3. A media tour, in which an author does local print and broadcast interviews coast to coast, visiting a city per day

A regional campaign refers to publicity that targets a specific *region* or part of the country, such as the Midwest, the South, or northeastern seaboard. Regional campaigns have two blocks:

1. Print outlets, such as daily and community newspapers, multiple publishers, newsletters, and magazines
2. Broadcast media, like local network affiliate and regional cable television shows, and regional radio shows

A local or "market specific" campaign means publicity that targets one city. Local campaigns can consist of two blocks:

1. Print coverage, such as local daily newspapers, multiple publishers, weekly community papers, newsletters, and city journals and magazines
2. Broadcast placements, like network affiliate, regional cable, and local independent television shows, and local radio outlets

Grassroots campaigns are similar to local campaigns, except they target much smaller markets, such as rural towns and little villages scattered across the map. These campaigns can be made up of two blocks:

1. Print
2. Broadcast

Let's review briefly each campaign type and its building blocks. Because we are going to use these blocks later in the chapter to build hypothetical campaigns, I've assigned each block a letter name.

National

- National print **(A)**
- National broadcast **(B)**
- National media tour **(C)**

Regional

- Local print in markets that comprise target region (Midwest, South, etc.) **(D)**
- Local broadcast in markets that comprise target region **(E)**

Local/Market Specific

- Local print in one city **(F)**
- Local broadcast in one city **(G)**

Grassroots

- Local print in small town or village **(H)**
- Local broadcast in small town or village **(I)**

Building the Road to a Successful Campaign

Now that we've reviewed the basics, let's walk through a few examples to illustrate how this works. We're publicizing a book called *The Road to Fame*. Authored by a famous Hollywood agent, it's a career guide for young hopefuls who want to break into the entertainment business. The publisher has asked us to recommend a campaign strategy. Which combination of building blocks do we use?

The first thing we need to do is ask some key questions: What's the estimated initial print run for *The Road to Fame?* Where is the book most heavily distributed? What's the author's media experience and availability? What's the target demographic for this book? When is the book pub dated? The answers we receive will enable us to choose the proper building blocks.

After chatting with the publisher, we've obtained the following details: The estimated print run is 40,000 copies. The strongest lay down of the book is in New York and Los Angeles, the country's entertainment hubs. The author has extensive interview experience and has cleared his schedule to participate in the publicity process. The target demographic for this book is adults ages eighteen and up, ranging from struggling performance artists to future directors, producers, and agents who wish to enter the entertainment arena. The book is pub dated for June.

In this particular case, I'd recommend doing national and local print and broadcast out of New York and Los Angeles. If we look at it in terms of building blocks, that would be blocks **A, B, F,** and **G.** Though the initial print run is over 35,000 copies, and therefore qualifies the book for an author media tour, there are mitigating circumstances that make a tour a less viable option. For one thing, the books are most heavily distributed in New York and Los Angeles. The sell-in in other markets doesn't justify touring. Additionally, the majority of book buyers who fall within the target demographic live in those two cities. By concentrating our efforts on national and local television, radio, newspapers, and magazines out of these two markets, we maximize visibility to our desired audience. Since we've got a strong budget and aren't touring, we can utilize those extra dollars for promotions. Perhaps we could do a literary contest or personal appearances, among a myriad of other publicity-generating events.

Recipe for a Bestseller

Let's explore another example. We're publicizing a book on surviving infidelity, called *Caught in the Act,* written by a renowned marriage counselor. A native of Chicago, the author is eager to promote her book. The initial print run is 50,000 copies, with even distribution throughout the country. The demographic for this book is married women who have either committed adultery or been victimized by it.

Reflecting on the information we have, I'd suggest we do national print and broadcast, a ten-city media tour, and local Chicago print and broadcast. That would be building blocks **A, B, C, F,** and **G.** Let's examine why this combination makes the most sense.

Caught in the Act addresses a topic that affects millions of women all across the country. National print and broadcast coverage is crucial on several levels: it reaches massive audiences throughout the country, initiates a buzz about the book, and the subject is a juicy and publicizable one from the media's perspective. However, with an initial print run of 50,000 copies, we need more than just national exposure. National exposure can get the ball rolling, but we'll lose the momentum if we stop there. That's where the tour comes in. Once we get the author on national television and radio shows, and in big newspapers and magazines, we can use that visibility as a springboard for the media tour. The media tour heightens the excitement market by market and gives the author an opportunity to reach people on a much more personal level.

Rounding out the strategy is local print and broadcast interviews in the author's hometown, which is critical from both a marketing and human vantage point. Hometown PR at the end of a tour creates a huge local media blitz, which parlays itself into national exposure. Additionally, and probably most importantly, it's a terrific morale booster for the author, who is likely tired and running out of steam by the tail end of the campaign. The hometown hero's welcome gives the author a necessary emotional and spiritual lift that empowers him to keep the PR going.

As you can see with the example of *Caught in the Act,* national print and broadcast followed by a media tour, and culminating in hometown PR, is one of the old-fashioned meat-and-potatoes recipes for creating a *New York Times* bestseller. In order for this campaign combination to be effective, however, the following elements must be in place: an initial print run of over 35,000 copies, subject matter that is newsworthy and relevant to a broad audience, and strong author credibility and media savvy. Even with all those components, there are still no guarantees with publicity. But if you use your judgment and logically analyze the variables, you'll choose the most intelligent combination of campaign building blocks. After that, it's about perseverance, persistence, flexibility, moxie, timing, and yes, a little bit of luck.

The Incredible Expanding Campaign

Many authors adamantly believe that if their book isn't available all over the country, it won't be successful. That isn't true. Not every book should be widely distributed coast to coast right out of the gate. Often, an *expanding* regional approach that begins with clusters of grassroots markets graduates to groups of smaller-to-midsize cities and culminates with national lay down, and media offers the greatest potential.

Sometimes the publicist will be in a position to contribute early on, at the distribution phase. This is often the case with self-publishers, who bring in PR people as overall marketing consultants at the initial stage of a project. I've always enjoyed having that kind of input. Let's explore a hypothetical example of an expanding regional campaign, why it's the most effective blueprint of action, and the building blocks required to pull it off.

A moderately capitalized self-publisher has brought us on board at the developmental juncture to spearhead the publicity, public relations, and promotions for a landmark children's book. Entitled *Mommy Why Won't They Play with Me*, it targets children who get teased by their peers. Part motivational, part beautifully illustrated whimsical story, the book is designed as a companion and comfort to families with kids who are the classroom outcasts. The author is a third-grade teacher in a small midwestern town.

The publisher doesn't have the resources for a large initial print run. The first printing is five thousand copies. He's asking us to recommend a distribution strategy. Remember the old saying, "It's better to be a big fish in a small pond than a small fish in a big pond"? The same applies here. If the publisher scatters the five thousand copies in bookstores all across the country, the distribution is diluted. Even if all the books sold in one week, it wouldn't create a stir. A few copies would sell here, a few there, but these little blips wouldn't achieve a cohesive impact. The sales would go unnoticed by the marketplace and the press—not to mention, the book couldn't make any regional bestseller lists.

If, on the other hand, the distribution were concentrated in one specific region of the country, such as the Midwest, the sales would draw attention from both the media and the publishing industry, because the playing field would be smaller and under a larger microscope. It's simple logic. If twenty people attend a large party, no one notices when those twenty people leave. But if twenty people attend a small party, everyone comments when they walk out the door. With that understanding in mind, here's what I'd recommend to the publisher.

He should choose five grassroots midwestern towns that border each other and distribute one thousand copies of the book, through a limited number of bookstores, to each town. The author should do local print and broadcast interviews in these small markets, along with readings in hospitals, schools, and other nontraditional outlets. Each time the author makes these personal appearances, camera crews and photographers should be invited to attend and cover the events. Remember, we're talking little markets here, where a visiting author is often considered big news. The whole emphasis should be on selling through the initial five thousand copies. This increases the chances of the book hitting regional bestseller lists.

As soon as the five thousand copies are sold, we should issue a press release to all the local print in the distribution region, as well as the national publishing trades, especially *Publisher's*

Weekly, touting the story of how *Mommy Why Won't They Play with Me* is touching lives in the heartland. The goal is to get as many press clippings generated as possible, so we can enter into phase two of the campaign strategy.

Once we've secured industry and grassroots press, we need to assemble a video reel and clip book and target our next group of grassroots markets. The reel and clip book will entice producers and reporters in our next region. We should keep doing the campaign, region by region, until we've done two or three parts of the country, then begin increasing the size of the markets with each "minijunket" (concentrated press push). Instead of grassroots towns, we next choose five cities in the South or Northeast. An expanding regional campaign can include as many as five regions representing a mix of grassroots towns and larger cities, to as little as one or two regions. It all depends on budget and response. That's where the flexibility part of the job comes in. As soon as sales and media coverage begin to escalate, that's the moment when national distribution of the book and national media should kick in. In a nutshell, you start out in clusters of small towns, graduate to groups of reasonably sized cities, then use the excitement generated in these regions as catalysts to ignite national media and bookstore chain interest.

The expanded regional campaign is a systematic approach to building a book region by region, until it clicks on a national level. It's cost-effective because it's divided into several smaller print runs, as opposed to one large run at the onset. Additionally, it strengthens the book's bestseller-list potential. Also, because the campaign is spread out over an elongated period of time, it provides continued fodder for press.

Let's break down our campaign strategy for *Mommy Why Won't They Play with Me* into our basic building blocks. Though this campaign strategy may seem a bit complicated, it all comes down to mixing and matching our building blocks. We start with print and broadcast in one or two clusters of grassroots towns, move on to regions of smaller-to-midsize cities, until we've covered several concentrated areas of the country. Next, we parlay the grassroots and regional coverage into national print and broadcast. The combination of building blocks is: **H, I, D, E, A,** and **B.**

Tailored to Fit

Remember, constructing the right type of campaign comes down to three key components:

- Analyze the particular circumstances surrounding the book in question, i.e., print run, author expertise and media ability, marketing budget, and newsworthiness of the book
- Examine which campaign building blocks would be most effective
- Assess how those building blocks should be mixed and matched for maximum results

For example, with *Caught in the Act,* we chose to utilize national print and broadcast as the springboard for local print and broadcast, as well as a tour. However, with *Mommy Why Won't They Play with Me,* we're starting with a grassroots and regional push as the stepping-stone to national attention. Just knowing what building blocks to use isn't enough. You have to have a construction plan.

What if you've got an author who's a wonderful interview but doesn't come across on television? Despite all the coaching in the world, she isn't comfortable in front of a camera. There's no such thing as an author or book that isn't publicizable. You have to be willing to tailor the campaign to fit the situation. A romance writer I've represented for years falls into this category.

Ebullient, articulate, with a wonderful sense of humor, she's a natural on radio. Whenever she does live radio with call-ins, the telephone board lights up with eager fans anxious to talk with their literary hero. When we first started working with this writer, we analyzed which blocks should form the base of her campaign. Since she adores radio and likes print, we did a coast-to-coast blitz, in which we booked telephone interviews for her with the top twenty radio stations in the country and the big daily newspapers in each of those markets. The result was terrific. It was an effortless and enjoyable experience for her, and we generated the necessary coverage to galvanize book sales. Our building blocks in this case were **E** (radio only) and **F.**

Once you determine which building blocks are appropriate for a particular campaign, you can begin to erect a sound strategy. Choices abound. For example, say you're publicizing an adventure novel written by a retired shark hunter. You might choose national print and broadcast, a ten-city tour, and local media in the author's hometown. Instead of pitching the book as a straight feature, you may decide it would be more enticing to the media to create an essay contest in conjunction with the book. The key is knowing exactly what coverage you want to achieve, how you want to accomplish it (i.e., the angles), and why this is the best method.

Continuing on the subject of radio, remember the old saying: *Radio sells books.* There are a multitude of reasons why. Radio interviews give authors significantly more airtime than television. The average television interview is three to twelve minutes, whereas a typical radio interview is twenty minutes to an hour. Radio audiences are big book buyers, especially listeners who follow AM talk. Keep its power in mind when devising campaign strategies.

Campaign of Tomorrow

There's one more type of campaign I'd like to address in this chapter. It's still comprised of our core building blocks in terms of the "what," but the "how" is different. Satellite campaigns are becoming more and more popular as a time- and cost-effective way to generate television and radio coverage nationwide. Earlier in this book, we talked about satellite interviews as an alternative, if it's not logistically possible for an author to do an in-studio interview. Satellite tours fall along the same lines. Let's use our example from earlier in this chapter, *Caught in the Act*.

We had decided the best blueprint of action for this book would be national print and broadcast, a ten-city media tour, and hometown interviews. What if the author couldn't travel due to a hectic schedule? We could use the same building blocks, but instead of sending her to the tour cities, she could do the interviews via satellite. In chapter 12, I discuss satellite tours in detail.

Common Sense and Ingenuity

Here's the bottom line on understanding the different types of campaigns and knowing which is best for you. Carefully examine the issues intrinsic to a literary launch, including such variables as:

- Initial print run
- Budget
- Author expertise and interview ability
- Target demographic
- Distribution details
- Newsworthiness of the subject
- Timelines
- Logistical concerns (such as author availability)

When you're confident you've considered the necessary components, begin assembling the building blocks of your campaign.

How will you know what makes the most sense? Logic. If you've got a book that's highly publicizable, the rule of thumb is to start out with national media, then segue into a tour or local press. On the other hand, if you're promoting a book that's more obscure or targets a narrower demographic, you may want to start out small with grassroots and local media before pitching national print and broadcast. Some books are best served by an aggressive regional campaign. Think about how publicity, public relations, and promotions can be tailored to enhance the strengths and compensate for the weaknesses of each specific book.

I'd like to share a final secret with you about campaign choices. Be resourceful. For example, if you're publicizing a book that could benefit greatly from a media tour, but the publisher hasn't allotted the budget for it, you can generate similar excitement by doing radio and newspaper phoners in ten or twenty markets, plus national television. No matter *what* obstacle is placed in front of you, stop for a moment, analyze all the elements, ponder each of the building blocks we've discussed, then unleash your creative acumen and engineer a campaign.

Occasionally you may have to go out on a limb in support of a daring idea. Take the risk! Publicity is about courage and imagination. The rest is academic.

Our next chapter focuses on the art of writing a press kit. Stay tuned!

How to Write the Perfect Press Kit

A PRESS KIT IS TO PUBLICITY WHAT THUNDER IS TO LIGHTNING. Without it, a campaign has no voice. In this chapter, we're going to explore in detail what a press kit is, its function, and how to create one. The press kit is an intrinsic element of any public relations effort and isn't relegated only to literary campaigns. However, for the purpose of clarity, I'm narrowing our focus to writing press materials for books.

A press kit is a package or folder containing information specifically formatted for the media that illuminates the newsworthiness of the book and author. If you're pitching a producer or reporter, the first thing they're going to ask for, if you haven't sent it already, is a press kit. I can't emphasize enough the vital importance of the well-written press kit. It establishes the precise positioning of the book and author that you want presented to the press, provides an overview for interviewers who will not have had time to read the book, reinforces the media contact's initial impression of the publicist's professionalism, and documents exactly how and why this book is a story that needs to be covered.

Shoddy, sloppily written press kits that don't have an edge do *infinite* damage to a campaign. Yes, writing the perfect press kit is a painstaking and time-consuming process that demands a profound creative stamina. But it's well worth the effort.

A standard press kit contains the following components:

- A press release that positions the book as news
- An author bio skewed to reinforce credibility
- Suggested interview questions designed to ignite provocative discussions and cover areas not addressed in the press release
- A topic suggestions sheet for print and broadcast media that highlights different angles and story ideas
- Select excerpts from the book
- A personalized pitch letter
- Photos and B-roll
- Author print and video clips
- Other specialized pieces, depending upon the type of book and subject matter

Let's go through each of these pieces one at a time. A quick note—at the end of this chapter, I've provided actual samples of press kits for both fiction and nonfiction that you should find very helpful. While I can give you a foundation in this chapter on the ins and outs of how to write press kit materials, the samples will give you a more comprehensive and cohesive understanding.

The Press Release

The press release is the most important part of the press kit. It positions the book and author to the media. A press release is *not* a book report. Though it should describe what the book is about, that description must be presented from the perspective of why and how the book is *news*. Though each publicist has her own style and approach, a standard press release is two to four pages, double-spaced. A press release is comprised of three primary parts: the tag FOR IMMEDIATE RELEASE followed by a colon, written all in caps and bolded in the upper-left-hand corner of the first page, and directly across in the upper-right-hand corner, the publicist's contact information, which includes her name and telephone number, written in upper and lowercase; two or three spaces underneath is the headline, which is single-spaced, in bold, all in caps; two to four spaces under the headline is the press kit body, double-spaced, with four spaces between paragraphs (i.e., two returns). The headline can be one-, two-, or three-pronged, separated by semicolons, depending upon the length and style of the release. The book title, as it appears in the headline, should be italicized. If it has a subtitle, the subtitle should be underlined. Here's an example of the format.

FOR IMMEDIATE RELEASE: Contact: Publicist Name
Telephone number

NATIONALLY RENOWNED CHILD PSYCHOLOGIST REVEALS CUTTING-EDGE RESEARCH IN LANDMARK NEW BOOK ON RAISING KIDS;

BUILDING HEALTHY FAMILIES, BY DR. JOY SANDERS, REDEFINES PARENTING FOR THE NEW MILLENNIUM;

One of the country's most respected and celebrated parenting experts . . .

The headline in our example above is two-pronged. Speaking of headlines, there are a few details I'd like you to note about the example above. Though it makes a general statement about the book's contents, it's presented in the context of *news*. The words "reveals," "cutting-edge," "landmark," and "redefines" are all buzz words that reinforce newsworthiness. Also, pay attention to how the author is introduced. The phrase "nationally renowned" emphasizes author credibility. The headline of a press release is critical. It will either draw in the reader (i.e., media contact) or turn him off. Personally, I spend an enormous amount of time writing the headline. Sometimes the headline will take me three or four hours to write and the body of the press release itself much less time. Bear in mind, however, what I mentioned moments ago. Each publicist has her own distinct writing style. My business partner, Lissy, for example, will often jot down a general idea for the headline, move forward with the body, and then go back and edit the headline after the body is completed. No matter what style you develop, the most important thing to remember is that the press release telegraphs to the world whether or not the book is news. Make the creative commitment to do it right.

Headlines that Focus and Spin

Always interview the author *in depth* before sitting down to write the release. Be aware of any publicity obstacles up front, such as author credibility issues or subject matter, and use how you position the book and author in the press release as a means to navigate those hurdles. For example, say you're publicizing a book about recovery from incest written by a newspaper reporter. The author isn't an academic expert on the subject, nor is she a victim. You have two challenges with this press release: first, author credibility, and second, sensitivity of the topic. If you approach the press release with the proper kind of creative thinking, you can nip these two potential problems in the bud.

Your headline might read something like this:

WOMEN IN RECOVERY FROM INCEST REACH OUT TO HELP OTHER VICTIMS THROUGH LANDMARK NEW BOOK;

DADDY RAPED ME: TRUE STORIES OF PERSONAL TRAGEDY AND TRIUMPH, **COMPILED BY CRITICALLY ACCLAIMED JOURNALIST ABBY SMITH, REDEFINES THE MEANING OF HOPE;**

Analyzing this headline, you can see clearly how we used it to help overcome the hurdles of author credibility and topic sensitivity. The headline positions the incest victims who contributed to the book as "women in recovery," which achieves two goals:

- It puts a positive spin on a delicate subject by reinforcing the healing element
- It places the burden of credibility on the book's contributors rather than the journalist who compiled the stories

The author's expertise is spotlighted in the context of her being "critically acclaimed" in her own arena. By positioning the "women in recovery" as the experts on incest, and the author as an authority on finding stories, the headline succinctly and subtly eliminates both initial obstacles. Also, note the buzz words "landmark" and "redefines," both of which connote *first* and/or news.

A quick comment on fiction. If you're writing a press release for a fiction title, it's the same creative process as nonfiction. Again, it shouldn't be a book report, but should briefly describe the book from the vantage point of its newsworthiness. For example, you're publicizing a novel about shark hunting written by a retired shark hunter. Your headline might read:

INTERNATIONALLY RENOWNED SHARK HUNTER RELIVES SOME OF HIS MOST TERRIFYING MOMENTS STARING INTO THE JAWS OF DEATH IN HEART-STOPPING NEW THRILLER;

FIN **BY DIRK WILLIAMS IS A DEEPLY PERSONAL ADVENTURE INTO THE MIND AND MEMORY OF ONE OF THE WORLD'S MOST DARING MEN;**

In this case, the most newsworthy component of the book is the author's credibility. His novel emanates from personal experience. The headline emphasizes that credibility, while still spotlighting its value as a thrilling literary ride.

What, Why, Who, How?

Now that we've talked about headlines, let's address the body of the press release. Once you've got your headline down, simply follow it logically, weaving in details that reinforce the positioning. Every press release should tell the media contact:

- What the book is about
- Why it's newsworthy
- Who the author is
- How the author is an expert on the subject matter

Every press release doesn't have to provide this information in the same order. It all depends on the tease in the headline. The rule of thumb is to present the body of the release in the same order mentioned in the headline. Take a peek at the samples in the back of this book.

One last note on press releases. Be honest! Though you can and should use buzz words that indicate news, such as "landmark," "pioneering," "trailblazing," "cutting-edge," "historic," "unprecedented," "unparalleled," etc., be sure that whatever verbiage you choose *accurately* reflects the truth. The easiest way to use buzz words is to think of them as exciting synonyms, rather than stand-alone phrases. For example, instead of using the word "unusual," you may wish to substitute "pioneering." I always tell my NYU students that a press release should have sizzle, but only to draw attention to the meaty substance. If it's all sizzle and no substance, it isn't a good release and will undermine media confidence in the publicist. Don't cry wolf with press releases. Do, however, be creative and diverse in how you choose your words.

Targeting the Author Bio

The author bio is the next most crucial component of the press kit. A well-written author bio should be one or two pages, single-spaced. As with the press release, you need to conduct a comprehensive interview with the author, during which you extrapolate vital nuggets that justify her credibility as a *definitive authority* on the subject of the book. An author bio shouldn't be a general summary of who the author is but, rather, a carefully structured positioning piece that tells the story of the author from the perspective of his or her expertise. At the end of this book, I've provided several actual samples of author bios to give you some ideas.

Constructing an interesting and newsworthy author bio is an art form in and of itself. I developed the following outlined process, which I hope you'll find helpful.

STEP 1: Interview the author at length. Areas for questioning could range from his academic expertise, professional experience, and major life events to hobbies, personal convictions, and anecdotal memories.

STEP 2: Assimilate all the data you've acquired from the author interview and analyze what this information tells you about the author as a whole. Explore how you can transform this information into an intriguing identity for the author that cross-promotes the book.

STEP 3: Decide how you think the author should be positioned to the public, review your opinion with the author, then begin writing the bio.

I've always found the best way to structure an author bio is to start out with a general positioning statement about the author that describes who they are as a person, then segue into specific facts that reinforce the first statement. Let me share with you an example.

Presenting a Role Model

Several years ago, I was asked to represent one of America's most beloved romance writers, Candace Camp. Her publisher wanted a tag for her, an identity that would be unique to her image, in much the way Stephen King is known as the King of Horror. I spent a couple of days with Candy, talking for hours about her life, interests, and career as a writer. Several details about her struck me. Full of sunshine and smiles, she had the warmest and most infectious giggle I'd ever heard. A dedicated mom and wife, in the morning while her daughter was at school and her husband at work, she would write her steamy novels. Then, in late afternoon, she turned her computer off and her oven on, becoming the perfect homemaker. The other fascinating component about this woman's full life was that her husband was an ex-priest.

Candy and I had so much fun together. After I left, I sat down with all my notes and began playing with verbiage. What was it about her that was different? How could I define her to the public in a way that would truthfully depict her character, while still being provocative to the media? Then the idea hit me. I crafted a bio in which I described Candy as "Romance Writing's Wholesome Mom Next Door." The juxtaposing of her wholesome image with the sultry, sexy novels she penned made for a great story. Candy loved the positioning because it presented her as a role model for any woman who didn't want to be pigeonholed as one-dimensional.

The bottom line on the author bio is that it should be a ministory that introduces the author as a fascinating and newsworthy individual with an expertise all her own. It positions the author in the same way the press release positions the book.

Suggested Interview Questions

The next piece in the press kit is Suggested Interview Questions, a list of ten to twenty questions. The purpose of Suggested Interview Questions is not to provide the media with a list of questions that the author would like asked. The real function of this piece is twofold:

- To address issues that, due to time and space restrictions, couldn't be covered in the press release
- To provide devil's-advocate questions that show the media that the author welcomes animated exchanges and doesn't shy away from aggressive debate

So often, publicists will write soggy suggested interview questions that have no edge to them at all. Producers and reporters don't need a publicist to educate them about what to ask. They do, however, appreciate questions with a surprising twist or a little fire to them. At the back of the book are several samples of questions that you can refer to.

Topic Suggestions Sheet

Next item—the Topic Suggestions Sheet! I have to admit this is one of my trade secrets. A Topic Suggestions Sheet lists different show and article ideas for media contacts, tailor-made for their needs. It can be formatted in many different ways. I always prefer to list each topic idea in bold print, single-spaced, and double-spaced between topics.

Let's use *Building Healthy Families,* the hypothetical sample from earlier in this chapter, to illustrate the idea. The topic one-sheet for this book might read:

BUILDING HEALTHY FAMILIES

Parenting in the New Millennium—The Ten Secrets for Raising Healthy Children

What To Do When Saving the Marriage Can End Up Meaning Neglecting the Kids—One of America's Top Parenting Experts Offers Step-by-Step Advice

Two-Career Families—The Risks and Rewards—Leading Expert Shares the Bottom Line on this Prevalent Concern

---

You get the idea. The Topic Suggestions Sheet can be as long as the imagination is fertile. The more ideas you give the media, the stronger your likelihood of coverage. If you're doing a sheet for a fiction title, the core elements remain the same. Position the author as an expert, personal story, or both, and list ideas for shows or articles in which the book could be logically cross-promoted within the context of the subject.

Select Excerpts

Now we've come to my very favorite press kit piece—Select Excerpts. Often, interviewers will not have had time to read the book in its entirety. They base their interviews on whatever they've gleaned from the press kit. The Select Excerpts piece provides a direct line to the author's voice, how she thinks and communicates. What I normally do is highlight newsworthy passages as I'm reading the manuscript or galley. Then, when it comes time to do this one-sheet, I transfer the highlighted sections.

How do you know what to excerpt? Here are some guidelines: Whether it's fiction or nonfiction, you want to look for quotes that are controversial, poignant, surprising, dramatic, or revealing. I usually do ten to fifteen excerpts, ranging from one to five sentences each. They should represent a diverse cross section of thoughts pertaining to the subject of the book.

The Personalized Letter or Memo

Each press kit should also have a personalized pitch letter. We talked at length about pitch letters in chapter 6. I'd like to review some key points. A good pitch letter is always personalized. As I explained earlier, I detest generic pitch letters. Why? When you're pitching the media, you're asking them to consider what you have to say. The very least you can do is address them by name. Though mass mailings are part and parcel of the PR business, there are ways to personalize pitch letters that are time- and cost-efficient.

First of all, as discussed earlier, you should always pre-pitch before you send a pitch letter. That means calling the media contact on the phone, letting them know briefly, in a sentence or two, what you're sending, and asking them to stay on the look-out for it. When you sit down to do your mass mailing, instead of writing a pitch letter in formal letter format, do a memo. Eliminate the "TO" part, and just use the "FROM" and "RE" parts, but with the order reversed and using "TOPIC" rather than "RE." I've included several samples at the back of this book, but here's a bird's-eye view of what I mean:

TOPIC:

LEARN THE SECRETS TO SUCCESSFUL PARENTING IN THE NEW MILLENNIUM—RENOWNED EXPERT, DR. JOY SANDERS, AUTHOR OF *BUILDING HEALTHY FAMILIES*, AVAILABLE FOR INTERVIEW

FROM:

(Publicist's Name and Contact Number)

You can mass-print these pitches and still personalize them. Simply handwrite in the upper left- or right-hand corner of the memo a short, friendly note to the contact, such as, "Thanks for taking the time to chat with me. Let's talk again soon," or just "Let's talk soon!" When the media contact sees the handwritten note, she'll feel acknowledged as a person. That's so important. The above example is how I normally pitch memos, but there are infinite variations. Play with different ideas and structures until you find the one that most fits your own personal style.

The main objectives of a pitch letter or memo are fourfold:

- Make the media person feel singled out
- Use bullet points in the body of the letter or memo to indicate exactly what the author will talk about
- Describe in vivid, succinct detail how and why the author is a good interview
- Explain in a few sentences how the author's message will impact his or her audience or readership

If you can keep those four elements in mind, you can craft ingeniously written pitches.

Photos and B-Roll

The next items needed in the press kit are author photos and B-roll. The photos should be 8″ × 10″ in size. I always suggest enclosing one color photo and one black-and-white. An important detail about author photos—make sure the photo is *current*. I can't begin to tell you what a major mistake it is to use an old author photo in a press kit. It gives the media a completely inaccurate visual perspective of the author. Nothing is more embarrassing for an author than to see a look of thinly concealed shock on a producer's face, followed by the words, "Oh, you look younger in your photo."

We've talked about B-roll before. B-roll is video footage used to enhance an interview. For example, if you've written a pasta cookbook, ideal B-roll might be footage of you cooking at a famous Italian eatery. There are three types of video formats: quarter inch, which is standard VCR tape size; half inch, which is larger and often used as a master; and beta. Most producers prefer B-roll on beta; however, it's always good to check, before doing any interview, which format they'd prefer for the B-roll. Sometimes, an EPK can be used as B-roll. An EPK, or Electronic Press Kit, is a video version of the press release. For example, an EPK of a cookbook might feature a few segments with the author preparing one of the recipes in the book. It also might contain vignettes of the author being interviewed or, perhaps, sitting in her study, writing. In essence, it's a visual bio that focuses on the book as the primary theme.

Clips

No press kit is complete without print and video clips! Some authors will have old magazine and newspaper articles in which they're featured, as well as clips of television interviews. You should review all the print and video clips and choose those that showcase the author from the most diverse and provocative vista. Once you've chosen several television clips, go to a professional dubbing facility and ask them to edit a clip reel.

The video clip reel is crucial to any author campaign. Without it, you won't be able to secure national television interviews. Producers need two things before they'll commit to putting an author on a talk show. First, they must preinterview the author by telephone to make sure she is aggressive and responsive. Second, they want to see video footage of the author on other television shows, to ensure that when placed in front of a camera, the author doesn't freeze. Additionally, a clip reel indicates whether or not the author is telegenic (i.e., looks good on camera). As you accumulate print and television coverage during the campaign, the print clippings should be added to the press kit on an ongoing basis. The best television interviews should also be edited into the clip reel.

The Evolving Press Kit

A press kit is not a static fixture in a campaign. A smart publicist knows that the press kit, just like the campaign itself, needs to grow and evolve with each moment-to-moment accomplishment. As a publicist, you have to stay on your toes, monitoring print and broadcast coverage. When your stack of clippings exceeds twenty articles, it's time to issue a press release that spotlights the book's continuing success. Or perhaps you just booked your author on a major network television show. Any milestones, whether they be publicity related or sales driven, should be shouted from the hilltops via a press release issued to the publishing trade and select sectors of the general consumer populace.

On average, when I'm working on a book campaign, I issue a new press release every six to eight weeks, highlighting all recent achievements. Sometimes it isn't just news about the book that warrants a new press release. Say, for example, you're publicizing a book about teen violence written by a renowned child psychologist. If something happens in the news, such as a high school shooting or a debate in congress on gun control, you could issue a press release indicating that you have one of the foremost experts on the subject, who could bring a fresh and intriguing perspective to the issue. This is a great tactical maneuver for garnering author press. That's why I keep emphasizing throughout this book to pay attention to the news, read the papers, watch TV, and listen to the radio. When a major story breaks, producers and editors are clamoring for experts from all sides and walks of life. The minute you see an opportunity, seize it. Write a press release positioning your author as a definitive authority, then send it to every news desk at every paper and television station you can. It can alter the course of a campaign and transform a moderately successful book launch into an historic campaign.

A few final notes about press kits. Take the time to be ingenious and imaginative. A brilliant press kit can't be written in two hours. It demands consideration and analytical thinking. The press kit is the voice of the campaign. It's the first word to the press and the public. Make it count.

Be prepared when you interview the author. Read the manuscript! So many publicists write press releases based on the flap copy from the book. Nothing angers me more! It's inconceivable to me that a publicist would or even *could* publicize a book he hasn't read. After you've read the manuscript, obtain a copy of an old author bio, past clippings, and any other information you can get your hands on. Do as much research about the author in advance as you can, so when you interview her you have an intelligent point of reference. It will also make the author feel important that you've taken the time to do this extra work. A press kit is the lifeline to a successful campaign. *Respect its power by making it as powerful as you're able.*

Little details make a large impact. Always spell check. Typos can render even the best press kits impotent. Make sure the grammar and sentence structure is correct. Pay attention to how the kit flows. Is it clear and understandable? Are there enough support materials (video, photos, etc.)? Is the headline a grabber? If you were producing a television show or editing a newspaper, would this press kit make you want to interview the author? The answer to that question should tell you everything you need to know.

Blanco & Peace Enterprises LTD.
Chicago • Los Angeles • New York

FOR IMMEDIATE RELEASE   Contact: Jodee Blanco
                                                      312.573.2070

BOB ZMUDA, GUERRILLA COMIC ANDY KAUFMAN'S WRITER AND CLOSEST FRIEND BREAKS HIS TWENTY YEAR SILENCE, DIVULGING THE TRUTH BEHIND THE HEADLINES SURROUNDING HOLLYWOOD'S MOST BIZARRE FUNNY MAN;

THE EMMY-AWARD WINNING PRODUCER AND FOUNDER OF COMIC RELIEF AND EXECUTIVE PRODUCER OF MAN ON THE MOON, THE UPCOMING MILOS FORMAN JIM CARREY FILM ABOUT KAUFMAN, SETS THE RECORD STRAIGHT IN CANDID AND PROVOCATIVE NEW MEMOIR;

***ANDY KAUFMAN REVEALED: BEST FRIEND TELLS ALL*, TO BE PUBLISHED LATE SUMMER BY LITTLE, BROWN AND COMPANY ALREADY HAS INDUSTRY INSIDERS BUZZING;**

Andy Kaufman, best known for his portrayal of sweet-natured mechanic Latka Gravas on the television series TAXI, was arguably one of the most ingenious and controversial entertainers of his time. More behavioral scientist than comedian, Kaufman boldly redefined the boundaries of entertainment, pushing the limits between a performer and his audience to the brink. Whether he was the teary-eyed child-man interviewing his hero Howdy Doodie, the sexually aroused intergender wrestling champion who often bedded his female opponents, or the bombastic lounge lizard singer Tony Clifton who poured a bowl of raw eggs over a stunned Dinah Shore in front of a live studio audience, Andy Kaufman broke all the rules.

Now for the first time, Andy's closest friend, writer, and co-conspirator, Emmy-award winning producer Bob Zmuda, who helped Kaufman engineer some of the most bizarre antics in show business history, breaks his twenty-year silence about the truth behind the headlines. In his new memoir ANDY KAUFMAN REVEALED: Best Friend Tells All (Little, Brown and Company; September 7, 1999; $24), Zmuda chronicles with brutal honesty and unprecedented insight the method and sometimes madness of Kaufman's legendary manipulations, and how these two fearless renegades hood winked an entire nation.

Drawing from his and Andy's experiences in Hollywood's inner-sanctum, deeply personal conversations spanning a decade of shared tragedies and triumphs, and clinical analyses from leading psychologists, Zmuda deftly reconstructs the real story that until now has never been told. He paints an illuminating portrait of a complex, often misunderstood loner who seldom ventured out of his room unless it was to jar millions of television viewers with his calculated lunacy or to satisfy his myriad sexual fetishes.

Zmuda describes how Andy made his living straddling the thin line between genius and insanity, and how he transformed that ability into a radical new genre of entertainment called Kaufmanism, which has influenced the likes of such comic luminaries as Robin Williams, Jim Carrey, Michael Richards, David Letterman, Lilly Tomlin, John Belushi, among countless others. He explains how Andy's contagious obsession with the Houdini like art of smoke and mirrors became the genesis for Kaufmanism, pranks of mythic proportion that to this day still have many people fooled.

In ANDY KAUFMAN REVEALED, Zmuda finally confesses the juicy details of these grand scale hoaxes, including: convincing a bus full of unsuspecting passengers that they were inhaling toxic fumes, thus sparking a mass coughing fit that resulted in a rush of ambulances and fire trucks to the scene; sabotaging a live network broadcast that sent an incensed cast of actors storming off stage and a deluge of press demanding Kaufman be banned from television; engaging Tony Clifton, Kaufman's infamous alter-ego, who in reality was a disguised Zmuda, to orchestrate a mystifying guest swap on both the David Letterman and Merv Griffin shows that caught these good-humored hosts completely off-guard; and their historic Carnegie Hall show where they bussed the entire audience to a secret location for milk and cookies; among many others.

Zmuda also delves into Andy's highly-publicized foray into professional wrestling and explains how they turned his off-beat obsession into one of the strangest cross-over careers in celebrity history. He discloses the truth about what really happened between champion Jerry Lawler and Andy Kaufman on that fateful day when Kaufman was hospitalized for a life-threatening neck injury, and the notorious confrontation that followed on The David Letterman Show that sent security guards scurrying onto the set. In addition, Zmuda talks openly about their creation of The Intergender Wrestling tour in order to satisfy Andy's peculiar need to wrestle women for sexual stimulation. In fact, Zmuda describes how he used to force Andy to tape himself down before each match to hide his aroused condition from the camera.

In perhaps what is one of the most formidable testimonials to the appeal of the anti-hero, Zmuda relates the astonishing origin and rise of Tony Clifton, an obnoxious, foul-smelling, middle-aged lounge lizard character whom Andy metamorphosed into when his dark side felt playful. He recalls some of Tony Clifton's most hair-raising exploits among which include: being bodily thrown off the Paramount lot after terrorizing the cast and crew of TAXI; opening for Rodney Dangerfield and so insulting the audience that they began to hurl any and all debris they could find to drive Clifton off-stage; and many others. For the first time in over twenty years, Zmuda also reveals how he and Andy engaged Hollywood's top make-up artists to help them perpetrate the perfect illusion—convincing the public, media and entertainment industry that Tony Clifton was really Kaufman. In actuality, it was Zmuda. Their ruse was so effective that it even fooled a top Las Vegas showgirl. The woman was sleeping with Tony Clifton believing it was Andy Kaufman, when all along it was Zmuda with whom she was having the affair.

In addition to reliving many of their greatest adventures in ANDY KAUFMAN REVEALED, Zmuda also talks openly about how Andy lived in a world of his own, often disconnected from reality. He documents: Andy's consuming devotion to Transcendental Meditation (TM) and how he believed it had taught him to levitate; his incomprehensible decision to moonlight as a busboy for minimum wage, even though he was making hundreds of thousands of dollars during the day starring on Taxi; his childlike fascination with hardcore prostitution and his successful personal challenge to bed nearly sixty hookers in one week; and his unsettling hygienic hatha yoga rituals that included swallowing twenty-five yards of cheesecloth for the purpose of internal flossing.

In ANDY KAUFMAN REVEALED Zmuda offers a rare and intimate perspective on the real individuals beneath the personas of some of America's most famous celebrities. He shares compelling behind-the-scenes stories about: Elvis Presley; Andy Warhol; Richard Burton; Judd Hirsch and the cast of TAXI; Deborah Harry, Dick Van Dyke, Johnny Cash, Jim Henson, Jay Leno, Kris Kristofferson, Gilda Radner, Pat Benetar, Eddie Murphy, Lorne Michaels, among countless others.

Through deeply personal diary entries, Zmuda also chronicles the disturbing last days of Andy Kaufman, his heroic struggle to cheat terminal cancer, and the public hysteria that erupted over the belief that Andy had faked his death. "To this day I still suffer the loss of my best friend," states Bob Zmuda. "Andy Kaufman's life was a courageous and brilliant testament to those kindred artists who pushed the limits higher and higher through their art."

Bob Zmuda is the recipient of an Emmy, numerous Ace Awards, the highly-coveted Justice In Art & Media Award (JAMA), and is a Grammy nominee. He is the founder, creator and executive producer of the highly successful Comic Relief broadcasts on HBO, annually hosted by Billy Crystal, Robin Williams, and Whoopi Goldberg, the largest gathering of comedians in the world, which has raised over 50 million dollars for homeless men, women and children.

For television, he produced and wrote: "A Comedy Salute to Michael Jordan," along with the Emmy nominated "A Comedy Salute to Andy Kaufman" both for NBC; "Hurricane Relief," with Gloria Estefan and Paul Simon for Showtime; "Baseball Relief" for Fox; and "The American Comedy Festival" for ABC. He hosts a 26-part series on Comedy Central and recently executive produced the "NFL Comedy Blitz" for CBS. He is currently producing a documentary on Andy Kaufman for A&E's Biography series, to air in Fall '99.

On the film side, Zmuda is currently co-executive producing with Danny DeVito's Jersey Films, MAN ON THE MOON, a biopic about Andy Kaufman directed by Milos Forman, starring Jim Carrey, Danny DeVito and Courtney Love, with Paul Giamatti portraying Bob Zmuda. It is due for release from Universal Studios in Fall of this year. Additionally, he is producing together with Jim Carrey an explosive documentary that chronicles the lengths Carrey went through to get inside the mind and body of Andy Kaufman. Other film credits include: PUNCHLINE with Tom Hanks and Sally Field; also DC CAB and BATMAN FOREVER, both for director Joel Schumacher. Bob Zmuda is energetic, articulate, and a wonderful raconteur. He is available for interview.

###

Blanco & Peace Enterprises LTD.

Chicago • Los Angeles • New York

JUICY CELEBRITY STORIES FROM
ANDY KAUFMAN REVEALED BY BOB ZMUDA

In ANDY KAUFMAN REVEALED Zmuda offers a rare and intimate perspective on the real individuals beneath the personas of some of America's most famous celebrities, sharing such behind-the-scenes nuggets as:

* Elvis Presley stopping his henchmen from man-handling a sixteen year old Andy Kaufman who had been laying in waiting in a kitchen cupboard in the bowels of the Hilton Casino in the hopes of meeting his idol–The King;

* Andy Warhol's dinner with the equally odd Andy Kaufman, during which the silence was deafening, until both eccentrics discovered their shared obsession with their childhood hero Howdy Doody;

* Richard Burton's humiliation and scathing glare when a young Bob Zmuda, sitting in the front row for his performance of Equus, fell asleep and began snoring loudly in the middle of the actor's most dramatic soliloquy;

* TAXI star Judd Hirsch's love-hate relationship with Andy that almost drove him to strangle Andy Kaufman, much to the support of the other cast members;

* Rocker Deborah Harry's and Andy's bitterly disappointing Broadway debut;

* Dick Van Dyke's loving support of Andy and his undeterred loyalty in the face of controversy;

Other celebrities featured include Jim Henson, John Belushi, Jay Leno, Kris Kristofferson, Gilda Radner, Eddy Murphy, among many others.

Blanco & Peace Enterprises LTD.

Chicago • Los Angeles • New York

BOB ZMUDA

A BIOGRAPHY

Savvy, imaginative and irreverent, Bob Zmuda has built a life and career out of doing what many might label the impossible. Often compared to showman P.T. Barnum by his peers for his intrinsic understanding of what makes an audience tick, Zmuda continues to boldly redefine the parameters of entertainment. Never one to impose limits on his creative instincts or shy away from a challenge, he has become one of comedy's most respected and celebrated visionaries, with a history of achievements spanning nearly three decades in the business.

Born and raised in Chicago, Zmuda came of age during the turbulent 60's, when daring, alternative forms of theater were just beginning to infiltrate the mainstream. Fueled by an innate need to open minds and challenge the norm, he utilized cutting-edge performance art as a vehicle to arouse people out of their complacency. At the young age of seventeen, he had founded his own guerrilla theater group, the politically charged No Name Players.

Deeply committed to his responsibility as an activist and his career as an actor, Zmuda continued to explore innovative avenues for effectively integrating both missions. Throughout the late 60s and early 70s, he immersed himself in the underground theater movement, experimenting with game and street theater, improvisation, psychodrama, among other avant-garde genres. One of Zmuda's early influences was the legendary Viola Spoolin, who empowered him with the insight to perceive acting as a cultural catalyst. Determined to experience as many diverse disciplines as possible, Zmuda also studied directly under luminary Lee Strassberg, and was a student at the prestigious Carnegie Mellon University.

It was then he met Chris Albrecht, now President of Original Programming for HBO. Together, the two young hopefuls moved to New York, where destiny led them to the Improv, the oldest comedy club in America. There, they cut their teeth in the world of stand-up comedy, working alongside fellow struggling comics such as Jay Leno, Richard Lewis, Richard Belzer, Larry David, Freddie Prinze, to name just a few.

During this period, Zmuda met guerrilla comic Andy Kaufman, whom he would later write for and produce. Together, they forged one of the most successful and talked about alliances in comedy history, perpetrating pranks of mythic proportion on the public, entertainment industry and media, that to this day still have many people fooled. In fact, these grand scale hoaxes would launch a comedy movement called Kaufmanism, influencing the likes of such artists as David Letterman, John Belushi, Michael Richards, Lily Tomlin, among countless others.

In 1985, one year after Kaufman died of lung cancer, Zmuda held a memorial for his best friend that would become the genesis for Comic Relief on HBO, the largest gathering of comedians ever assembled in the history of show business, hosted annually by Billy Crystal, Robin Williams, and Whoopi Goldberg. Comic Relief, for which founder and executive producer Bob Zmuda received an Emmy Award, an Ace Award, and the Justice In Arts & Media Award (JAMA), has raised over 50 million dollars for homeless men, women and children.

One of television's most prolific forces, Zmuda also produced and wrote: "A Comedy Salute to Michael Jordan," with Patti LaBelle and Spike Lee and the Emmy nominated "A Comedy Salute to Andy Kaufman" with Michael Richards, Gary Shandling and Carl Reiner, both for NBC; "Hurricane Relief," with Gloria Estefan and Paul Simon for Showtime; "Baseball Relief" with Sharon Stone and Jerry Seinfeld, for Fox; and "The American Comedy Festival" with Dan Ackroyd and John Goodman for ABC. He hosts a 26-part series on Comedy Central. He recently executive produced the "NFL Comedy Blitz" with Kelsey Grammer and Ray Romano for CBS, and is currently producing a documentary on Andy Kaufman for A&E's Biography series, to air in Fall '99.

On the film side, Zmuda is currently co-executive producing with Danny DeVito's Jersey Films, MAN ON THE MOON, a biopic about Andy Kaufman directed by Milos Forman, starring Jim Carrey, Danny DeVito and Courtney Love, with Paul Giamatti portraying Zmuda. It is due for release from Universal Studios in Fall of this year. Additionally, he is producing together with Jim Carrey an explosive documentary that chronicles the lengths Carrey went through to get inside the mind and body of Andy Kaufman. Other film credits include: PUNCHLINE with Tom Hanks and Sally Field; also DC CAB and BATMAN FOREVER, both for director Joel Schumacher.

In September, Zmuda's first book *ANDY KAUFMAN REVEALED: Best Friend Tells All*, will be published by Little, Brown and Company.

Bob Zmuda is energetic, articulate, and a wonderful raconteur. He is available for interview. B-roll and video reel of Zmuda available upon request.

Blanco & Peace Enterprises LTD.
Publicity • Public Relations • Promotions

March 17, 1997

Rhonda Shear
USA Up All Night
1230 Avenue of the Americas, 3rd Floor
New York, NY 10020

Dear Rhonda,

Thank you in advance for reviewing this correspondence. Enclosed are press materials on one of the most intriguing and provocative up-and-comers in the literary and film worlds, Jay Bonansinga.

A born maverick, Bonansinga deftly challenges conventional wisdom on the fine line between good and evil. He blends the plot-weaving acument of Dean R. Koontz with the fiercely dark characters reminiscent of a David Lynch or Quentin Tarantino film. One doesn't read Jay Bonansinga. They experience him.

An energetic and cutting-edge interview, he is disarmingly candid. Not shy about expressing passionately felt personal opinions on taboo subjects, Bonansinga, challenges traditional ideals and methods, taking even the most adventuresome of imaginations on a thrill ride. On the visual side, his intense renegade look carries with it a mysterious appeal. That, combined with Bonansinga's off the cuff slant on today's "hot topics," can consume an audience's curiosity and capture their attention.

In fact, Jay's been capturing a lot of attention lately. With three critically acclaimed books already under his belt and a fourth one in the works, Jay is igniting a real buzz in the literary community. Hollywood insiders are also taking notice of this prolific young mind. His original screenplay MANSLAYER, bought by Kushner Locke International, is currently in pre-production with Mary Lambert (PET SEMETARY) directing. His first book, BLACK MARIAH has been optioned by New Line Cinema with George Romero slotted to direct. THE KILLER'S GAME, his newest novel, a throat-grabbing thriller hot off the presses this month has also been optioned by New Line Cinema and developed into a major motion picture screenplay.

THE KILLER'S GAME offers a fascinating window into the soul of the professional assassin. Career hit man Joe Flood, nicknamed "Slugger," a living legend in his field, is diagnosed with cancer. Flood, determined to die by the sword and not at the debilitating hands of his illness, puts out a contract on his own life, inviting the cream of the crop of professional killers to best him at his own game. An hour before the deadly "contest" is set to begin, Flood discovers his doctor's office made a teeny tiny mistake. The lab goofed. Joe is fitter than a fiddle. There's only one problem. He can't call off the "hit parade." Once a contract is in motion, it cannot be rescinded. With the will to live his only weapon, Joe is forced to prove that he's still the best.

I'd love to speak with you more about Jay Bonansinga. If you have any questions please do not hesitate to give me a call at 312/573-2070.

Sincerely,

Neal Silverman

Blanco & Peace Enterprises LTD.
Publicity • Public Relations • Promotions

FOR IMMEDIATE RELEASE

Contact: Jodee Blanco
Neal Silverman
312/573-2070

LITERARY RENEGADE JAY BONANSINGA BLASTS OPEN A WINDOW INTO THE PROFESSIONAL ASSASSIN'S SOUL, WITH HIS NEWEST THRILLER *THE KILLER'S GAME*;

HOLLYWOOD INTEREST ALREADY ESCALATING;

Literary renegade Jay Bonansinga, whose work has always deftly straddled the line between social commentary and the thrill of the ride, has catapulted the velocity to dangerously high-impact with his newest and most enthralling yarn yet, THE KILLER'S GAME. Set against the blood-drenched, razor-edged backdrop of the professional hitman's intimate world, THE KILLER'S GAME provides a provocative window into the souls of people who exterminate human lives for a living.

When career assassin Joe Flood, affectionately referred to by his peers as "The Slugger," is diagnosed with a terminal disease, he puts out a multi-million dollar global contract on his own life. From covert C.I.A. operatives, mafia hitmen, and independent female "exterminators," to inner-city gang-bangers, homeless KGB agents, and free-lancing terrorist gun-slingers, every eliminator in the business jumps at the chance to see who can successfully take out the deadliest one of them all. Just as the wheels of this fatal *contest* are put into motion, he discovers that he was misdiagnosed! But it's too late to stop the hitman parade. Once a contract is initiated, it can't be rescinded.

357 W. Chicago Ave., Suite 400 • Chicago, IL 60610 312/573-2070 • FAX 312/573-1077
270 Lafayette St., Suite 1505 • New York, NY 10012 212/274-1616 • FAX 212/274-9876

As Joe and his girlfriend Maizie frantically race against time, struggling to snatch their lives back from the jaws of a living nightmare, Joe must taste the bitter, acrid reality of what it feels like to be the hunted instead of the hunter.

"I've always been fascinated by the paradox of the hitman's inner-life," reveals Jay Bonansinga. "Many real-life assassins have large families and lead double lives, keeping their homicidal vocations a secret...they go to church, love, cry, laugh, they even teach their children the difference between right and wrong," he continues. "THE KILLER'S GAME gave me the opportunity to sink my teeth into the fascinating aspects of that bizarre truth."

Early response to the book from both the publishing and entertainment communities has been overwhelming. THE KILLER'S GAME is also being published in the U.K., France, Germany, Bulgaria, and The Netherlands, and is available as a Dove Audio read by veteran character actor Robert Forster. On the film side, THE KILLER'S GAME has been optioned by producer Andrew Lazar (*Assassins, Bound*) and New Line Cinema. It's been developed into a major motion picture screenplay that has Hollywood insiders buzzing.

Author Jay Bonansinga is energetic and provocative. He is available for interview.

###

Blanco & Peace Enterprises LTD.
Publicity • Public Relations • Promotions

JAY BONANSINGA

When author and screenwriter Jay Bonansinga walks into a room, sparks fly. Erudite, imaginative, and outspoken, this literary renegade is generating a real buzz in both the publishing and entertainment communities. A born maverick, Jay challenges the traditional parameters of storytelling, deftly crafting turbo-propelled "mind movies" that race past the speed limit.

Also racing past speed limits is the growth of Jay Bonansinga's extraordinary career. His first novel, THE BLACK MARIAH (Warner Books), a haunting dark thriller, flew off shelves worldwide-including editions in the U.K., Germany, France, Japan, Spain, Italy, Hungary and Russia. Nominated for The Bram Stoker Award for Best First Novel, it was immediately optioned by New Line Cinema, with legendary director George Romero (*Night of the Living Dead, The Dark Half*) committed to direct. Bonansinga co-wrote the screenplay. His second novel, SICK (Warner Books), a breathlessly-paced erotic odyssey, voted One of the Top Ten Horror Novels of 1995 by Science Fiction Chronicle, was published in the United States, Canada, the U.K. Japan, France, Germany and Hungary, with foreign rights pending in numerous other international markets.

Bonansinga's third novel THE KILLER'S GAME (Simon & Schuster), is a throat-grabbing thriller hot off the presses this March. Already optioned by Hollywood wonderboy producer Andrew Lazar (*Assassins, Bound*) and New Line Cinema, the book has been developed into a major motion picture screenplay that has industry insiders buzzing.

In addition to his prolific stream of successes as an author, Bonansinga's scripts are also turning heads. MANSLAYER, an original screenplay, bought by Kushner Locke International, with Mary Lambert (*Pet Sematary*) directing, is currently in pre-production.

When Jay isn't immersed at his computer pouring out a book or screenplay, he's earnestly concocting an over-the-top short story, sure to engender goosebumps on even his most thickly-skinned of fans. An award-winning writer of short-fiction, he's been published in such hot underground publications as Grue, Cemetery Dance, and Outre, as well as anthologies like IT CAME FROM THE DRIVE IN, MISKATONIC UNIVERSITY, 100 LITTLE VICIOUS VAMPIRE STORIES, GHOSTCLIFF, among others. His articles and essays in the fields of horror, science fiction and suspense have appeared in FilmFax, Video Marketplace, Screen, American Fantasy, as well as many others.

357 W. Chicago Ave., Suite 400 • Chicago, IL 60610   312/573-2070 • FAX 312/573-1077
270 Lafayette St., Suite 1505 • New York, NY 10012   212/274-1616 • FAX 212/274-9876

"I don't want to engage audiences," says Jay Bonansinga, with a mischievous smile. "I want to *engulf* them, take them on a nail-biting roller coaster ride into the funkiest, unexplored regions of their own psyches,"he continues. "What makes a horror story or thriller *truly* scary and exciting for me is when it evokes a response in someone that makes them question their own perception of themselves."

Never one to rest on his laurels, Bonansinga is busily at work on his fourth novel, HEAD CASE, a shadowy tome of intrigue and suspense due out from Simon & Schuster in 1998. Jay Bonansinga lives in Evanston, IL with his wife Jeanne.

###

Blanco & Peace Enterprises LTD.
Publicity • Public Relations • Promotions

SUGGESTED INTERVIEW QUESTIONS FOR JAY BONANSINGA

1. I hear that you locked yourself up in a dank, dark shooting gallery with a bunch of edgy, gun-obsessed militia types in order to prepare for the writing of THE KILLER'S GAME. Could you tell us a little more about that, and how you came out of the experience unscathed?

2. Everyone is hot on the bandwagon about the over-abundance of violence in books, film and television, yet THE KILLER'S GAME is awash in tidal waves of blood and mayhem. How do you justify capitalizing on violence within a storytelling framework?

3. You're a self-proclaimed maverick and renegade with a pension for celebrating extremes in your work. Do you do that in your life, too?

4. THE KILLER'S GAME makes the art of assassination seem cool, hip, happening, hot. Doesn't that make you feel just a little guilty?

5. You're a respected and frequently sought-after expert on horror and science fiction. What is it about the dark side that lights up your imagination?

6. You've been quoted as saying that everything you learned about writing, you got from watching movies. Doesn't this raise eyebrows in the serious literary community?

7. You started out publishing very twisted, very dark horror fiction. Now you're in a much more commercial arena, writing mainstream thrillers. Was this a difficult jump?

8. I've heard that you consider yourself-- in your own words-- a "film school brat." Is this something that you've tried to cure in therapy, or is it an advantage for a novelist?

9. You seem to participate much more closely-- some might even say obsessively-- with the film adaptations of your work. Isn't this a somewhat masochistic exercise?

10. Aren't you terrified that one of the dark, homicidal creations that you traffick in will one day show up on your doorstep and break one of your kneecaps or something?

11. If you could meet an infamous killer from literature, who would it be and why?

12. What's next for Jay Bonansinga?

357 W. Chicago Ave., Suite 400 • Chicago, IL 60610   312/573-2070 • FAX 312/573-1077
270 Lafayette St., Suite 1505 • New York, NY 10012   212/274-1616 • FAX 212/274-9876

The Secret Art of Media Research

*Y*OU'RE ARMED AND READY WITH A FABULOUS PRESS KIT, JAM-PACKED with provocative angles, newsworthy hooks, and great story ideas. You're chomping at the bit to begin pitching media, to get as much exposure for your book as possible. Where do you go from here?

One of the most vital elements of any publicity campaign is sound media research. You need to know who to pitch and what they want if you're going to have any real chance at getting them to commit to an author interview. No matter how talented you are at selling story ideas to producers and editors, if you don't understand how to generate print and broadcast leads, you've entered the media marathon with two weak ankles. Media research is so much more than pulling databases or looking up names and numbers in *Bacon's* media guides. It's a methodical, highly creative process that demands persistence, pit bull–like aggression, attention to detail, and a relentless investigative instinct.

Slow and Steady . . .

Everyone automatically assumes that the most important characteristic of a good publicist is courage. While an ability to take risks is crucial, it pales in comparison to curiosity. A publicist who turns over every stone and looks under every rock will get much more media coverage in the long run. It's like the old fable of the tortoise and the hare. The publicist who rushes through the media research phase of the campaign is like the hare, who's so focused on the finish line that he underestimates the race. The publicist who takes the time to research which media is the most appropriate to pitch may be slower out of the gate, but in the end will win countless more interviews for his author. With these thoughts in mind, let's explore the nuts and bolts of media research.

The Thrill of Discovery

I've always loved doing media research. A lot of PR people find it tedious, but I get such a kick out of discovering new media outlets. The key is knowing where to look. As we discussed earlier in this book, there are a boatload of media guides published that provide detailed information about every print and broadcast outlet in the world. I've worked with all of them and have found *Bacon's* directories to be the best. *Bacon's* directories are available in several volumes and also on CD-ROM. They're divided into television, radio, newspapers, and magazines. Television, radio, and newspapers list by state and region, with separate sections on national outlets. Magazines are listed alphabetically and cross-referenced by subject category.

PR newsletters are also terrific. *Bulldog, Partyline, Contact,* and *Lifestyle* are just a few of the countless newsletters available to publicists that list the most updated information about the media, including breaking news about the industry, staff changes, beat reporters seeking experts for stories, and specials currently in production, among other coverage opportunities for authors, celebrities, and experts. Keep in mind, however, that a good publicist should use media guides and newsletters as a *starting point only*.

Speaking of starting points, media research begins at home. Watch TV, read the newspapers, listen to the radio. Expose yourself as much as possible to all the media you can. There's nothing more effective than a publicist pitching a reporter she's read, a television show she's watched, or a radio show she's heard. These give her the power of the audience's perspective. Though you can't listen to every radio or TV show in America, or read every newspaper or magazine, once you become familiar with different formats and sensibilities of shows, as well as sections of newspapers and magazines, you'll experience a whole new level of confidence and professionalism when you pitch.

Analysis and Planning

Step two of media research is an honest analysis of the book and author. You need to establish realistic guidelines for yourself. For example, if you've got an author with a severe speech impediment, you wouldn't do extensive research on radio shows, but might focus more on viable print outlets. Conversely, if you're publicizing a book on a lighthearted topic and the author is wonderful with a microphone, you may want to concentrate on radio and television instead of print, which usually requires a harder news angle.

Let's look at another example. You're publicizing a novel with a strong New Age spin. The author is articulate and electric on camera. If I were doing this project, I would research magazines, television and radio shows, cable networks, and holistic writers, among other media that specialize in New Age audiences. I wouldn't eliminate mainstream media, but I would do a lot of extra research, trying to unearth every possible New Age outlet that I could.

The bottom line is that once you've established your campaign strategy, research media that *supports* that strategy. Don't go off on tangents that will irritate the media and have you chasing your own tail. If you're publicizing a book on hair and makeup tips, it wouldn't make sense to spend a lot of time researching the assignment reporters at network news shows, because they wouldn't perceive this topic as a breaking story. However, if you had a feasible pitch in mind that you think might work for the health reporters on the network news desk, you'd be smart to take a leap of faith. Just make sure when you're doing media research that you recognize what's realistic and what's not. That doesn't mean not to go after long shots. It just means that you should be clear about the difference so you can exercise sound judgment in what you pitch to whom and how much energy you spend. Energy, like money, should be invested wisely, both at the research and implementational stages.

Gather Your Resources

Once you've determined the categories of media you wish to research, you're ready for step three. It's time to hit the resource manuals and the phones! In earlier chapters in this book, I review how to use *Bacon's*. I'll briefly reiterate it here for clarity. On the television side, national television is divided by network, syndicated, and national cable networks. All the national television listings are alphabetical and in the front of the guide. Local television is divided into two categories. Regional cable networks are delineated alphabetically by state in the front of the guide following the national section. Local broadcast television is listed alphabetically by state and city/town.

Radio is laid out just like television. National radio listings are in the front of the guide, listed in two categories: network and syndicated. Local radio is listed alphabetically by market and station call letters.

The newspaper guide is arranged slightly differently. The front section lists all daily newspapers alphabetically by market. The second section outlines all weekly community papers and multiple publishers alphabetically by state and township. The end of the guide provides a comprehensive breakdown of national papers, syndicated columnists, wire service bureaus, and beat writers, among other national print outlets. The magazine guide lists publications by subject matter and cross-references alphabetically.

Media research is, in large part, a communication process, because once you look up all the necessary information in *Bacon's* guides, you've got to explore your options further. I'm going to illustrate what I mean by walking you through a typical example.

Media Research, Step by Step

We're publicizing a book entitled *The Road to Riches,* a how-to business book for entrepreneurs, written by a well-known corporate renegade who started his own company and has since made millions. We've narrowed down our research strategy to national print and broadcast business media. I always like to search broadcast first, as it is usually the most time-consuming component of the research phase. I whip out *Bacon's Television* and first review network, syndicated, and cable network shows. I photocopy all those pages, highlight what seems to be the most appropriate outlets for my author, then begin telephoning the contacts listed. Bear in mind, if you're a seasoned publicist, you probably already have many contacts of your own, but that doesn't exempt you from the research phase. It gives you an advantage, but you still have to roll up your sleeves like everyone else.

What should we ask when we get a contact on the phone? I'll be very specific here. Let's say we're contacting network cable shows and have just telephoned the producer listed for a weekly show called *Business First.* After several messages back and forth, we finally get the producer on the line.

"Hello, my name is Jodee Blanco, from Blanco & Peace, and I'm updating my media lists, as I have someone soon to be available for interview. Do you have a few seconds? Thanks so much. Are you still the contact for *Business First?* What types of stories do you like, and what's the format of your show? What stories are you working on now? This is the list of other business shows I have for your network. [Read list.] Do you know if I've missed anything? Thank you so much for taking the time to chat with me. I really appreciate it."

Producers, as long as they're not on deadline, will respond with courtesy to those questions because they understand exactly what you're doing. Sometimes, you may be stumped because a producer will be impatient or unwilling to help you. When that happens, simply call the programming department and ask what shows are currently in production and who the contacts are.

I've got another great trick, which we touched upon in chapter 3. Remember what we discussed about in-house and outside productions? Often, broadcast and cable networks will air shows that are produced by independent production companies. When you contact the programming departments, it's always a good idea to ask them what specials are in development or production, as well as what series are being independently produced. Programming directors are usually cooperative, and this kind of data is invaluable. Remember, if you're good at media research and tenacious, one contact name on a page in *Bacon's* should create a minimum of five to ten new leads. The rules for researching radio are the same as television. Speak with producers first, and if you feel you're not getting enough specifics, have them transfer you to programming.

Researching print is similar. Most media guides will give you the names of the beat writers at each newspaper. In our example, *The Road to Riches,* the natural contact to call first would be the business editor. Here are some of the questions you would want to ask him:

Are you still the business editor for this paper? Who are your section's beat reporters? Are there any freelance writers you work with frequently whom you'd recommend I pitch stories to occasionally? Are you currently working on any feature stories about self-made millionaires or entrepreneurs, as I may have someone who would be a great expert? Are any of your business columnists syndicated? Are you competitive with any other publication in your market, and if so, what's your position on first print and exclusivity?

You may not be able to ask all these questions, as editors and reporters have tight timetables, but you should have an idea now of how media research works. On the magazine side, the same applies. Once you have your lists of targeted magazines, call reporters and editors, inquiring about beat writers, stories currently in the hopper, and policies on competitive publications, among other data that will empower your pitch.

Creating a Database

Let's back up a minute and review where we're at. You've completed the campaign strategy and know exactly what categories of print and broadcast media you want to pitch. You've gone through the television, radio, newspaper, and magazine guides, photocopying all the pertinent pages, and have highlighted potential appropriate coverage targets. You've telephoned each and every contact and followed up on new leads. You feel confident and energized, knowing that you have a strong media hit list that's updated to the minute. Now what?

Having an organized database is a powerful weapon in public relations. Everyone has his own preference in terms of how he would like to structure and format his database. It doesn't really matter whether you're an Apple or PC fan. Databasing is more about logic and simplicity than anything else. I'm going to share with you how Blanco & Peace databases media. Keep in mind that part of the fun is developing your own system and style. Hopefully my thoughts will give you a basic guideline from which to start.

Each campaign should have its own media database. For *The Road to Riches,* I'd suggest dividing the database into three sections: national television; radio; and print. If the author were touring, I would do a separate section for each city. The wonderful thing about databasing media is that it gives you long-form media lists that you can pitch from, as well as corresponding labels for mailings. When Blanco & Peace enters media into databases, we include the following information:

- Media outlet (network, syndicator, newspaper or magazine, etc.)
- Name of show or section of newspaper
- Contact name
- Phone number
- Fax number
- E-mail
- Address

Sometimes we annotate the entries with other specifics, such as deadlines and story preferences, among other details.

I can't emphasize enough the importance of staying on top of databases. When a contact name changes or a show alters its format, take the time to amend your booking sheets in longhand, and update the computer database at the end of the campaign. It saves so much time later on.

Staying Flexible

Another element about media research and list compilation is flexibility. Don't assume that the database you assemble at the beginning of the campaign won't expand and evolve once pitching is underway. As you pitch, you'll uncover new leads, which you'll need to notate and act upon. Additionally, a smart publicist piggybacks breaking news whenever possible. That means that in a moment's notice, you may have to generate a whole new category of media lists to accommodate a piggyback opportunity or capitalize on a newsworthy development in the campaign.

For example, recently, one of the novelists my firm represents signed several precedent-setting deals with prominent Internet companies to promote her books online. We immediately began researching the Internet writers at the top daily national papers, syndicated cyberspace columns, Internet magazines, and television and radio shows that cover Internet news. We crunched on the research, because we wanted to issue a press release while the story was still hot. Within two days, we had a target hit list from which we were able to generate significant coverage.

Tricks of the Trade

I'd like to share some of my trade secrets for media research. Maps! If you're doing a grassroots campaign for an author, one of the best media sources in the world is a basic map. Say, for example, you're sending an author on a five-city tour. Look for the names of small towns that border the bigger tour cities, then check *Bacon's* for media in those markets. Another great trick— the entertainment trades. *Hollywood Reporter* and *Variety,* as well as *Broadcasting and Cable,* and *Electronic News* cover television, cable, and radio. You should make a point of reading these trades at least once or twice a week. You'll get information on new shows, staff changes, trends, and heaps of other items that will give you a heads-up on new media opportunities.

Here's a fun one—*TV Guide!* Every week, I read *TV Guide* cover to cover, listing by listing. Sometimes new shows will pop up that missed *Bacon's* deadline. Also, *TV Guide* tells you what guests are being featured on which shows, enabling you to analyze interview booking patterns of certain producers. On top of that, *TV Guide* provides a bird's-eye view of competitive time slots between talk shows. Again, it's so crucial to be aware of the media, what's hot, what's not, which shows are neck and neck in the ratings war, which newspapers are breaking the biggest stories, and what start-up magazines are gaining momentum, among other industry insights. The more you know, the more educated your pitch.

Another secret? Chambers of commerce. Every regional market has a chamber of commerce. Most of them maintain updated media lists. The people who work in these offices are warm and friendly and always open to helping PR firms. You can buy a list of chambers all across America, or simply call information and ask for the number. They're a wonderful source for information.

Along the same vein, media escorts are tremendously helpful with media research. Though we'll talk more about media escorts in the chapter on tours, media escorts are men and women who work specifically with touring authors. When an author is in a specific market, usually the publicist will hire a local escort to accompany the author to interviews and troubleshoot on-site whenever necessary. These escorts know the regional media in their towns inside out and have personal insights about producers, reporters, and even on-air personalities that can prove immensely beneficial to a publicist.

Whenever my company plans an author tour, my staff automatically makes two phone calls in each market. They ask the media escorts to send their own media lists, and then check in with the chamber of commerce for copies of its lists. Between our own database and these supplemental lists, we enter the pitching process with confidence and knowledge.

Media Kit Mailing

After the initial media research and databasing is complete, your next step is the mailing. Since you will have spoken to as many of the contacts as possible, the pitch memo can be personalized. Media mailings cast the first impression. Beautiful, well-written press kits with an intelligent pitch memo set the stage for future communication between the media contact and the publicist. The media mailing should include:

- Press kit with all relevant pieces
- A copy of the book
- The pitch letter or memo

Packages should be sent priority mail (guaranteed to arrive in three days) or first class. Don't cut corners on mailing costs. If you do, what you'll really be cutting is the producer or reporter's image of the campaign.

I always recommend using Jiffy Bags or padded white envelopes for press kit/book mailings. There's nothing more offensive than a rumpled up press kit accompanying a damaged book. I also have a stamp I had specially made that says in big, bold, capital letters: OPEN IMMEDIATELY, DEADLINE MATERIAL ENCLOSED

You have to understand that producers, reporters, and editors receive on average dozens of book mailings a week. They can't possibly sift through all of them. The packages that are clean and crisp looking, and distinguished by a stamp or sticker indicating newsworthiness, are the ones that get opened and the contents actually read.

Another thing to remember with mailings—make sure everything is spelled correctly on pitch letters and labels. Nothing turns off media contacts more than if their name or the call letters of their station is misspelled. Don't be careless. A little typo can undermine your credibility. That may seem severe, but I've spent twenty years socializing with media people, and I know what angers them. When you spell their names wrong, it's a sign of sloppiness and disrespect. Take the time to do it right.

We've talked about this before. Pre-pitch contacts *before* you do a mailing. It will motivate the contact to keep an eye out for the package and will predispose them favorably to the story ideas it contains. Also, it will save on budget. Mass mailings sent without pre-pitch calls waste so much money.

Overcoming Obstacles

The media research and mailing process is a vital component of the publicity campaign. So often, publicists generate the same old media lists for every book, never bothering to tailor-design a database for each project. That kind of laziness damages opportunities.

I understand that a lot of the problem isn't just laziness, it's time constraints. Publicists are overworked to the gills. Many of them simply don't have time to do fresh, updated media lists for each campaign. If that's the case, there are several solutions.

College interns are quality, inexpensive labor. Most students would give their eyeteeth to do a publicity internship, as they know it's a tough industry to break into. If the publicist lays out what needs to be researched, the intern can do the footwork.

Sometimes, it can be a time management issue. For example, prime pitching time is always from 10:00 AM to 3:00 PM. In that time frame, you can access contacts coast to coast. From a biological perspective, those are prime energy hours. Get to the office a little early and research media in Eastern and Central time zones before 10:00 AM, and stay late a few nights to research media in Pacific and Mountain time zones after 3:00 PM. Once you learn to lay out your day, you'll find there is ample space to do media research. And it's *so* important.

One last item, and it's something I say to my staff continually. *Look beyond the obvious.* When you're researching media, think creatively. Seek the unanticipated opportunity. For example, let's say the author of *The Road to Riches* is a gourmet cook in his spare time. Research culinary magazines. You could pitch them on doing a story about the millionaire entrepreneur who dons a chef hat after 5:00. Imagine the angle that no one else would consider, figure out which media would be most appropriate to pitch, research the outlets, then go for it big!

Next chapter: the ins and outs of pitching media.

The Ins and Outs of Pitching Media

*Y*OU'RE READY TO START THE MEDIA PITCHING PROCESS. THIS IS ONE of the most intricate and complex elements of publicity and public relations. There's a psychology to selling story ideas that transcends everything you think you ever knew about sales. Though pitching is an acquired skill, some people have a natural flair for it, while others struggle to master its myriad challenges. No matter which category you fall into, my goal is to turn you into a lean, mean pitching machine! Let's get started.

Improvise!

One of the questions I'm most frequently asked by college students interested in a public relations career is, "What's the best course to take to prepare me for the publicity world?" You may be surprised by my answer: improvisational theater. Why? Pitching media requires a razor-sharp response mechanism. The muscle that monitors response is honed by activities such as improvisational theater and extemporaneous speaking, among other forms of presentational challenges that demand on-the-spot, quick thinking.

Let me give you an example. You're pitching a romance author and think you have the lifestyle writer from *USA Today* on the phone. Full of effervescence and energy, you're talking away, trying to persuade the reporter to interview your author. Suddenly, the reporter cuts you short and says, "I don't know why you're talking to me. I'm not the lifestyle writer. I edit the food section for the paper." If your *"response-ability"* is well practiced and you can respond on a dime, you'll turn this fumble into a touchdown.

Here's how I would improvise in this situation. "As a matter of fact, you're precisely the person I want to be talking to . . . who better to chat with about a romance writer than the food editor . . . my author can provide your readership with a whole new take on food, sharing intimate secrets about great romantic local restaurants, as well as dozens of ideas for sumptuous aphrodisiac meals." You get the picture. No matter what response a media contact gives you, if you're good at improvisation, you're never tongue-tied in the clutch. Remember what we talked about in chapter 2 on front- and side-door pitching? Cultivating your response mechanism enables you to side-door pitch on the spot.

One of the most challenging aspects of publicity today is getting media contacts on the telephone. With the onslaught of voice mail, many producers, reporters, and editors rarely even pick up their phones, and there are no more secretaries to schmooze in order to inspire those return calls. As a result, publicists have to be more on their toes than ever before. That means if you get a media contact on the telephone, you probably won't have the luxury of getting them back on the phone anytime soon. It's now or never. If you can't switch angles in midstream or shift gears in a blink, you diminish your booking capacity by 70 percent or more. Publicity isn't for the weak-kneed. It's for the silver-tongued.

The Power of Words

Another inside perspective on pitching? Vocabulary. I can't tell you how critical it is to utilize a broad spectrum of words when you communicate with press. First of all, if you speak with a rich vocabulary, it inspires immediate respect. This is especially true when you're cold-pitching a reporter or producer. When a publicist has a strong sense of language, it captures the attention of the media person and motivates them to concentrate on what you're saying.

How do you begin increasing your vocabulary? There are several tricks. One of the greatest resources is *The Synonym Finder,* published by Rodale Press. Easier to use than a conventional thesaurus, it's terrific for boning up on new words. Each week, choose ten new words that you rarely, if ever, utilize in day-to-day conversation and consciously make the effort to substitute these words for phrases and expressions you would normally use. You'll notice a colorful change not only in how you speak, but in how others pay attention to what you say.

For example, you're writing a pitch memo and want to get across to the media that your author is "full of energy," "intelligent," and a "terrific interview." Rather than describe your author with such predictable and unimaginative phrasing, why not try something like "this author is ebullient, erudite, and a brilliant raconteur." You're getting across the same message, but instead of using a bicycle to get where you're going, you've gotten behind the wheel of a Ferrari. *Present it the way you want it perceived.* If you communicate an idea, whether it be on paper, in person, or by telephone, be authoritative, confident, and articulate. Vocabulary is an intrinsic element of those characteristics. The respect and attention you elicit will surprise you.

The Power of Silence

Another great pitching secret is that *silence is power.* I learned this lesson from my dad when I was very young, and it has served me well in my professional field. How often have you talked with someone or had a salesperson pitch you on a product, and every other phrase out of his mouth is "um," or "ya know." It's human nature to fill uncomfortable silences with sounds. Nowhere is this truer than during a sell. Think about your own experiences. You're pitching a reporter or producer on a specific book, and suddenly you don't know what to say next. Rather than hesitate and gather your thoughts, you utter "well, um . . ." until you figure out your next sentence. Nothing commands attention more than silence. If you're pitching a media contact and you're at a loss for words for a moment, don't fill the silence with grunts and nonwords. It diminishes your power. Simply close your mouth, take a deep breath, gather your thoughts, then continue speaking. This is so important. Be aware of when you say "um" and "you know," and try consciously to stop yourself. You'll discover that this little exercise in self-discipline will revolutionize your communication skills. Remember, present it the way you want it perceived. If you want a confident, enthusiastic response from someone, it's incumbent upon you to establish and maintain the tone.

No is No Answer

We've talked about this in previous chapters, but it certainly bears reemphasizing. If you're pitching a contact and he's telling you that he doesn't have any interest in your author, he's not saying "no" to *you,* he's saying "no" to your *pitch.* What does that mean? *Turn it around!* For instance, rather than just accept their "no" and hang up, seize the bull by the horns, and enlist curiosity as your weapon. Say to your contact, "I understand this isn't a story you personally can pursue at this time, but are there any other stories you or perhaps a colleague are working on in which my author could be included as an expert or resource?" Don't go blindly into that dark night of disinterest. Turn the contact's lights on, make him help you identify other potential leads. Media people understand that a book publicist's job is to generate interview opportunities for authors. If you're friendly and respectful, yet maintain a subtle, but distinct, assertiveness in your voice, the contact will be more than accommodating.

What should you do if a contact says "no," and isn't willing to share helpful information about other people who might be interested in your author? Try this approach: Nothing disarms an irritable media person more than a publicist who gently, but with integrity, calls him on his rudeness. For example, you might say to a short-tempered or ill-mannered media contact, "Gee, I'm sorry, I must have caught you at a bad time, as you seem a little out of sorts ... . when would be a good time to get back to you, as I really do need to talk with you?" Nine times out of ten, this statement will take the wind out of his sails, and he'll give you an alternate day and time to reach him. I'd also suggest faxing or e-mailing a quick note, thanking him for scheduling an opportunity to chat. This way, you've reminded him in print, as well as ingratiated yourself further by acknowledging their kindness. Little gestures can have an infinite impact.

Getting a Commitment

Publicity is riddled with dilemmas. One of the most common is that you'll pitch a contact, and he'll be deeply interested in book-ing an author, but for some reason won't commit. You'll keep get-ting answers like, "Yes, I really want to arrange an author interview, but I'm just not sure yet. Can you touch base with me next week?" Then, you call back a week later, and the contact still doesn't have a definitive answer, yet continues to wave the carrot, until you think you're going to scream. Let me first explain, from the con-tact's perspective, what's really going on. If you're pitching a pro-ducer, reporter, or editor and you're getting put off like this, it usually means that the contact wants to confirm the booking, but must convince someone above him. Frequently, with television, a segment producer will be gung ho for an author, but the host will be lukewarm. Media contacts don't keep publicists hanging for fun. They're usually caught in the middle themselves.

Here's a wonderful solution that continues to work for me almost without fail. Tell your contact that you'd like to set up an informal telephone conversation, similar to a preinterview between him and the author. Explain that there are no strings attached, and if he or the host/boss aren't absolutely blown away by this author, that you'll pick up your marbles and go home. If you've media-coached your author properly (which we'll review in detail in the next chapter), she will be able to sell the booking through.

A couple of tips on this technique: Make it exceedingly clear to your contact that this telephone conversation with the author is just an exploratory chat, and he shouldn't feel any pressure or obligation. If you don't position it this way, he'll be less likely to do the call. Also, make sure you explain to the author exactly the purpose of the phone call. Don't mislead her. Most importantly—and I can't reinforce this enough—confirm the telephone conversation like you would any other appointment. Set up a day, date, and time, and issue a friendly confirmation memo. You never want to leave off casually with the contact and author, encouraging one to call the other whenever convenient. This doesn't work, because if one should catch the other off guard, it could blow the whole thing. Always control communications between authors and media contacts, so that both parties are rested, ready, and assured each other's full and undivided attention.

The Courage to Change

Another valuable insight about pitching is the flexibility factor. If you're pitching a television producer on booking an author, and he doesn't think the author is appropriate for the television show, but would be great for the host's morning radio show, shift gears and push that opportunity. It seems like common sense, but when you're in the clutch and the pressure's on to generate interview opportunities, sometimes it's hard to see the forest for the trees. For example, say you're pitching a media tour, and you've got a tentative schedule of days and dates for each city. If a big television show can only do your author on a specific date and it means you have to change the tour schedule, do it. When you're pitching, there's no such thing as "set in stone." You have to use your judgment. If a major national booking comes through, it may mean rescheduling several local interviews. It can be so easy to panic. Picture it. You've been pitching *Sharon Osbourne* for months. Suddenly, the producer calls and says that there's an open spot the next day. You've confirmed five other interviews for the author tomorrow and don't want to cancel at the last minute. What do you do?

First, breathe. Second, think logically. Third, analyze exactly what's booked for tomorrow. Are the interviews live, taped, radio, television or print? The taped radio interviews can be rescheduled. You may be able to do the live radio interviews by telephone. Print could also be done by phone. The local television shows will probably have to be rescheduled. Should you reschedule everything each time a national booking comes through? No. But what you should do is carefully examine what's at stake, look at it from all sides, then make a decision. If you're not flexible in your thinking, you can lose major opportunities.

Giving Contacts What They Need

We've been exploring the larger elements of pitching. Now I'd like to address some of the more subtle nuances specific to book publicity. As I've mentioned throughout this book, media contacts receive hundreds of literary pitches a week. If you want to grab their attention, you've got to be able to see the world from their vantage point. When you pitch a producer or reporter, always sell your author from the perspective of how she will empower the show's audience. You never want to start a pitch conversation with the words, "I've got an author . . ." The secret to effective pitching is selling the media contact on how you can help them, not on why they should help you. When you start out by saying, "I've got an author," the connotation is that you want the media to do you a favor by booking her. Instead, start out with, "I've got something you may be interested in that affects countless people in your audience."

Let me show you what I mean. You're pitching a book on divorce, *Irreconcilable Differences,* written by a famous divorce attorney, that advises people on how to choose a good lawyer.

Here's how you might want to pitch this book to a national television producer: "Imagine how many people in your audience are struggling with the possibility of divorce or have loved ones facing the big D word . . . I've got someone who could provide your audience with vital, little-known information that could impact their lives . . . in fact, he's even written a book on the subject, and his name is . . ."

As you can see, I lead the pitch with how this subject affects the audience, then I bring in the author as an expert, then I mention the book as a credibility-fortifying vehicle. Pitching is the most aggressive form of subtlety in business. You have to be aggressive in *what* you sell, but subtle in *how* you sell it.

To reiterate, when you pitch, always remember that the media's job is to empower its audience with information that either entertains or illuminates. Your media contacts don't care if you have an author you need to book. That's your problem. What they do care about is how this author can help them fulfill *their* responsibility to their audience. If you keep this in mind every time you pick up the phone to pitch someone, your success ratio will shoot through the roof.

Sometimes a media contact will be wishy-washy about arranging an author interview. He'll tell you he wants to confirm something, but can't right now for a number of reasons, ranging from studio time, deadlines, and potential breaking news to pending staff changes or sometimes even the weather. When this happens, realize that the reporter or producer isn't trying to jerk you around. He's simply not in a position at that moment to do what you need him to do.

A marvelous technique for getting around this obstacle is what I call "penciling in." Tell the media contact that you completely understand where he's coming from, but what about if he would just "pencil in an interview date and time?" Explain that you're clear this would be tentative only and that you'll confirm it definitively closer to the date. Reassure him that you recognize you'll have to be open and flexible. This method works on several levels. Once an interview is penciled in, the media person feels more of an obligation to come through, which gives you better leverage with him psychologically. It's much easier to convince a media person to reschedule something he's already tentatively committed to.

Pitch Terminology

Before we conclude this chapter, I want to review with you several key terms that relate to pitching: "hook," "peg," "angle," and "spin."

The media *hook* is the part of the pitch that will grab the contact. Let's say you're pitching a novel on sharks written by a retired shark hunter.

The obvious hook for this book would be that the author is writing from actual personal experience. The *peg* is the time component. In other words, when you pitch a story, you have to know when you want the story to run and have a specific reason why. For example, you've pitched *USA Today* on interviewing the author of the shark book. Of course, you want the article to hit when the book is released. Therefore, the peg is the book's release date. The peg is a critical component of publicity.

Remember when we talked about the word "evergreen?" To refresh your memory, an evergreen is a print or broadcast story that the media gets in the can and sits on until they have a hole in their schedule and need a filler piece. Stories that don't have pegs attached often become evergreens. It's vital that when you pitch media, you're crystal clear about the peg. The peg could be a release date, an event, a holiday that the story ties into, an anniversary, birthday, or any other time factor that locks the media into airing/running the piece within a certain window.

We've explored the word "angle" before, so we'll just briefly revisit it here. The *angle* of a story is the focus. Different pitches have different angles. For example, several years ago, I represented a *New York Times* best-selling romance writer named Jennifer Blake. The quintessential Southern Belle, she led a full and interesting life, which afforded us a great many angles to work with. That's why it's always so important to interview your authors in depth before you strategize their campaigns. The more information they give you, the more fodder you have to develop diverse angles.

Jennifer was a potpourri of exciting elements. She loved to cook and could whip up a gourmet meal in moments. We were so impressed with her culinary acumen that we pitched the food angle to a national television show, which booked her on the spot. She talked about her newest novel while whipping up one of her delectable dishes for the audience. Another angle we used for Jennifer was her acumen as a decorator. She lived in a nineteenth-century plantation that she and her husband had lovingly renovated. We pitched the lifestyle writers at several daily papers on interviewing Jennifer about her home and how her experiences beautifying it helped to inspire her literary work. Angles should be infinite. As a publicist, creating angles is the lifeblood of what we do. One last note on angles, which we've mentioned earlier—*look beyond the obvious.* There's always another idea just waiting to be found.

"Spin" is a term that relates closely to positioning. The best way to explain it is to show you. Let's say you're publicizing an autobiography by a well-known stand-up comedian, and you want to pitch the *Wall Street Journal* on the author's little-known achievements as an entrepreneur. You'd *spin* the pitch to emphasize his successes in business, rather than his experiences as an entertainer. Spinning means presenting the positioning from a specific perspective in order to generate a particular response. Spinning isn't lying. It's about emphasizing and de-emphasizing certain elements of a pitch, based upon whom you're pitching and their particular interests.

Improving Your Odds

Pitching is so much more than selling. There's a psychology to it. There's a lot of rejection to it, too, which you can never, ever take personally. Let me put it to you this way: If you pitch an author to thirty newspapers and confirm three interviews, you're doing wonderfully! It's all a matter of odds. That's why the media research phase is so vital. The more outlets you unearth, the better your odds are at generating more coverage for the author. You simply can't allow yourself to get discouraged. Selling stories to the media takes intelligence, persistence, courage, creativity, and heart. You have it in you. The secret is being willing to unleash it.

Next chapter, how to be a fabulous interview!

How to Be an Exciting Interview for Print, Television, and Radio

*P*UBLICITY SELLS BOOKS. THAT MEANS IT'S INCUMBENT UPON AUTHORS to master the media gauntlet, or their books will never reach full sales potential. Look at it this way. Let's say Tony Bennett is booked to do a concert at Carnegie Hall. No matter how wonderful a performer he is, or how many fans he has, if the public isn't told that he's going to be there, the hall will be empty. People can't buy tickets for an event they don't know about. It's the same thing with publishing. You may have a book on the retail shelves, but if no one is aware your book is available, how is it going to sell? Authors *must* understand and embrace the publicity machine, or they cut their careers off at the torso. With that said, let's examine what it takes to be a great interview.

The Big No-No

We'll start with the most important rule. Don't continually say "in my book" during an interview. You can mention it once. More than once, you risk never being asked back by that outlet again. Why? When an author is booked to do a media interview, he's welcomed as a guest because he's an expert on the subject he's written about. The media will promote the book for him. If it's television, the show will edit in a still of the book on the screen. Usually, the host will also hold up the book at the end of the author's segment and recommend to the audience that they buy it. If it's radio, the host will mention the book several times throughout the broadcast. If it's print, the publication will either print the front cover or run the title and publishing information in the article.

The worst thing an author can do is to keep reminding the audience he's there trying to hawk his book. It's classless and infuriates producers and reporters. Believe me, I understand how hard it is to keep from mentioning it. It's even more tempting if you feel your interviewer hasn't lived up to his promise to promote the book.

Should that be the case, there are two solutions. During a commercial break, simply ask the host if he could remember to promote the book. If you don't have that luxury because you're only on for a quick segment, go ahead and say something like, "Thank you so much for allowing me to come and chat on your show. I care so much about this subject; in fact, that's why I wrote my book. . . ." Usually, most interviewers won't put you in the latter position. The media is gracious about promoting books. The secret is to confirm how the book will be promoted *before* you go on air. Make your requests ahead of time, and confirm it in writing if you can. That way, there will be no uncomfortable moments during the interview.

Now that I've laid out the big interview no-no, I want to walk you through the interview process, step by step.

Step 1: Background Information

The first component of a good interview is knowing as much detail about the interview as possible. For example: What angle was the interview booked on? How long is the interview scheduled for? Is it live or taped? Is it a feature, or are you being interviewed as an expert on a particular subject? Are there any items of specific interest to the interviewer that you should focus on? What's the specific audience demographic (young, old, female driven, etc.)?

The more you know going into an interview, the more power you have. Nothing feels worse than walking into an interview unprepared. If you're a publicist, take the time to brief your author. If you're an author, make the time to listen.

Step 2: The Look

You know the old expression, "If you look good, you'll feel good"? Well, nowhere does that ring truer than in an interview. Remember, present something the way you want it perceived. If you want to be perceived as conservative, dress the part. If, on the other hand, you're interviewing with a hip, young outlet like MTV, perhaps you'd prefer to present a more casual appearance. The bottom line on attire and image is this: Choose an overall look that you're comfortable with, then adjust it subtly based upon the media outlet you're interviewing with and its specific demographic. I'd suggest working with image consultants. They're worth their weight in gold.

There are several rules of thumb on dressing for interview success that you should know. Never wear plaid or any other busy patterns; they wreak havoc with the camera lens and distract viewers from the content of the interview. Wear solid colors, and avoid yellows, grays, whites, and muted pastels, which can make you look pale and sickly, even if you're feeling great. Don't wear anything tight or uncomfortable that needs periodic adjusting, such as short skirts, shirts with bulging buttons, ill-fitted collars, etc. If you fidget with your clothing during an interview, it diminishes the impact of your message. Also, don't overdo accessories. Large pins, big earrings, and other clumsy pieces of jewelry take attention away from you. Accessorize to complete a look, not define it.

Make sure your hair is off your face. Sophisticated styles are all well and good, but if you're constantly futzing with your hair or brushing it away from your eyes, it will get on both the audience's and the interviewer's nerves. If you're mature and have a lot of gray, you might want to consider a henna rinse. Gray hairs stick out like sore thumbs on television. If you're completely gray, that's one thing, but if you have dark hair with a smattering of gray, it can be distracting when seen through a lens. Remember, the camera exaggerates every feature, good and bad.

One last note on appearance—grooming. Make sure your nails are clean and manicured, your clothing is freshly dry-cleaned and unwrinkled. Don't wear anything with stains, no matter how small. The camera picks up *everything*. Be honest with yourself about what's flattering on you and what isn't. If you can't be objective, ask a friend or, as I mentioned before, an image consultant. Untucked shirts, stained garments, snug sweaters on overweight bodies, and gaudy makeup can put you behind the eight ball before you've even picked up the pool cue. Appearance counts. Make yours speak volumes.

Step 3: Make the Audience Love *You*

This may come as a surprise to you, but there's a psychology to utilizing media interviews to sell books. Let me tell you how it works. When an author does a television interview to promote her book, two events happen in the mind of the viewer—that is, the potential book buyer. First, if the viewer likes the author, feels a kinship with her, it will motivate him to continue paying attention to the segment. If for any reason the author is unappealing to the viewer, no matter how wonderful the author's message is or how fascinating the information, the viewer will change the channel. The gut reaction of the viewer to the author is what motivates the viewer to go to the bookstore. Once he's in the store, it's the content of the book, cover copy, and overall look that will make him buy it. It's very important you understand these two psychological steps. Too many authors do media interviews without taking seriously the likability factor. It's a mistake.

Several years ago, I did a publicity campaign for an author who had written a book about surviving widowhood. Though she was a wonderful woman, she came across cold and indifferent on the air. I explained to her that when she was asked about her late husband during an interview, she had to show genuine emotion and let the audience know that even though she had moved on and was remarrying soon, that he would always hold a place in her heart. The author, however, was uncomfortable sharing her feelings because she was concerned it would offend her fiancé. While I understood her plight, book buyers did not. She did an hour interview on a huge national television show, and rather than boosting sales, it sparked returns. Why? The author's unwillingness to talk openly about her feelings and pay honor to her late husband's memory on the air translated to the audience as uncaring. Nothing could have been farther from the truth about this author, who was loving and genuine to the core. But it just goes to show you that audiences are sensitive. Part of being a successful author is realizing that when you give media interviews, you must be aware of how your gestures, demeanor, and outlook will be perceived by the viewers. Otherwise you do yourself a disservice that can hurt book sales.

Along the same lines, body language is critical. Some authors try to look relaxed during an interview. Be careful here. This is especially true for television. You'll normally be seated on a chair or couch. You should sit straight and project your energy forward. That doesn't mean to lurch. It just means to sit erect, and when you do gesture or move for emphasis, lean slightly forward. Why? If you lean back in your seat, it translates to the audience that you're disinterested in your own interview. Certainly that isn't your intention, but again, reality and the perception of reality from a camera lens are often not consistent. Be aware of your body language, and you'll always be in control of visual perception.

One last item. If you're like me and talk with your hands, make sure you gesture beneath your chest. If you gesture in front of your face, it's distracting and will take away from the potency of your message.

Step 4: Handling the Interview

Don't shy away from the word controversy. If you've written a book on a meaty subject, chances are you'll find yourself in an interview situation that demands you take a position. That's OK. In fact, it can be wonderful for book sales. The trick is knowing the secrets for controlling the interview so that the atmosphere only becomes as heated as you want. There are certain interview formats that lend themselves more readily to the controversial spin. Probably the most typical are cable network roundtables, network morning shows, and prime-time newsmagazines. If you find yourself in the hot seat, go with it. If you try to fight it, the host or other guests will nail you. Here are a few secrets.

Always be firm, respectful, and energetic. You can't be attacked if you don't waffle in your position. When an author is wishy-washy during a tense interview and keeps changing perspective, it makes both host and audience lose faith in the author's sincerity. Take a position and stick with it. It demonstrates honesty and integrity. If the subject is a real hot button, like abortion, capital punishment, women's rights, etc., don't be afraid to voice your perspective. Just remember these tips.

Know as much about the subjects that are going to be discussed on the show as possible. Ask the producer about the topics and intended direction of the show during your preinterview session over the phone. Be prepared with the points you want to make, and be able to support those points with hard facts. During the interview, it's always a good idea to acknowledge the opposing perspectives without giving your own ground. For example, you might say something like, "I respect your passion on this subject, as I am equally as passionate on the topic; however . . ." (then introduce or reiterate your perspective). Being strong doesn't mean being a jerk. Maintain your opinion, support it with hard facts, and treat the interviewer and other guests with respect.

Sometimes you can be in an interview situation that grows dull and lifeless, and you need to create a spark. One of the best techniques for infusing a gray interview with color is to ignite a debate. You might say to the host, or other guests if it's a round-table, "This brings up an interesting point. What about . . ." or "What do you think of this . . ." Wield this sword prudently, how-ever. Be sure that whatever kindling you throw into the fire, you are well versed on the facts. Don't be an Archie Bunker. Know your stuff on the subject, or don't bring it up.

Another trick of the trade is understanding the subtle nuances of adjusting your demeanor and approach to a subject, based on the format of the interview and the synergy between you, the host, and other guests. For example, if you're the expert on a one-hour syndicated talk show like *Oprah,* or a similar format, it's keenly important that you jump in whenever you feel you need to make a point. Don't wait for the host to ask you a question. Contribute openly and spontaneously to the show.

On the other hand, if you're being interviewed on a late-night, one-on-one type format like *David Letterman* or *Craig Kilborn,* after your interview segment is completed, usually you'll remain onstage but will simply change seats to allow for the next interview to take place. In that situation, you wouldn't want to jump in and interrupt the flow of the other person's interview.

Bridging Techniques

Another critical component of "giving good interview" is being fluent in the language of bridging techniques. Often, you'll be in the middle of an interview, and you'll be asked a question that you don't want to answer or the interviewer will try to take you in a negative direction. Always remember one thing—pay atten-tion because this is so important—*You're the one in control of the interview, not the interviewer. You're the one with the answers. The interviewer only has the questions. It's the person with the answers who ultimately manages the interview.*

Interviewers will sometimes try to spice up the conversa-tion with abrasive or aggressive questions. You have to keep your cool, remember that *you're* the one in control, and start bridging. Here are some examples of bridging techniques:

"I'm so glad you asked that question; it reminds me of . . ." (then simply change the direction of the interview anywhere you want it to go).

"That's a terrific question, very insightful, but before I delve into the answer, let me make this point . . ." (same thing here, now you can change the focus of the interview).

There are dozens of bridging phrases. Others include: "I can't answer that, but I can say this . . ." and "That's a brilliant question, but let's consider this issue from another vista . . ." You'll come up with your own bridges as well. The point is that you always acknowledge the intelligence of the interviewer, then take the interview where you want it to go.

Eye Contact

We should discuss a few more crucial items: eye contact and camera acumen. When you're doing television, it can be disconcerting because of all the cameras. Don't worry about looking into the cameras. The general rule of thumb is simple: Look into the eyes of the person you're talking to. If you're doing an interview with a live audience, sometimes it's impactful to make eye contact with the audience. Before you give an interview, take a few moments to chat with the producer, and ask him about the camera setup, the best way to make eye contact with the audience, and if there are any other technical details you should be aware of. The producer will appreciate your thoroughness, and it will increase your confidence and comfort going into the interview.

Keep It Simple

Here's a bit of advice I can't emphasize enough. When you give interviews, speak clearly and use accessible language. One of the biggest mistakes authors make—and believe me, it's a doozy—is that they use technical terminology and other lofty language that completely alienates their interviewers and audiences. Academics and other professional experts tend to fall into this trap more readily than novelists. Let me give you an example that, to this day, still makes my stomach lurch.

Several years ago, I represented a globally renowned psychiatrist. The top-rated network prime-time newsmagazine in the country assigned its star anchor to interview him about his newest book. Though this author had written numerous textbooks, this was his first commercial title. He was excited about the interview, but concerned because all his colleagues, many of whom looked down upon mainstream media, would be tuned in when the piece aired. The camera crew and anchor came to his office to tape the interview. We were supposed to tape for one hour, then the show would edit it down to a twelve-minute segment. The taping ended up going a painful five hours. Why? My author refused to speak in plain language. He riddled his answers with psychobabble and sophisticated medical terminology that even the interviewer couldn't grasp. He was so fixated on appearing intelligent in front of his colleagues and proving to them that he hadn't "sold out" his expertise just to promote his book that he nearly sabotaged the interview. I can honestly say it was one of the most frustrating experiences of my career. When the segment finally did air, my author came off as aloof and arrogant. The interview didn't make a dent in sales. In fact, if anything, it damaged sell-through. The moral of this story? Speak elegantly, but simply. I don't mean to talk down to a host or audience as if they're children. But when you do an interview, use conversational terminology and language. Pretend you're chatting with an intelligent, educated next-door neighbor, and you can never go wrong.

The Perfect Guest

Being a savvy interview is as much about instinct as learned skill. Be aware of the mood of each interview, whether it be radio, television, or print. Speak clearly and elegantly, using understandable, accessible language. Practice your bridging techniques so that you're ready for any curveballs. And always, *always* treat your interviewer with respect.

Now you should be well on your way to being a lean, mean, interview machine! Next chapter, the Author Tour. Stay tuned . . .

The Author Tour

Y OU HEAR AUTHORS TALK ABOUT IT ALL THE TIME. "I'M GOING OUT on tour this month." What exactly does that mean, and why do they do it? How does it get done? Earlier in this book, we chatted briefly about the author tour. In a nutshell, a tour is when an author visits a city a day and does media and personal appearances in each.

An author tour can be an effective marketing tool. The average tour is anywhere from five to twenty-five cities. Authors do interviews all day long in a city, then in the late evening travel to their next scheduled city. Author tours are grueling for both author and publicist. They demand patience, stamina, and quick thinking. I've been booking, managing, and going along on tours for the better part of fifteen years. I know the grind. In my mind, there are two kinds of authors in this world: those who can handle touring and those who don't have what it takes. If you're one of those writers who doesn't believe you're cut out for the road, perhaps by the time you finish reading this chapter, you'll have a new, empowered outlook.

Let's talk about why publishers tour authors. You remember what we learned about sell-in and sell-through. Author tours are wonderful for reinforcing both. If the bookstores know that an author will be touring, they make sure they have plenty of copies of the author's book in the stores in the tour markets. On the sell-through side, author tours are good, old-fashioned grassroots marketing. Yes, national television is important, but nothing motivates sales more that when an author comes to someone's hometown. There's just nothing quite like it. That doesn't mean, however, that every book should automatically be toured. There is a broad spectrum of elements that must be considered before deciding upon an author tour. Authors have a tendency to believe they should tour no matter what, and when their publishers don't agree, they become angry and disillusioned. The truth is that sometimes a tour doesn't make sense, and there might be other, more worthwhile strategies. The secret is learning how to make sound judgments in this area.

Who Should Tour?

Let's start out with the basics. Obscure, noncommercial books don't tour well. If a book is narrow in subject matter, too technological or ethereal, or targets too specific a demographic, touring is not the answer. Those kinds of books are best served by aggressive niche campaigns, in which you publicize directly to the special interest audiences most likely to buy the book. For example, if you're publicizing a book of German literature translated into English, rather than tour the author, you'd be better off researching German-American organizations, language clubs, universities, and other entities who would have a vested interest in the subject. Once you've compiled a healthy target list, you could pitch them on personal appearances, as well as setting up interviews with print media outlets that reach this demographic. If you tried to tour this author, it wouldn't work because it's too specific a subject, and tours require more universal topics. Think of it this way: If the local radio station in Columbus, Ohio, or Des Moines,

Iowa, wouldn't be interested in the author or topic, then you shouldn't consider a tour.

In addition to the content of a book, you have to analyze the author's ability as a spokesperson. Is the author a good interview? Is he telegenic, energetic, and willing to endure the long hours and infinite stream of last-minute changes that are part and parcel of any tour? If the author is unwilling or unable to embrace the rigors of the road, don't do a tour.

Once you've made an honest assessment of the author's road warrior factor and whether or not the book itself is publicizable, then you need to examine the distribution element. The rule of thumb followed by most publishers is that, if the initial print run of a title is over 35,000 copies, then a tour might be warranted. The number of tour cities is usually based on the advance orders.

For example, an initial print run of 35,000–40,000 could warrant a four-to-six-city tour. A run of 40,000–50,000 might motivate the publicity department to do a seven-to-eight-city tour. A nice, healthy print run of 50,000–60,000 would make a good argument for a ten-city tour. With anything over 60,000, you should negotiate as many tour cities as you can. Realistically, ten cities at 60,000 copies, twelve cities at 65,000–75,000 copies, fifteen cities at 75,000–100,000 copies, and twenty cities and up for any initial print run over 100,000 copies borders somewhere on average.

Do keep in mind, however, that all publishers have their own criteria for touring authors. And each book has its own unique set of circumstances that need to be considered by the publisher before committing to a tour. For example, a publisher may have a book in which the advance orders are only 15,000 copies, but the author is especially dynamic and promotable, and the subject of the book is a cultural hot button. In a situation like this, the publisher may do a tour, even though, typically, a modest print run such as this wouldn't justify it. There's really no concrete formula for determining whether or not a book tour is the best publicity route. You have to look at all the elements involved and make a logical decision based upon an honest read of the circumstances.

Let me share another example with you. I worked with a globally renowned marriage counselor who had written a book on relating to the child in your mate. The book was pithy, informative, and well written. Initial print run was upwards of 60,000, and the publisher was eager for me to book the author a fifteen-city tour. I, on the other hand, tried everything I could to dissuade the publisher from a tour. Why? Though the author was a brilliant scholar, he had all the energy and dynamism of postnasal drip. Worse, the poor guy hated doing interviews and got so nervous in front of a camera that his teeth would chatter. The publisher was convinced that with some media coaching, everything would be fine. I coached the author and sent him out. Our strategy was to begin with national television and then move into the tour cities. Lo and behold, after his first national interview, the producer called and berated me. "He's so stiff, he made the host uncomfortable during the whole show; that guy should not do television." Needless to say, we canceled the tour. Instead, I booked dozens of print interviews for the author. He loved doing them and the book sold very well without the tour.

The moral of the story is this: Don't automatically assume that you should tour a book just because the print run is strong. Conversely, don't assume you shouldn't tour a book because the print run is weaker. Look at all the elements and decide from there. I will tell you one thing, though. A tour is *never, ever* justified if there are less than 10,000 copies of the book in the stores, or even available online.

If you're unsure whether or not a book tour would be effective for a particular title, ask yourself the following questions:

- What's the initial print run of the book?
- Are there any parts of the country where distribution is strongest that the author could tour to?
- Is the author promotable and a solid interview?
- Is the subject of the book appealing and interesting to a mainstream, grassroots audience?

- Is it a book that local media would be inclined to cover?

The answers to these questions will guide you to the right decision.

It's All in the Timing

Now that we've looked at how to judge whether or not a book tour is the answer for you, let's examine the timing of a tour. The best time for an author to tour to local markets is within three to five weeks of ship date. Most publishers ship books from the warehouse two to three weeks prior to pub date. For example, if a book is pub dated March 1st, that means the books would have shipped out to the stores in early to mid-April. It's always best to leave enough time for the books to ship, arrive, and be placed onto the shelves. So if pub date is March 1st and books ship in mid-April, the tour would ideally begin the second week in March. Bear in mind, however, that publishers' schedules can vary. It's always best to ask your publisher when books are shipping, and plan the tour for three to five weeks after that date.

Steps to a Successful Tour

Now I'd like to get into the nitty-gritty of planning and scheduling a tour. I'm going to walk you through the process in stages. Ideally, you need six months to book a tour from start to finish. It can be done in less, but the more time you have, the better. Heck, I've pulled together tours in one or two weeks. The bottom line, however, is that four to six months to prepare everything is always the best bet. If it has to be done at the last minute, make sure you work with a seasoned professional who knows the ins and outs of the game.

Step 1: Read the Manuscript and Interview the Author

Obviously, as we've discussed throughout this book, these tasks are absolutely basic to tailoring any publicity campaign so that it fits the author, and the book, like a glove.

Step 2: Choose Your Markets

Once you've done your reading and interviewing, analyze which tour cities would be most appropriate. For example, if it's a novel that takes place in New England, perhaps you'd want four or five cities on the Eastern seaboard. Brainstorm with the publisher's sales force which markets would benefit the book most. A good tour market is judged according to quality and quantity of local media, number of bookstores, and population density. Tour markets are divided into two groups: primary and secondary. Primary markets are the top thirty cities in the country. Secondary markets are smaller cities.

Sometimes it makes more sense to do a tour comprised only of secondary markets, because the author gets more coverage as a big fish in a smaller pond. In other cases, major markets are the best strategy. Again, you have to look at all the elements, and then make a decision. I'll give you a hint: You can always choose the markets you think best and then pre-pitch the media by telephone. Based on the initial responses you get, you can substitute cities. Tours are never set in stone. The more flexible you are, the better media you'll get.

Step 3: Get Organized

Once you've read the manuscript, interviewed the author, and chosen the tour cities, you need to do your structural setup. Make one manila folder for each tour city. Inside each tour folder will be the media contact sheets, copies of media labels, media leads, and all other information specific to that particular tour city. *I can't emphasize enough how vital it is to maintain neat, organized tour folders, one for each tour market. If you don't, the tour will fail before it begins!!!* On the outside of each tour folder, staple a tour booking sheet. Let's look at a sample booking sheet, and I'll describe it simply for you now.

Author __John Smith__

Title __Love Potions__

City/Date __Chicago - Mon. Dec. 9__

Hotel/Escort __Drake - Jo dee Blanco__

TIME	SHOW	ADDRESS	CONTACT/COMMENTS
Arrive 8:15ish 8:30-9:00am LIVE	WGN AM "Rick Kogan Show"	435 N. Michigan Ave Chicago 60610	Rick Kogan 312-222-5555
9:30 -10:00am	Sun Times feature	at Drake Hotel 140 E. Walton	Denise O'Neil 312-810-0764
11:30 -1:00pr	Book Signing at Barbara's	North Wells and Schiller	Barbara Smith 312-573-9090
Arrive 2:15 pm 2:30-3:30p	Chicagoland Cable "Books Today"	276 N. Lake Shore Drive	Susan Moritz 312-961-3434
4:00 -5:00p	Chicago Tribune	at Pump Room - Ambassador East Corner of Goethe and State	Bill Harlman 312-333-0404

A tour booking sheet is divided into columns. It looks like a calendar page from a day planner. On this sheet, you write down all confirmed author interviews for that city. Morning interviews are written at the top of the sheet, afternoon interviews in the middle, evening interviews on the bottom. You get the idea. The point of these booking sheets is that, by glancing at one, you can assess immediately, just from a visual perspective, where the schedule for that day has holes and what media you need to fill in. You should never put two days on one booking sheet. If a day is jam-packed with interviews and you can't fit them all on one sheet, staple a second sheet at the bottom of the first sheet and continue working your way down. If you add a second sheet, you may have to rewrite the bookings so that it lays out properly and isn't confusing. Take a peek at the sample sheets at the back of the book. This is a straightforward method that saves enormous time and prevents countless mistakes. It's always best to have booking sheets stapled to the outside of each manila folder and to write in bookings by hand. The problem with booking via computer is that, when a media person calls, they won't have time for you to boot up to the right page. You need to be able to grab the tour folder for that city, flip to the booking sheet, and start writing in the information.

Step 4: Localize Your Press Kit

Once you've prepared all your tour folders, you're ready to write the press kit. Make sure you provide as many angles as possible. It's always smart to localize tour kits. For example, have specific pitches for the Midwest, East Coast, West, and South. One of the biggest challenges for publicists is convincing local media in tour markets of the local relevance of a book or author. You can combat this problem by weaving local hooks into the press kit as it's being written.

Step 5: Mass Printing

Once the press kit is written, submit it to the author and publisher for their approval. When you've obtained their changes, create the finalized draft of the press kit, and print at least thirty press kits for each tour market. For example, if you're doing a ten-city tour, print 300 kits.

Step 6: Media Research

Now you're ready to begin media research. If you've pre-pitched some of the tour markets, you'll already have a heads-up on the research side. You'll need to create a media database for each tour city. If you already have databases for some of the tour cities, you'll need to update them. To refresh your memory on how to do media research, consult chapter 9. A brief reminder: Look up radio, television, and print outlets in each tour market in *Bacon's;* photocopy the pages; then begin calling outlets, verifying the contact information.

Step 7: The Initial Mailing

Once you have the media research and database completed, generate the labels, and do the initial media mailing. The mailing should include a copy of the galley (or book, although usually bound books aren't available until much later), the press kit, and a personalized pitch memo. I always recommend that tour mailings go first class. Anything cheaper is less reliable and gives off the wrong image.

If you're pitching national media as well, you should do the national mailing, too. There are two ways you can incorporate national media into a tour. Sometimes, it's best to lead with big-gun television and radio (most of these shows are out of New York, Washington, D.C., and Los Angeles), which creates a pre-tour buzz. In other cases, it's more effective to start with the tour, and then follow with national coverage. The latter is most beneficial when an author is less well-known, as the grassroots coverage they obtain on the road increases them as a media commodity to the national producers.

You should allow one business week for the mailing to hit.

Blanco & Peace Enterprises LTD.
Publicity • Public Relations • Promotions
Chicago • Los Angeles • New York

"MAN ON THE MOON" PRODUCER BOB ZMUDA TELLS-ALL ABOUT ANDY KAUFMAN

Who: Bob Zmuda, creator and founder of
              Comic Relief, author of "Andy Kaufman Revealed:
              Best Friend Tells All," and executive producer
              of the upcoming bio-pic film about Kaufman
              "Man on the Moon," starring Jim Carrey

What: Bob Zmuda is signing his new book
              "Andy Kaufman Revealed: Best Friend Tells All"
              and will also be talking about exclusive
              behind-the-scenes nuggets from
              "Man on the Moon"

Where: Book Soup
              8818 Sunset Blvd.
              West Hollywood, CA 90064

Date: Wednesday
              Sep. 29, 1999

Time: 8:00–9:30 pm

Contact: **Tod Dell'Aringa/Jodee Blanco**
              Blanco & Peace
              312.573.2070

Step 8: Begin Pitching!

An ideal tour schedule includes a minimum of five interviews per city, representing a solid cross section of live and taped television and radio placements and one or two good print features. You always want a combination of live and taped coverage, because it gives the illusion that the author is in the city for much longer than a day. Think of it this way: An author does a live radio and television show in the morning, which enables her to promote her book signing later that day. They do a taped piece and newspaper interview, which hit several days after they leave. Each tour city should be like a mini–media blitz. By combining taped and live coverage, you can create that effect, as well as maximize attendance at autographings.

When pitching, the secret is to book anchor shows in each market first. Anchor shows are the live network affiliate television morning shows or noon news, and live AM radio morning, afternoon, or evening drive shows. It's always easier to book everything else around the live anchor shows. Once you've confirmed the anchor bookings in each market, then go back and fill in the schedules. Sometimes, you won't get five interviews in a city, but you should have at least three interviews to justify the author traveling to that city.

Tips Regarding Scheduling

When you're booking the schedule, make sure you leave at least fifteen to twenty minutes for travel time between interviews. If you're unsure about how close one interview is to another, you can ask a media escort (we'll talk about escorts in a second) or call the local chamber of commerce. Usually, fifteen to twenty minutes is a reliable window.

Remember, when you confirm an interview, be sure to repeat all the details to the contact as you're writing them down, then repeat them again before you hang up. Those details should include:

- Media outlet (e.g., television network, radio station, or newspaper)
- Name of show or newspaper section
- If the interview is live or taped
- Studio address and address of interview, if interview is taking place on location
- Full name of contact
- Main office phone number of contact
- The main twenty-four-hour studio line
- Time of interview
- Duration of interview
- Requested arrival time of author (most media contacts like authors to arrive at least fifteen to thirty minutes in advance for radio and television interviews)

It's critical that all this information gets written down directly onto your booking sheet for that city. Don't write down interview information on a scrap piece of paper or notebook and then transfer it onto the booking sheet. This is a big no-no, because you could end up booking interviews that overlap. Keep your tour folders with booking sheets close to you and organized at all times, so when you talk with a media contact, you can pull out the appropriate folder quickly and efficiently, and jot down the information right onto the sheet.

Bear in mind that throughout this whole process, media contacts will lose books as well as request additional copies. On top of that, it's tough to reach people, so you'll be faxing and e-mailing notes to producers and reporters constantly, urging them to call you back. Booking a tour is a time-consuming job. You've got to stay calm, and be aggressive and creative.

Blanco & Peace Enterprises, LTD.

PUBLICITY SCHEDULE FOR NAURA HAYDEN, AUTHOR OF HOW TO SATISFY A MAN EVERY TIME AND HAVE HIM BEG FOR MORE

(SENT VIA MODEM)

Contact: Jodee Blanco
312/573-2070
Jennifer Crawford
312/573-2070

<u>Sunday, March 7th</u>

Naura, please take a cab to La Guardia. Keep your receipts and Kensington will reimburse you. Thanks!

Depart New York (La Guardia)	5:59 pm
Arrive Pittsburgh	7:35 pm
US Air #3131	

Pittsburgh escort: Sandi Kopler 412/486-5804

Sandi will pick you up at the airport. She will be waiting for you at baggage claim holding up a copy of your book. If for some reason you don't see her, take a cab directly to your hotel and call her at home from there. We don't anticipate any problems with your airport pick-up, but we always like to lay out back-up scenarios just to be safe.

Hotel: The Westin William Penn
530 William Penn Place
Mellon Square
Tele: 412/281-7100
Confir# 747040316
Direct Billing Contact: David Sins
Rate: 185.00

Note: This applies to all your hotels—direct billing has been confirmed through Mona, your travel agent. However, if there is any problem, we give you the names of all the contacts at the hotels who confirmed your direct billing status so that you can ask for them personally if you need to.

That's it for today. Get a good night's sleep. Tomorrow's schedule is on the following page.

Monday, March 8ᵗʰ

PITTSBURGH

(Additional confirmed media interviews in Pittsburgh completed today: WPIT AM (Sportsfan Network) Lynn Cullen Show)

Sandi will pick you up this morning.

Your first interview is by telephone.

Arrive 10:15 am   WPXI TV (NBC)
10:30-11:30 am   "Cullen on Cable"
LIVE IN STUDIO   11 Television Hill
                                    Pittsburgh
                                    Contact: Brian Abzanka
                                    Host: Lynn Cullen
                                    Tele: 412/237-1259

1:00-2:30 pm   Pittsburgh Post Gazette
                                    feature interview
                                    34 Boulevard of the Allies
                                    Pittsburgh
                                    Contact: Mary Uricchio
                                    Tele: 412/263-1582

Note: We're trying to schedule an evening drive for this afternoon. More on that later.

Note: Before you leave your hotel for the interview below, pack up and check out. You will be going to Cleveland via car service directly from your last interview tonight.

Arrive 9:50 pm   KDKA AM (NBC)
10:00-11:00 pm   "Mike Romiga Show"
LIVE WITH CALL IN FOR ONE HOUR   1 Gateway Center
                                    Pittsburgh
                                    Contact: Chris Bailey
                                    Host: Mike Romiga
                                    Tele: 412/575-2240

Monday evening, March 8th continued...

After your interview at KDKA, a car service will drive you from Pittsburgh to Cleveland. Sandi Kopler, your escort, has facilitated the arrangements. She has already put the car on her credit card which will be billed back to Kensington later. The cost of car service should be $334.00, which includes gratuity.

Arrive Cleveland

The car service will be taking you directly to your Cleveland hotel. There will be a message for you there from your Cleveland escort confirming what time she will pick you up in the morning. You should also feel free to call her when you arrive. Don't worry that it's late. She knows you're getting into town late and is aware you may call her when you arrive.

Cleveland escort: Mary Kay Maxson and/or Marilyn Strauss 216/831-0301

Hotel: Ritz Carlton
1515 West 3rd Street
Cleveland
Tele: 216/623-1300
Confirm# 80816368
Direct Billing Contact: Diane Bravo
Rate: 129.00

That's it for today. Get a good night's rest. Tomorrow will be magic!

Tuesday, March 9th

CLEVELAND

Your escort will pick you up this morning.

Arrive 6:50 am	WZJM FM (ABC)
7:00-7:45 am	"Big Dave & Lou Lou"
LIVE IN STUDIO	2510 St. Clair Avenue
	Cleveland
	Contact: Kim Johnson
	Hosts: Dave Eubanks, Lou Lou
	Tele: 216/621-9300

Note: This is the number one rated morning zoo show in Cleveland. Knock 'em dead!

Arrive 9:30 am	WEWS TV (ABC)
10:00-11:00 am	"The Morning Exchange"
LIVE IN STUDIO	3001 Euclid
	Cleveland
	Contact: Laura Wadsworth
	Host: Robin Swoboda/Mark Johnson
	Tele: 216/431-5555

Note: This is the leading network affiliate morning show in Cleveland. It's legendary in this market. The time you're on is of course dependent upon how the interview goes as well as news of the day. Be your natural ebullient self and see where it takes you on-air. Normally, this show gives authors a couple of good, healthy segments. It can be longer though. Just play it out.

Noon-1:00 pm	Cleveland Life Newspaper
	Feature interview
	Over lunch—you need to swing by
	the paper and pick up the reporter
	and go to lunch somewhere near the
	paper that's easiest for the reporter.
	1729 Superior Avenue
	Cleveland
	Contact: Shelby Shockley
	Tele: 216/771-5433

Note: This is one of Cleveland's leading weekly papers. It reaches a diverse demographic.

Cleveland schedule continued on the following page:

CLEVELAND, Tuesday, March 9th continued...

Arrive 3:15 pm	WZAK FM (ABC)
3:30-4:00 pm	"Woman to Woman"
TAPED	2510 St. Clair Avenue
	Cleveland
	Contact/Host: Kim Johnson
	Tele: 216/621-9300

Before your next interview, please check out of your hotel and bring your bags with you. You'll be driven to Columbus directly after the below interview.

Arrive 5:45 pm	WAKR AM (ABC, AP)
6:00-7:00 pm	"The Phil Ferguson Show"
LIVE IN STUDIO	1795 West Market Avenue
	Cross streets: Hawkins & Market
	Akron Radio Center in Akron
	Contact/Host: Phil Ferguson
	Tele: 330/865-7888

Car service will drive you to Columbus. Your Cleveland escort has facilitated all the arrangements for your car service. Kensington is being billed directly through the escort service. This car service should run about $300.00.

Columbus escort: Cathy Fisher 614/457-2137

Hotel: Hyatt Regency
250 North High Street
Columbus
Confir#2770887
Tele: 614/463-1234
Direct billing contact: Jim Davis

When you arrive at your hotel, there should be a message from your Columbus escort with your pick-up time tomorrow morning. If you don't receive a message, call her when you get in this evening.

That's it for today. Tomorrow's schedule on the following page.

Wednesday, March 10th

COLUMBUS

Your escort will pick you up this morning. Knock 'em dead today.

Arrive 6:50 am
7:00-7:45 am
LIVE IN STUDIO

WHOK FM (AP)
"Ric Night & Mark Danzier"
1 Nationwide Plaza, 2nd floor
Columbus
Contact: Ric Night
Hosts: Ric Night/Mark Danzier
Tele: 614/225-9465

Note: This is a popular country station. You'll reach a lot of homemakers driving their kids to school who need advice on making their marriages work.

Arrive 8:15 am
8:30-8:40 am
LIVE IN STUDIO

WTVN AM (ABC)
"Bob Connor Show"
1301 Dublin Road
Columbus
Contact: John Corbey (also hosting)
Tele: 614/486-6101

Note: This is the leading AM station in the market. John Corbey is subbing for Bob Connor today. Here's how this whole thing works. You're doing another interview with the same station this afternoon. The first interview is shorter, during which time you need to plug your longer interview for tonight. FYI—John Corbey really wanted to interview you for a long format piece, but couldn't because he has to sub for the morning guy today and a woman is actually subbing for his show tonight. So in essence you'll be on his show this afternoon, but will interviewed by his sub, who normally hosts a show called Chick Talk.

Arrive 9:50 am
10:00-10:30 am
TAPED IN STUDIO

WOSU AM (NPR)
"Morning Edition" (NATIONAL)
2400 Olentangy River Road
Columbus
Contact/Host: Ellen Rogers (or Tom)
Tele: 614/292-9678

Wednesday, March 10th continued...

Noon-1:00 pm	Columbus Messenger Company Feature interview to appear in: Eastside Messenger Madison Messenger Southeast Messenger Southwest Messenger Westside Messenger Over lunch—you need to swing by the paper and pick up the reporter and go to lunch somewhere near his office that's convenient to him. Contact: Dan Trittschuch Tele: 614/272-5422

Note: This interview is with a multiple publisher. It will appear in all of the paper's editions listed above.

You've got the rest of afternoon to yourself.

Arrive 5:50 pm 6:00-7:00 pm LIVE IN STUDIO	WTVN AM (ABC) "John Corbey Show hosted by Jane London from Chick Talk" 1301 Dublin Road Columbus Contact: John Corbey Tele: 614/486-6101

Note: In between these two interviews you should check out of your hotel, as you will be driven directly from your next interview to your hotel in Dayton.

Arrive 9:50 pm 10:00-11:00 pm LIVE IN S TUDIO	WTVN AM (ABC) "Steve Cannon Show" 1301 Dublin Road Columbus Contact: B.J. Patton Host: Steve Cannon Tele: 614/486-6101

Wednesday evening March 10th continued...

Your escort has arranged for a car service to drive you to Dayton. The escort is taking care of the bill and will submit an invoice to Kensington.

When you arrive Dayton, there will be a message for you waiting at your hotel from your Dayton escort with you pick-up time for tomorrow morning. If for some reason you don't receive a message, call her when you arrive tonight. Don't worry about waking up these escorts. They do this for a living and they understand the demands of tour schedules.

Escort for Dayton and Cincinnati: Kathy Tirschek 513/522-6771

Hotel: Crowne Plaza
        130 Shipyard Drive
        Dayton
        Tele: 843/842-2400
        Confir# 63119618
        Direct Billing Contact: Joe Moore
        Rate: 109.00

That's it for tonight. Tomorrow's schedule on the following page.

Thursday, March 11th

DAYTON/CINCINNATI

(Also confirmed in Cincinnati and already completed: <u>Cincinnati Post</u>)

Your escort will pick you up this morning.

Note: Dayton and Cincinnati essentially border each other. In order to accommodate the media in these markets, we're combining the cities as one. This makes travel more convenient and it also helps increase the blitz affect.

Arrive 6:45 am	WGTZ FM (CBS)
7:00-7:50 am	"Z93 Morning Show"
LIVE IN STUDIO	717 East David Road
	Dayton
	Contact: Kim Farris
	Hosts: Sean Roberts, Kim Farris
	Tele: 937/294-5858

Note: This is the leading morning zoo type show in the market. You're hitting prime morning drive. Go get 'em!!!

Arrive 8:30 am	WTUE FM (ABC)
9:10-9:30 am	"Kerrigan & Christopher Show"
LIVE IN STUDIO	101 East Pine Street
	Dayton
	Contact: Pat McCrotch
	Host: Steve Kerrigan/Chris Geisen
	Tele: 937/224-1137

Note: You need to be by a telephone for your next interview. DO NOT USE A CELL PHONE FOR RADIO PHONER INTERVIEWS. Ask your escort to suggest the best place for a phone. Perhaps you could go back to your hotel, do the below interview from there.

If you recall, you had a phoner scheduled with a Chicago radio station from this morning. The producer rescheduled the phoner for March 25th (details to come separately) due to a last minute change in the host's schedule. This will give you a chance to get an earlier start on your drive to Cincinnati.

After the above interview, check out of your hotel. You may want to have a nice lunch, too. Now, your escort will drive you to Cincinnati.

Thursday, March 11ᵗʰ continued...

Hotel: Hyatt Regency
      151 West 5ᵗʰ Street
      Cincinnati
      Tele: 513/579-1234
      Confir# 2852181
      Direct Billing Contact: Ray Alfred
      Rate: 157.00

Remember, your escort in Cincinnati is still Cathy, your escort from Dayton.

Arrive 12:50 pm 1:00-2:00 pm LIVE IN STUDIO	WCIN AM (ABC) "1480 Talk with Lincoln Ware" 3540 Reading Road Cincinnati Contact: Alicia Reese Host: Lincoln Ware Tele: 513/281-7180
Exact time to come LIVE IN STUDIO	WLW AM "The Bill Cunningham Show" 1111 St. Gregory Cincinnati Contact: Rick Wallberg Host: Bill Cunningham Tele: 513/241-9597

WLW carries the basketball games and right now we're in the process of the NCAA playoffs. Bill is getting back to us on exactly when he can do the interview. The time is contingent upon the basketball broadcast.

Friday, March 12ᵗʰ

CINCINNATI

Your escort will pick you up this morning.

Arrive 8:10 am   WKRC AM (ABC)
8:30-9:00 am (or longer)   "Morning Show with Jeri & Craig"
LIVE IN STUDIO   1111 St. Gregory Street
                                        Cincinnati
                                        Contact: Jeri Tolliver
                                        Host: Jeri Thomas/Craig Kopp
                                        Tele: 513/852-1650

You can have a leisurely breakfast, then check out of the hotel.

Depart Cincinnati   2:55 pm
Arrive La Guardia   4:59 pm
Delta #174

Please take a cab back to your apartment. Keep all your receipts, then submit them to Kensington for reimbursement.

Congratulations on a job well done! Get some rest this weekend. Next week continues the adventure!

###

Step 9: Confirmation Sheets

Make a note of every new interview you confirm. At the end of the day, before you leave the office, write out confirmation sheets to each contact. I've included some samples of confirmation sheets at the back of the book. Briefly, a confirmation sheet should include all the pertinent interview information, including day, date, time, interview location, author name, and title of the book, as well as your contact information. You should fax the confirmation sheet, then call to verify it was received. After you've filled out all the confirmation sheets, do a memo for the publisher or distributor, outlining each confirmed booking. It's critical that the bookstores know that the author will be doing these interviews; otherwise, you run the risk of the stores not having enough copies of the book when the interview coverage hits.

Step 10: Travel Arrangements

Tours are executed in legs. Each week is considered a leg of a tour. When you've got the media for the first leg booked (usually about three to five days ahead of time), it's time to book the travel and hotels. *Do not try to get discount airline fares. It will cost you so much more money in the end, because discount fares are subject to many restrictions, and author tours are riddled with last-minute schedule changes. Travel must be booked around media. Media cannot be booked around travel.*

After you've confirmed all the media for the first leg, communicate to the travel agent the flights and hotels you need. You should work with a travel agent who specializes in tours. Most publishers have lists of them. Record labels also maintain databases of tour agents. Once you've arranged all the travel and accommodations, the next item is media escorts.

Booking Media Escorts

Media escorts are local public relations people who specialize in author tours. They'll pick up the author at the airport, get her settled into her hotel, and accompany her to all her interviews. I can't tell you what a godsend these people are. They know all the local media in their markets and can troubleshoot if there's a problem. Local media escorts run anywhere from $150 to $300 per market (or more, if the escort accompanies the author for two or three long days), and they are worth their weight in gold. In fact, my firm won't book author tours unless the publisher or author writes the escorts into the budget. There's simply too much at stake to attempt a tour without them. Too much can go wrong not to have them on your side.

The best escort organization in the country is the Promotion Network, headed up by veteran escort Emily Laisy. You'll find contact information for Emily in the Resource section at the end of this book, and you can call her any time, day and night, read her off a list of cities, and she'll make sure you have an escort in each one. She also does a monthly newsletter that's very helpful to publicists.

Step 11: Keeping Track of the Details

Now that you've got all the media booked and the travel, accommodations, and escort taken care of for the first leg, it's time to enter the schedule into the computer. I'm a stickler about comprehensive, detailed schedules. I've included several samples at the back of the book. Reviewing my samples will teach you all you need to know about how to draft an interview schedule. Suffice it to say that the more details you provide, the better. There's a reason for this. When authors are on the road, the situation can be nerve-wracking and taxing. They need to have all the details of their tour right at their fingertips. That includes:

- Flight numbers, departure and arrival times
- Record locator numbers and office and emergency numbers of the travel agent
- Hotel names, addresses, phone numbers, and confirmation numbers

- Media escort name, plus home and cell phone numbers
- Complete interview schedule, with pickup times, interview duration, angle the interview was booked on, name of interviewer, location of interview, media contact phone number, and studio hotline
- Demographic information about the outlet
- Travel time between interviews
- Suggestions on when to eat and pack
- All other pertinent logistical details

Never write out more than one day per page on a tour schedule. If a day is very long, you can use as many pages as you want, but don't ever put more than one day on a page. Otherwise, reading the schedule becomes too confusing. Also, make sure, if you're the publicist who booked the schedule, that every phone number you have is on that schedule. When an author is on the road, he should be able to reach his publicist, travel agent, and media escorts twenty-four hours a day. As I told you, a tour is a full-time job. If you're an author and are considering doing a tour, or a publicist who's booking the tour, respect each other, and realize that, for the duration of the tour, you're road warriors and need to be ready for anything. Period.

Step 12: Update Constantly

Once the first leg of the tour is typed up and printed out, copies need to be faxed to the publisher, author, and media escorts. As changes occur—and *they will*—make sure all adjustments are entered into the computer, and new, updated schedules are printed and issued to all relevant parties. Confirm verbally each interview twenty-four to forty-eight hours before the author hits that city. This is urgent. You may have confirmed the interview when you booked it, and sent a written confirmation and verified its receipt, but media moves like lightning, and news stories are breaking every minute. If you don't call a day or two before the author arrives in the tour city and confirm directly with the contacts for each interview, you risk losing the bookings. When I say verbally confirm these interviews, I don't mean leave a voice mail message with your media contact. I mean get the person or his assistant on the phone, confirm the interview, and document in your notes that you did it. Media coverage that isn't confirmed doesn't count.

As you're managing the first leg of the tour, you're probably also still booking interviews for the second and third legs. Doing a tour is a juggling process. You've got to be on your toes. Always make sure that every outlet has a copy of the book, and if it's television, verify that they're editing in a still of the book. Pay attention to detail. Stay organized.

Step 13: Debriefing

When the tour is completed, go back and communicate with each of your contacts, and obtain as many clippings and video and audio dubs as possible. One of my favorite tricks is to arm my authors with tons of blank video- and audiotapes when they go on tour. Often, if an author gives a producer a tape and asks for a dub, he's more than happy to oblige. For those who won't, you can follow up later.

The Cost of Doing Business

Now that we've reviewed the steps of pulling off an author tour, let's look at the financial side. Tours are expensive. Let's break down an average ten-city tour.

Author travel and accommodations	$2,000 per city
Media Escorts	$275 per city
Media Mailings	$2,700
Phone and Fax	$2,700
Press Kit Production	$650
Misc.	$700
APPROXIMATE TOTAL HARD COSTS FOR TEN-TO-TWELVE-CITY TOUR, NOT INCLUDING PR FIRM MONTHLY RETAINER FEE:	$31,500

The above numbers are hard costs only and do not include a monthly fee for a publicity firm. If you're a publisher and are attempting to book a tour yourself, you can expect the above hard costs, give or take a couple of thousand dollars, depending on if and how you cut corners. If you need to hire a publicity firm to spearhead the tour, most firms charge anywhere between $3,000 and $8,000 a month to book a tour, depending upon the number of cities, client expectations, and how much lead time they're given.

Becoming a Road Warrior

Now that you've got a handle on how to execute the logistics of an author tour, let me share with you some of the intangibles that you're unlikely to glean from a book or classroom. The best way to truly comprehend the rigors of a tour is to go on the road with the author. Nothing is more illuminating than seeing for yourself what it feels like to function on almost no sleep, rush to one interview after another, and run from airport to airport every day with barely enough time to eat, shower, iron your shirt, call home, check your e-mail, or just breathe evenly. I can't begin to tell you how important it is for a publicist to experience the road at least once.

There are so many reasons why going on tour with an author offers such an advantage. For one thing, authors tend to complain often and loudly when they're touring. Some of the complaints are legitimate. Some aren't. Even seasoned road warriors, familiar with the grind, get tired and cranky, especially toward the end of a tour when their nerves are frazzled. If an author knows his publicist has accompanied touring authors in the past, he'll be more responsive to her authority because he'll realize she can genuinely empathize with how he feels. In addition, the publicist will know which of his complaints need to be addressed and which are just the author blowing off steam.

I've gone on tour numerous times with authors. It gave me such an edge. I went on the road with a film and television producer who had written his memoirs. We did fourteen cities in fifteen days. It was really tough. He had interviews scheduled from 5:30 AM until almost midnight every day, with flights in between. Tempers flared more than once. I remember one morning in particular. This author was an unusually heavy sleeper—I always made sure that, at each hotel, he would receive two wake-up calls. The final week of the tour we were in Chicago. He had a live national television interview scheduled for 6:00 AM. I was down in the lobby at 5:30, our prearranged pickup time. 5:45 came and went. No author. I called his room repeatedly. No answer. By now, I was concerned that my interview schedule may have actually killed the guy! Death by media blitz.

Desperate to quell my concerns that something was terribly wrong, and equally determined not to miss this great television opportunity, I called the hotel manager and asked him to send a security guard to the author's room. The manager, who by now was worried that I may have a heart attack, graciously obliged. I waited nervously in the hotel lobby. Five minutes later, a slightly bedraggled, moderately irritated author walked out of the elevator. "Where were you?" I asked, ready to pound him over the head with a copy of his own book. "I'm sorry," he replied sheepishly. "I must have accidentally pushed the do-not-disturb button on my phone." Lesson learned? Always make sure the author checks his phone before he goes to sleep to make sure that the ringer is on, that it's plugged in, and that the do-not-disturb button is off!

Though the above story is certainly funny, it proves a point. Whenever I tour an author, I always tell the author to call me at home right before going to sleep. That's why I make this request. In addition to finding out how the day went, it gives me an opportunity to review the wake-up time and make sure all systems are go. I never would have known the importance of communicating with the author late at night, without this road warrior experience.

Often, when I work with young publicists, they'll ask me why my tour schedules are so detailed. In fact, some have even used the word "anal." "Why do you tell the author when to eat, sleep, and pack?" they ask. "Isn't that basic common sense?" Yes, one would think so. I used to think so myself, until I went on tour and learned differently—the hard way. I was touring with a former football player. We had ten cities in ten days. He had interviews back to back. Several times, we missed flights because we thought we would have time to run back to our hotel and pack after the last interview of the day, but needless to say, we miscalculated. Food presented a similar problem. I hadn't written in meal times on the schedule. As a result, on more days than I care to remember, we ended up grabbing protein bars on the fly because I hadn't factored in lunch or dinner. At the tour's end, we were sick and tired. Once again, I learned my lesson. Now, every schedule I make up has specific times and locations for each meal. If a day is exceptionally tight with media, I instruct the media escort to prepare nutritious box lunches and to bring snacks along, so the author can eat in between interviews.

You see why experiencing the road is so crucial? Little things make an infinite difference, especially when you learn them firsthand.

Another reason why going on tour is an asset is the media-relations perspective. When you accompany an author on tour, it gives you the invaluable opportunity to meet key local media contacts in person.

I'm not saying that every time you send out an author you should go yourself. What I am saying is that you need to make it a point to go on tour at least once or twice. The rewards are great.

One last note about tours: Whether you're an author or a publicist, there are several tricks of the trade you should know before hitting the road that will make the tour much easier. I've outlined them below.

- Don't overpack. Bring a few outfits that can be mixed and matched, preferably fabrics that don't wrinkle. Men, don't feel compelled to wear suits. Nice shirts and/or sweaters with casual tailored pants are fine.

- Bring a compact clothes steamer for stubborn wrinkles and a small can of instant stain remover.
- Pack a small alarm clock and use it as backup to hotel wake-up calls.
- Carry small plastic bags of nuts, dried berries, trail mix, and protein bars, so that you have energy food right at your fingers.
- Bring two pairs of shoes only—one for dress, one for travel.
- Make sure you have a beeper and a cell phone with nationwide service on you at all times. Media schedules can change at the drop of a hat, and you need to be reachable twenty-four hours a day, seven days a week.
- Ask your media escort to bring video- and audiotapes to all your broadcast interviews, so you can obtain dubs on the spot.
- Have postcards made of your book cover—the front is the actual front cover, the back of the postcard is the actual back cover copy of the book plus your Web site address. You can give these postcards to people as you meet them in each tour market.
- Bring an expenses envelope with you and every time you pay for something, put the receipt in the envelope—this will make submitting expenses to your publisher easier and cleaner.
- Begin your tour on a Tuesday instead of a Monday each week. That way, there will be no Sunday emergencies when people aren't in their offices.
- Hire a college intern to send out thank you notes to key contacts in tour markets: bookstore personnel, producers, reporters, editors, etc.

A final note on publicity tours. A publicity tour is worth its weight in gold. The ideal tour consists of live and taped media, personal appearances, and bookstore signings. Just make sure, however, that a tour is the best bet for your book. They aren't for everyone. In the next chapter, we're going to examine the money side of book publicity. How much should you spend on publicizing your book? How can you maximize results out of a minimal budget? More ahead!!!

You should now feel confident and ready to experience the wonderful adventure of a book tour. Remember: Keep your sense of humor. Don't let small things bother you. Communicate at least three times a day with your publicist!

Happy road wars!

The Money Perspective

*I*T'S TIME FOR US TO EXPLORE HOW TO MAXIMIZE PUBLICITY EXPOSURE with a minimal budget. How much does publicity cost? What elements are the most and least expensive? Is there any way to cut corners without diminishing results? In this chapter, we're going to examine these and other key questions.

Publicity itself is free. *Generating* the publicity is where the cost comes in. Communication expenses, such as telephone bills, mailings, messengers, and overnight services; supplies, like press kit folders; photocopying and other production expenditures; video dubbing; and travel are among the most typical expenses associated with a standard publicity campaign. If you're doing a tour, it dramatically increases all of these expenses, because you're creating publicity in a multitude of markets.

Determining Your Budget

Every campaign is different in terms of how much each of the above costs will run. The key is to understand the *process* for determining a realistic budget. In this chapter, I'm going to walk you through the budgeting process step by step, then share some suggestions on promotions and other cost-cutting vehicles that enrich a campaign without emptying the bank account.

Step 1: Initial Analysis

You need to ask yourself the following questions:

- What are the advance orders on the book?
- What's the initial print run?
- What's the distribution scenario?
- Are there any pockets of the country where distribution is more concentrated?
- Is this book the first in a series, or is it a one-shot?

Understanding the exact circumstances of the book is critical to making sound judgments about budget.

Let's examine each of these questions one by one. As we've mentioned in previous chapters, the advance orders on a book determine initial print run. If the advance orders are 35,000, then initial print run should be approximately the same number. Distribution is also critical. There have to be books available to the end user (book buyer) in order to warrant publicity. With the proliferation of the Internet, it's not always urgent that books be in retail outlets, because consumers can purchase titles from e-tailers. However, bookstore availability is still the better option if you're seeking to hit the *New York Times* bestseller list, as titles sold exclusively via the Internet aren't tracked by the *New York Times*.

Where the book is distributed is also an issue. Some books have a regional tie-in, due to subject, author recognition, or location of publisher. You need to incorporate the geographic component of a campaign focus into the budget. For the most part, regional publicity efforts are less expensive than broad national campaigns. Another detail to consider when analyzing a budget is whether or not the book you're publicizing is a single title or the first in a series of titles. Sometimes, if you're launching a series, even though the initial print run may be modest on the first book, it's worth it to stretch the budget because you're looking at a long-term return on your buck.

The bottom line on step 1 of determining a budget is that you must ask yourself the proper questions and be realistic about the answers. Once you've accomplished this part of the process, you're ready to move on to step 2.

Step 2: The Formula

Every publisher approaches budgets a little differently. They all have their own tried-and-true equations for assigning dollar amounts to marketing campaigns. The money allotted to publicity is often miniscule at best. That's why it's so important that publicists be as creative and imaginative as possible. Though there are a plethora of different mathematical formulas for determining the marketing budget by title (i.e., per book), on average, most publishers are in the same ballpark.

Here's a basic breakdown of a typical formula. Lee Thompson, one of the most respected and successful marketing directors in the business and a colleague of mine at NYU's Center for Publishing, teaches this formula in her marketing class. The following is a hypothetical example, based on a hardcover trade title priced at $24.95.

	Retail Price $24.95
Using an average discount to the bookstore of . . .	50%
The bookstore makes . . .	$12.47
From the retail price of . . .	$24.95
Subtract the bookstore discount of . . .	−$12.47
The publisher nets . . .	$12.48
Based upon an Advertising/Promotional/ Publicity budget of 10%, the allowance per book is . . .	$1.24
Multiply the above by the initial print run . . .	10,000 copies
The budget is . . .	$12,400

As you can see by looking at these numbers, unless you're publicizing a book with a large initial printing, the publicity budget is usually small. There are, of course, exceptions. But for our purposes in this chapter, I want to focus on the typical scenario, as that's what most of you who are reading this book are probably encountering. Remember earlier we talked about getting publicity placements confirmed in advance so that sales can utilize this information to galvanize sell-in (i.e., advance orders)? Now you understand exactly why that's so important. Once you've assessed what your allotted marketing budget is, you have to decide how much of that will go towards publicity.

We'll use the above example of a $12,400 budget with an initial print run of 10,000. Let's say the book we're talking about is a nonfiction title called *Hazard,* a memoir of a retired fire chief, who describes what it's like to risk one's life for a living. Based upon earlier discussions we've had about advertising versus publicity, we'll assign the bulk of the $12,400 to publicity, as publicity is traditionally more effective selling this genre of books than advertising. It's also much more cost-effective. We'll allot $2,400 for a small sell-in ad in *Publisher's Weekly* and for the production of one hundred galleys of the book (galleys cost about $15 to $20 apiece). The remaining $10,000 will be used exclusively for publicity. Our next step is determining what the publicity campaign will be and estimating costs.

Step 3: Determining the Campaign Based on Budget Allotment

We've got $10,000 to spend on *Hazard*. An author tour is out, because there aren't enough copies of the book available to warrant the expense; plus, a tour costs a minimum of $1,500 a city, and that's if it's done in-house. If a PR firm is hired, it's more expensive. Taking into consideration the subject of the book, and the publicizability factor of the author, our best bet would be to anchor the campaign on national print and broadcast media and local author publicity. Let's break that down into specifics, then estimate the cost in step 4.

The author can do national print interviews, such as newspapers, wire services, magazines, and syndicated columnists, either by telephone from his home or in person with the local stringer for whatever publication it is. It doesn't require travel. National radio interviews can also be done by telephone. National television is where travel comes in. As we discussed in previous chapters, most national television shows are produced out of Los Angeles and New York, with the exception of *Oprah*. Though a satellite interview might be an option, you can be sure that some travel will be required for national TV.

Let's say we book the author on a major network television show out of New York, then pull together a solid media schedule for him while he's there that includes national cable interviews, a national newspaper, several New York dailies, and a few morning and evening drive radio programs. The goal would be to get the author as much media exposure as possible, in order to maximize the expenditure of the trip. Then don't forget, we're also doing local author publicity, which, despite the fact it doesn't include travel expenses, still has costs attached to it.

Step 4: The Breakdown

This expense breakdown is based on an in-house or author-implemented campaign and does not include costs of an outside PR firm. (All costs are estimates.)

A) Production of Press Kit
Number of kits needed for campaign	100
Printing cost	$300
Press kit folders	$200
Approximate total cost	$500

B) Mailings
Number of books to be mailed with press kits	75
Cost of mailing books	$300
Number of galleys to be mailed with press kits	75

Cost of mailing galleys	$300
Approximate total cost	$600

C) Overnight Mailings and Messengers

Number of press kits with books to be overnighted and/or messengered	25
Cost	$500
Number of press kits with galleys to be overnighted and/or messengered	25
Cost	$500
Approximate total cost	$1000

D) Long Distance Telephone Bill

Monthly charges for calling New York, Los Angeles, and author's local market	$500
Approximate total cost for four-month campaign	$2000*

You want a high phone bill, because the higher the phone bill, the more calls that are being made for the book.

E) Supplies for Campaign

Jiffy bags for mailings	$200
Video dubs for national television	$1000
Author photos (includes photo shoot and duplicates for press kits)	$500
Approximate total cost	$1700

F) Author Travel and Accommodations

New York, two days and two nights for media interviews

Flight**	$1000
Hotel	$800
Meals	$200
Car service/taxi	$200
Media escort	$400
Approximate total cost	$2600

**Cheap flights don't work when traveling for media, because they don't allow for last minute changes—media travel requires full-fare bookings.

G) Miscellaneous Expenses

Includes such expenses as obtaining video dubs of television interviews done in New York and hometown market, and a clipping service to round up all print coverage that runs

Approximate total cost $1000

H) Local Author Publicity Expenses

Includes such expenses as parking and media escort $200

TOTAL ESTIMATED
PUBLICITY EXPENSES FOR *HAZARD* $9,600

That leaves $1,200 remaining in the kitty. Let me tell you from experience that $1,200 will get spent more quickly than you can bat an eye. National television shows reschedule frequently, not to mention requesting guests at the last minute, creating more travel and accommodation expenses. There are always unexpected expenses tied to a publicity campaign. It's always good to leave a little elbowroom when you're estimating budgets. The numbers I've shared with you above are on the high side, but still realistic. Imagine, this budget is for a book that's being publicized in-house or by the author. If you were to bring in an outside PR firm, you would have to factor that into the budget as well. In our last chapter, I'm going to review how much PR firms cost and how to know when it's time to go outside for publicity help. For now, let's continue looking at general budgeting issues.

Step 5: Monitoring the Impact of the Campaign on Sales and Adjusting Budget

Publishers tend to be conservative in budget allotments, as indicated by the typical formula used for determining budgets. Therefore, it's crucial that sales be continually and closely monitored, because when a publisher sees that publicity is propelling both sell-in and sell-through, the company will pump more money into the campaign. Traditionally, publishers take a look-see attitude about budgets. They assign a dollar amount to the publicity campaign, then wait to see how events unfold. If they recognize that publicity is truly making a difference, often, they will increase the budget.

For example, my firm recently worked on a campaign for a celebrity memoir. Initially, the budget allowed for national print and broadcast out of New York, his hometown of Los Angeles, and Chicago, where he grew up. We blitzed these markets, generating so much media coverage that within three weeks of pub date, the book had already gone into its third printing. The publisher immediately responded by sending the author on a ten-city tour. This is not an isolated incident. It's called "chasing a book when it's running."

For a book to be successful, it needs a strong initial publicity push. Once that's achieved, the book will either catch on through word of mouth and build, or not. If it does start to "run" (i.e., move off the shelves with velocity), the publisher will "chase" it up the hill, infusing more dollars into the campaign, supporting it with increased advertising, publicity, and in-store promotions. Bear in mind, however, that the majority of books don't "run." Most books see a modest entrée into the stores and then sell over time. Publicity is critical to both types of books. Those that need to be chased require a fast, firm publicity hand. Those that seep their way into the public consciousness need a committed, tireless publicity hand, holding fast to the helm. That's why monitoring the impact of a campaign is so important. You have to see how and where the campaign is working to determine if and how additional monies should be spent.

The best way to monitor a campaign is to ask the sales department for information. If you're with a large publisher, your editor can always access this data. Publishing is a numbers game. You have to physically analyze the correlation between sales patterns and publicity coverage. No publisher is committed to a book's failure. Like you, they want the book to succeed.

The Golden Tortoise

Then you've got the books that start out slow and never run, but reach the finish line doing a slow trot. One of my favorite examples of what I've always called "golden tortoises" (in honor of my favorite, "The Tortoise and the Hare") was John Bradshaw's book, *Healing the Shame that Binds You*. I was the publicist for that campaign early in my career. The wonderful thing about being green in a job is that even though you may not intuit all of the opportunities, you also don't see any of the obstacles. This book was tricky to publicize because the concept of "shame" was difficult to translate into verbiage that would be newsworthy to the media and accessible to audiences. On top of that, John Bradshaw was still learning the ins and outs of giving great media interviews. Our three strengths were that the book was brilliant, John had a companion television show airing on PBS, and he and his publisher, Health Communications, were deeply dedicated to putting this title on the *New York Times* bestseller list.

We started out methodically, booking John on one or two big national television interviews a week. We filled in with radio and print phoners, systematically hitting one city at a time, until we'd created publicity in the country's top thirty markets. Unlike a "blitz" campaign that ignites a book that "runs," we were like the tortoise. Each month, we added a few more strides to our marathon, making sure our steps were steady, strong, and focused.

It took nearly a year, but *Healing the Shame that Binds You* hit the Number One spot on the *New York Times* bestseller list and stayed there for weeks and weeks. Every book John Bradshaw wrote thereafter also hit the *New York Times* list. Additionally, he became such a captivating television interview that MGM gave him his own syndicated talk show. It just goes to prove that publicity operates on many levels, the most critical being the willingness of the author, publicist, and publisher to work together and not give up.

Publicizing Out of Season

One small insight that can save you much heartache if you're an author: Publishers release books by season, as we discussed in chapters 1 and 2. Once the season has passed for a book, the in-house publicity department must move on to the next season. That's the reality of the business. Accept it. That doesn't mean, however, that you should roll over and play dead. There are options. First, you can bring on a freelance publicist or PR firm to continue the campaign, or you can continue it yourself. Once the season has passed, it may be a little more difficult to obtain sales figures from your publisher, as the staff will be immersed in the challenges of the titles ahead of them. Respect the pressure they're under, and be elegantly persistent. Call your editor and see if he can help you. A word from your editor to the sales director will make a mountain of difference. As an author, you have to stay on top of your publisher, but there are ways to do it that are helpful to the book and not detrimental to your relationship with your house.

For example, when you ask your editor to fill you in on sales figures, tell them you want to keep the book alive and would like their suggestions on how you could best serve your book. Let them know you're willing to put the love and time in, and you'd be deeply grateful if they would let you know on a regular basis how sales are doing, so that you can budget your efforts accordingly. Publishers will respond to that positively. Remember, you can catch many more flies with honey than you can with vinegar.

Maximizing Coverage Per Dollar

Now that we've reviewed the five steps for determining a publicity budget, I'd like to address creative techniques for generating publicity that maximize both coverage and dollars. We've touched upon some of these ideas at length in previous chapters. You should peruse chapter 2, which delves into promotions tailor-designed for publicity purposes. We'll revisit the subject here, as it's so pertinent to budget.

One of the most cost-effective publicity secrets is promotion. You always want to do a promotion that enlists the participation of the general consumer, because from the media's perspective, anything the public does is news. Let's look at an example.

My firm did a campaign for a financial thriller set in Manhattan. We didn't have a large publicity budget to play with, so we had to be imaginative. The novel centered around a historic artifact unearthed at a construction site in New York. We were so impressed by the premise of the book that we constructed a promotion around it. We asked people in the Tri-State area to share stories of the most unusual item they'd ever found and how it impacted their life or the lives of others. The most inspiring entry would win a weekend for two at a resort located on a historic site in New England. We issued the press release to hundreds of media outlets throughout New York, New Jersey, and Connecticut, arranging print and broadcast interviews for the author so he could promote the contest and his book, which, of course, was the inspiration for the contest. The response was wonderful.

It was a keenly cost-effective promotion. The media hook was the contest, which didn't cost anything to do. The resort comped the winner's weekend package in exchange for the publicity exposure generated during the author interviews. The expenses were standard and kept to a minimum: mailings and communication expenses, and two short trips to New York. The first trip was for the author to give media interviews. The second was for the author to present the award to the winner, which was covered by the media.

Speaking of events, that's another great way to generate publicity for little money. Piggybacking events is a favorite trick among sharp publicists. Piggybacking is latching onto something that's already in the works as an opportunity to cross-promote a book. Let me give you a few examples. You're publicizing a book called *MOTHERHOOD—The First Nine Months,* written by a mother and psychologist, that offers techniques for dealing with the psychological hurdles of pregnancy. This book provides a myriad of piggybacking options. You could research whether or not there's a national organization of Lamaze instructors, and find out if they do an annual event and if they would be interested in having the author speak and sign books. You could offer to get media to cover the event, which would benefit the Lamaze group from a publicity standpoint. You could also contact the top ten obstetricians in the author's hometown, ask if they have any events, seminars, or conventions, and encourage them to invite the author as a special speaker.

The secret to piggybacking is having your pitch firmly in your mind. There are two elements to the pitch. The first is knowing exactly how the author's participation can benefit the organization or group. In other words, if they're doing something with your author, what's in it for them? Second, what do you want to get out of it in terms of publicity and promotion for the author? One hand helps the other.

One last cost-minimizing publicity secret—we've addressed it before, but it bears repeating—the telephone. Print and radio interviews can often be done over the phone. If you don't have a large publicity budget, try and set up at least one AM morning or evening drive radio interview and one good daily newspaper interview in twenty key markets. The trick to pulling this off is developing an intriguing local angle for each market, and scheduling the interviews so that the radio interview and the newspaper piece hit in the same week. This creates a mini-blitz effect and can really boost sales.

When it comes to budget and publicity, where there's a will, there's a way. The more imaginative you are, the better coverage you'll get.

Our next chapter is on cross-promotion, the ancillary picture, and what to do when something goes wrong. Stay tuned . . .

Beyond the Boundaries of Book Publicity: The Cross-Promotional and Ancillary Picture

*W*E'VE TALKED ABOUT HOW TO PUBLICIZE A BOOK. SOMETIMES, book publicity is part of a larger picture. For many authors, a book is a means to another end, and not an end in and of itself. People write books for many reasons. Entrepreneurs write books to reach new clients. Doctors and lawyers write books to build their practices. CEOs write books to increase corporate visibility. The bottom line is that not every author's *sole* objective is a successful sell-in and sell-through of their book. Frequently, they have a much larger agenda, and the book is a stepping-stone. When that's the case, you need to know how to maximize exposure for the book, while simultaneously utilizing it as the vehicle to create awareness for whatever else is on the cross-promotional agenda. Let me share a few examples to make this clearer for you.

The Book as Corporate PR

Several years ago I did a campaign for a brilliant young lawyer who specialized in protecting small investors from unscrupulous financial professionals. He had written a book on the subject, hoping it would heighten awareness of the issue, bring new

clients into his firm, and empower him to continue helping people on a much larger scale. For him, the book was a ladder to the
next level of his career. He wanted me to execute an aggressive,
multidimensional publicity campaign that would get him out on
the media circuit and communicate his message to potential victims of investment fraud.

I knew the moment he called that there was a much bigger picture at work here than straight book publicity. He sent me
a copy of the galley, which I read in earnest. Next, we set up an
appointment so that I could interview him and develop a blueprint of action. He explained that all across America, there were
thousands of unsuspecting men and women getting duped out of
their entire life's savings by sleazy financial professionals who
preyed on the weak and innocent, especially recent widows and
the elderly, among other groups. "There are so many victims out
there who don't know where to turn for help," he told me. "I
wrote my book to protect people, but my firm can help actual victims recoup their losses," he continued. "Writing a book enabled
me to make a difference on a larger scale."

Though this author cared deeply about the success of his
book, it wasn't his primary motivation. He wrote the book as a
publicity hook to galvanize awareness about investment fraud and
generate new clients. In a situation such as this, our goal for the
client was much broader in scope than a standard book campaign. The press kit included additional pieces other than the
book release and author bio, such as a backgrounder on the
client's law firm, professional highlights, and other details that
focused media attention on the firm itself. In this case, the book
itself was both the news peg and the hook.

When you're publicizing a company or service and a book
is the vehicle, the traditional rules of thumb about book publicity
don't necessarily apply. Take the example above. The point of
creating media exposure for the investment fraud book was to
boost the client's business. Therefore, even though the book didn't
have a large initial print run, and the sell-in was weak at best,

we still targeted major national media and toured to various cities, because the purpose was corporate PR more than sell-through of the book.

The Book as Public Awareness Catalyst

Let's look at another circumstance. You may recall several chapters back when we talked about athlete and actor Jim Brown, whose autobiography, *Out of Bounds,* I helped put onto the *New York Times* bestseller list. In Jim's case, the purpose of the book was threefold—to generate income; to function as his reentry vehicle, as Jim had been out of the public eye for many years; and most importantly, to lay the groundwork for the launch of his landmark rehabilitation movement, the AMER-I-CAN Program.

When I was assigned the book, I asked Jim, during our interview session, what specifically he wanted to achieve vis-à-vis the book. For him, the book was clearly a catalyst. We engineered his campaign with that in mind. All the press materials focused on the newsworthiness of the book, yet simultaneously alluded to the pending birth of the rehabilitation program. I arranged public appearance opportunities with government and community leaders, during which he could promote his book and cross-promote his efforts with convicts and other disenfranchised individuals. When we squeezed as much publicity juice out of the book that we could, we immediately stepped into high gear with the AMER-I-CAN Program, launching the second phase of our campaign.

Understanding Tie-In Publicity

Always remember that the secret to being a good book publicist is understanding all the elements and knowing how to fine-tune the positioning to achieve multiple goals. Nowhere is that skill more needed than in the cross-promotion game. Often referred to by publicists as "tie-in" publicity, there are a few rules of thumb that can help you to meet the inherent challenges head-on. First, always ask the author exactly why he wrote the book and what it is specifically he would like the book publicity to achieve, above and beyond book sales itself. Second, once you've established with the author his cross-promotional or tie-in agenda, you must weave that element into the overall PR positioning for the book.

For example, say you're doing a book about breast cancer prevention, written by a renowned oncologist who runs a series of clinics across the country. The author's goal is to utilize the book publicity as a springboard to promote her clinics. In this case, you could position the book as an awareness tool inspired by the clinics' commitment to empower women with life-saving knowledge.

Rarely is a book ever an end in and of itself. Usually, for an author, a book is a *means* to an end.

Entertainment Industry Cross-Promotions

Another cross-promotional situation that frequently crops up in book publicity is film and/or television tie-ins. There are several ways in which this can occur. The most common is when a book and film are released simultaneously, or a book is rereleased in paperback to coincide with a film launch.

Say, for example, you're representing an author who's written a novel about the Civil War entitled *Treacherous*. The hardcover debut was reasonably successful. It's now a year later, and a major Hollywood studio is releasing the film in six months. Your author consulted on the script. He has a sound relationship with the studio and production company, and the publisher is eager to capitalize on the film buzz to galvanize sales for the paperback, which will hit shelves right before the movie comes out. How do you facilitate an effective cross-promotion in which everyone benefits? There are three steps. Though I've used a film release as the example, the same steps apply to a television movie or program. The only difference with television is that instead of a studio, you'd be coordinating efforts with a cable or broadcast network and/or syndicator.

Step 1: Gather Information and Document Specifics

Communication is the key to cross-promotion. *Never* assume anything. Talk with the publisher. Ask all the pertinent questions. What's the initial print run? What's the publicity budget? In a perfect world, what would the publisher envision as ideal copromotions between itself and the studio? Once you have this data from the publisher's perspective, you can sit down with the studio's publicity and marketing departments and discuss how they and the publisher can work together. As book publicist, your role is to function as a communications conduit and neutralizer between the studio and publisher, and to implement a book campaign that complements, enhances, and supplements the marketing of the movie. The more synergy between the studio's and publisher's efforts, the stronger the sell-through will be on both tickets and books.

When you meet with the studio's publicity department, explore its campaign plan for the film. When does the department anticipate rolling out the stars of the movie for media interviews? Would it be possible to invite booksellers to attend select previews in key cities? When will the studio start running trailers for the film? (A trailer is a short commercial for the film that features moments from the movie.) When does the ad campaign go into high gear? What's the positioning verbiage for the film? You want to make sure that the positioning of the book supports the positioning of the film. Has any advance media interest been confirmed in which the author could possibly be included?

The bottom line in terms of working with the studio is to explain that you need to generate media interviews for your author and want to work in tandem with its staff to maximize opportunities. Perhaps your author could do a few interviews with the cast. Or there might be interviews you arrange for the author in which the cast could be included. Once again, everything rests in your willingness and ability to communicate. Let the studio know your objectives for the book, and work with it to ensure that both your agendas dovetail. The earlier you do these meetings the better. Ideally, you start talking with the studio six months before the film is out. Though campaigns vary from movie to movie, the average motion picture campaign begins about six months prior to release date. Studios, like publishers, have a lot on their plates and usually welcome the extra media coverage that book publicists bring to the table.

The key is to always let the studio and publisher know what you're up to. Don't go off on tangents. Discuss your target media list. Review timing. I've often found that it works well for the author to hit the media first, just before the film publicity machine with all the stars kicks in. Bear in mind, as I've mentioned before, that each campaign is different. It's up to you to communicate, so that everyone feels comfortable and in control.

Once you've established exactly what the book campaign will be and how the studio and publisher will coordinate efforts, draft a memo that outlines specifically all these items. Copy everyone you've met with, and update this memo each week with developments, adjustments, and new information. I can't emphasize enough how crucial documentation is. If you don't put it on paper, you could get caught in bureaucratic firestorms. Like my dad always taught me—document, document, and document!

Step 2: Materials Coordination

Typically, if the book is coming out one to three months prior to the release of the film, that's when the author would begin the media gauntlet. One of the biggest advantages of having the rerelease of the book close to the opening of the film is the availability of the trailer. A film trailer makes for great B-roll for an author interview segment. For example, if your author is doing an interview on a network morning show, the show could edit in a still of the book, as well as broadcast the trailer. It gives the audience a sneak peak of the film and enriches the viewers' perception of the book.

Once you've coordinated the campaign strategy with the studio staff, you need to ascertain what support materials they can give you. Perhaps they can offer you dubs of the electronic press kit and/or several different trailers. Conversely, you also want them to communicate with you about their publicity placements for the film. Encourage them to include the book whenever possible, and work with them on how they would be most comfortable doing that. Some studios prefer a supply of books that they can send directly to their contacts. Other studios would rather communicate contact information to the book publicist and have them deal directly with the media contact. I always push for the latter, as it's less complicated and provides greater coverage control.

Remember that you catch more flies with honey than vinegar. Treat the studios with respect, but also hold your own ground. You're not asking them for permission to publicize your book. You're asking them to work *with* you, so that both the film and book campaigns benefit one another and blend seamlessly.

Step 3: Implementation Communication

As you confirm coverage for your author, let the studio people know what interviews you've booked, what the spin of each interview will be, and when the coverage will run/air, among all other important details. Give them as much advance notice as possible, and review with them how they'd like the author to position the film during the interviews. After these conversations, issue memos reiterating what was discussed. Keep publisher and studio abreast. In return, ask the same of the studio. Tell your contacts there that you would like to know about all pending film coverage, so that you can get these media contacts copies of the book and offer them interviews with the author. Of course, there will be bumps along the way. Studio and publisher may not always see eye to eye. But if you make an effort to communicate, and encourage the same level of communication from everyone else, you minimize potential problems from the start.

Man on the Moon

Recently, I handled the publicity for a memoir about comic genius Andy Kaufman, entitled *Andy Kaufman Revealed: Best Friend Tells All*, by Bob Zmuda. It was an amazing cross-promotional odyssey, as the author was also coexecutive producer of the film, *Man on the Moon,* a biopic about Andy Kaufman, directed by Milos Forman and starring Jim Carrey, Danny DeVito, and Courtney Love. Originally, the film was scheduled for release in early November, exactly two months after the book launch. The studio was so excited about the film that they decided to make it their big Christmas movie and pushed back the release date to December 22nd. While it was assumed to be wonderful for the movie, I had serious concerns about how the new release date would impact the book, not to mention there would be a lot more competitive film product out there, where we would have had an open field in November. I was worried that the extra two months in between would generate book returns.

The author and I sat down with Universal Studios executives and shared our thoughts. They were wonderful and very supportive. They appreciated our continued communication and respected our dilemma. We were able to map out a media strategy in which Bob would give media interviews in late August and continue through late November, at which point the cast would start the media gauntlet. The studio and I coordinated efforts closely. Bob vigorously cross-promoted the film during his book campaign, and the studio returned the gesture during the film campaign. In fact, in late October, they even sent Bob out on tour, during which he hosted college screenings of the film at night and did media interviews promoting his book and the film during the day.

The secret to our successful publicity coordination was communication and documentation. Sharing beneficial information is a form of respect. When you give respect, it comes to you tenfold. That's the most important lesson you can learn about cross-promotion.

Publicity to Create Ancillary Demand

We've looked at how to coordinate publicity efforts for cross-promotional purposes. What about when you want to use publicity to *create* those opportunities in the first place? We briefly covered in chapter 2 how publicity can boost ancillary rights. It's time to explore this area in more depth.

Ancillary rights refer to alternative forms in which a book can be sold other than its original literary format, such as film, television, paperback, audio, and merchandising, among many others. Intelligently targeted publicity placements can have an immeasurable effect on ancillary sales. Let's look at each of the above categories in more detail and examine how publicity can generate activity.

Film

When the film rights to a book are sold, it typically happens in two phases. The first phase is the option, and the second is the purchase. A production company, studio, or sometimes even an actor will take out an option against a purchase price. Say, for example, you've written a novel called *Murder at Midnight*. A production company has offered a $100,000 option against a $1 million purchase price. In layman's language, what that means is the production company would give you $100,000 for the *option* of being able to make a movie of your book. Though option times vary, most options are for one year. During that year, you couldn't sell the film rights to anyone else. It's sort of like putting a hold on merchandise. After the term of the option, the production company would have to do one of two things: pay the purchase price minus the option money or take out another option. I have friends who are authors who have bought homes on options that never purchased out.

When the film rights to a book are optioned or sold, it provides a profound sell-in and sell-through advantage. Think about *The Horse Whisperer*. When Robert Redford purchased the film rights, it catapulted the book's visibility to unanticipated heights. Publicity can play a key role in helping authors galvanize early film rights interest. The motion picture industry has a plethora of trade publications. The two biggest are *Variety* and the *Hollywood Reporter*. The *Los Angeles Times* is also influential. If you've got a book that would make a good film, you need to find angles that would work for the entertainment trades.

If there isn't a feasible entertainment angle for the book that would hook one of the big trade publications, you should set your sights on genre-specific publications that are read by movers and shakers in the film arena. For example, if you're publicizing a science fiction title, pitch the top ten science fiction trade magazines on interviewing the author. So many of the producers who do science fiction and horror films read these magazines. They're listed in *Bacon's*. You can also go on the Web and find dozens. Personal appearances are also a wonderful opportunity for authors. Research the popular seminars and conventions for the entertainment industry, and contact their promotions people to explore possibilities.

You've heard me say it before: Where there's a will, there's a way. Read the entertainment industry trades, as well as the peripheral, subject-driven publications read by industry professionals. All it takes is one article to get the ball rolling.

Television

When we talk about dramatic rights, we're referring to both film and television. Television rights can include a weekly series, made-for-TV movie, miniseries, documentary series, or syndicated series. The list goes on and on. Publicity can help ignite a fire of early interest from the television community on two levels: trade and general consumer coverage. Like film producers, television executives read *Variety* and the *Hollywood Reporter*. There are also many other industry publications that reach decision makers in the television arena. You have to be creative when you pitch these magazines. Read them for a few weeks to get a feel for how they spin stories, then put your thinking cap on.

Remember what we talked about early on in this book: front-door and side-door pitching. Getting authors covered in entertainment trade publications requires a side-door approach.

Recently, I met with one of the top television executives in the country, who acquires books for miniseries. She and I had a long talk, and I asked her what influences her choices, above and beyond the content and quality of the books themselves. Her answer? Publicity. She told me point-blank that when a book has a buzz, when the author is out there doing media interviews, it can sway her if she's sitting on the fence about a particular title.

If you're publicizing a book you believe has strong television potential, include Los Angeles publicity in your marketing strategy. Blitz the Southern California market. Imagine all the producers you'll reach. Again, I can't emphasize enough—consider all the elements, and be proactively creative.

Paperback and Audio

Some book deals are hard-soft, which means the publisher will release the book initially in hardcover and later in paperback. Many houses also publish their own audio versions of their books. For authors who have hardcover deals without paperback or audio included, publicity can be effective in helping to sell those rights.

If you're publicizing a title that falls into the latter category, make sure you keep the publishing industry closely abreast of what's happening with the general consumer campaign. Stay in regular contact with the publishing trades, as they're the lifelines of information to the industry. For example, say you're publicizing a novel about divorce, and you get the author on *The Today Show* and *Larry King Live*. You should immediately issue a short press release to the publishing trades like *Publisher's Weekly,* and encourage them to spotlight this information in one of their columns.

In effect, you're actually managing two simultaneous campaigns. One is to the general consumer, which fortifies sell-in and maximizes sell-through. The other is to the publishing industry itself, which also increases sell-in, as well as catapulting paperback and audio rights potential to the next level. The more the publishing industry is aware of a general consumer buzz about the book, the stronger the title will be in terms of paperback and audio opportunities.

Merchandising

Merchandising in publishing means products that emanate from a book property. When we talk about merchandising, we're getting into the area of branding. Branding in publishing has always been prominent in children's books. Take, for example, Winnie the Pooh, Peter Rabbit, and Babar. Over the last few years, however, branding has become a whole new area in adult trade publishing. Look at John Gray and his book *Men Are from Mars, Women Are from Venus*. His publisher, HarperCollins, was brilliant. Through a deft combination of publicity, advertising, and relentless promotion, they transformed the book into a brand. There are *Men Are from Mars, Women Are from Venus* board games, calendars, videos—you name it. Additionally, their campaign enabled the author to successfully serialize the book, spawning a stream of exciting sequels.

Publicity captains the merchandising ship in publishing. Though campaign strategies vary from book to book, the fundamental rules remain the same if you want to brand a title.

When you launch the book, you must blitz the country with media coverage. I'm talking about generating extensive national print and broadcast coverage out of New York, D.C., Los Angeles, and Chicago, as well as sending the author on a ten- to fifteen-city tour. It's critical that you cluster all the media into a three-to-four-week period, in order to generate momentum. Here's where destiny comes in. Once you've implemented the media blitz, the book will either catch on with the public, or it won't. If it does, you segue into the next phase: advertising and promotion. That *doesn't* mean you stop creating publicity placements. On the contrary, you keep the publicity going via radio and newspaper phoners coast to coast, while simultaneously mounting an advertising campaign and in-store promotions. The secret to branding, which is the blood and soul of merchandising, is to perpetuate a consistent message about the book and author continually, through a diverse spectrum of media and methods.

Next chapter: what to do when you're faced with a publicity crisis. Stay tuned!

Crisis Management: What to Do When Something Goes Wrong

*Y*OU'RE SAILING THROUGH A CAMPAIGN. EVERYTHING IS MOVING ALONG as planned. You're securing a diverse array of media coverage. The book is selling through well. All of a sudden, your dream project turns into a nightmare. What do you do?

Crisis comes in many different shapes and sizes. It would be impossible to review every form of crisis that can arise in a book publicity campaign. What we're going to do in this chapter is examine the most typical kinds of crises literary publicists face and the necessary steps to pulling a campaign back on track.

The Credibility Crisis

One of the most common crises emanates from the author credibility factor. Remember, earlier on, we chatted about an author of mine who was pushing a relationship book in the middle of her third divorce. The media wanted to cancel interviews they'd confirmed with her because they couldn't come to grips with a couples therapist who kept getting divorced. The author and I turned it around by transforming the problem into an opportunity. We issued a press release positioning her as a true expert on the subject of love, because who better to know about successful marriage than someone who's suffered ones that weren't. You can't appreciate heaven, we told the media, unless you've genuinely known the rigors of hell. Our crisis response was so effective that all the media that canceled reconfirmed every interview, and within ten days, her book was on the *New York Times* bestseller list.

When a circumstance arises that puts an author's credibility on the line, you have to examine how and why his or her expertise is in question. Nine times out of ten, you can turn the negative into a positive. Let me give you another quick example.

I once did a campaign for a former Israeli spy who wrote a book in which he claimed to be the source who broke the Iran-Contra scandal to the press. Never in my career did I ever confront so many author credibility crises in one project. It was so ridiculous, it started to become almost cartoonish. I would pitch network television and major national newspapers and magazines. Reporters and editors would confirm interview times, and then twenty-four hours after they'd received my confirmation sheet, would call to cancel the interviews. They were always cryptic about why they were canceling, but a few of my media contacts, with whom I'd been working for years, explained the problem to me from their perspective. They confided in me that when they told their superiors they were interviewing this author, they were instructed to cancel, because numerous world governments, as well as media organizations, profoundly questioned the author's credibility. I tell you, it was unbelievable.

To this day, I remember making over 500 media calls in one desperate day, only to be told over and over again, "I'd love to do the story, but my boss says your guy is an unreliable source." Normally, I wouldn't have taken a campaign in which the author's authority was the subject of such heated debate, but neither the publisher nor I had any idea what we were getting into until long after we were there. I liked the publisher and couldn't turn my back on it. Besides, I've never been a quitter by nature.

What did I do? Exactly what I told you to do earlier in this chapter. I analyzed how I could turn the negative into a positive. I called one of my closest friends in the media, the Washington D.C., bureau chief for a major daily newspaper, and asked him if he'd like to do a story on my author, but from a very unusual spin. I shared details of what was happening and pitched him on doing a feature about the book campaign itself and why so many road-blocks besieged this author. "You don't have to say whether you believe this author or not. The article should focus on the question, Is this author the real thing, or not? Your readers will paint their own pictures." My friend loved the pitch and did a full-page feature with photo spread. The angle of the article was whether or not my author was being silenced because people were afraid of him, or stonewalled because no one believed him. The feature was so fascinating that it got picked up by the wire and ran in over three hundred newspapers worldwide.

You may be asking yourself, why would I want an article that emphasized how the media was questioning my author's credibility? First of all, I trusted the journalist I gave the story to and knew he would be fair. Second, I realized that unless we took the inside campaign story to the press, we would continue to hit roadblocks. The spin of the article focused on the intrigue and suspense. It was like James Bond with a reality twist. Did I take a bit of a chance? Yes. Did it pay off? Yes. *Intelligent* risk-taking is part and parcel of a professional publicist's arsenal of effective weaponry when confronted with a media crisis.

Controversy Over Content

Another common crisis in book publicity is content. Often the press kit can generate extensive media interest, then when reporters and producers receive the actual book, they choose not to interview the author. Why? There can be myriad reasons. Sometimes, certain relationship and sexuality books can be very graphic, and producers are concerned that the authors will get too specific about intimate issues on the air, making audiences uncomfortable. Many books in the science, technology, and psychology genres are geared towards a more sophisticated reader, and the media worries that the authors will speak over the heads of their audience.

I've publicized so many books in which I was forced to deal with this problem! I remember years ago representing a famous psychiatrist who had written a book about homosexuality and genetic research. As a publicist, it was my job to make the press kit as newsworthy as possible and to use accessible language that triggered media interest. This was such a hot topic that I faxed the press release to my key media contacts months before the book was off press to generate early interest. Within one week, every major network magazine show called to confirm an interview with my author. The moment they received the book, they all contacted me in a panic. "This book is written in psychobabble and medical jargon. How do we know your author will speak in plain English?" they argued.

If you're a publicist and are facing this type of dilemma, you've got to take the situation firmly in hand and manage the crisis from both the media and author side. First, I issued memos to each of the producers who had booked my author, reassuring them that he would be a provocative interview and would speak in conversational language, as if he were chatting with a neighbor. Then, I had a long and animated discussion with the author, explaining the media's concerns, and coaching him on how to respond to questions simply and elegantly. Last, to make sure all bases were covered, I arranged in-person preinterviews for the author with all the producers, so that they would be confident we wouldn't let them down.

Bumped by Breaking News

Another kind of crisis that hits many book publicists over the head is long-term preemption and bumping. When a huge news story breaks in the press that dominates public attention, unless your author is an expert on a related topic, he's sure to get bumped and/or preempted. Bumped means a confirmed interview is canceled because another story takes precedence. Preempted means an interview that's airing is replaced by breaking news. Since I've been a publicist, some of the huge stories that nearly derailed campaigns I was working on included the Gulf War, the Shuttle Challenger tragedy, the Monica Lewinsky scandal, the TWA crash, and the war in Yugoslavia, not to mention countless hurricanes and other natural disasters.

I can't tell you how many author tours I was in the middle of booking with authors literally out on the road, when suddenly, a huge story broke and all bets were off. There are only two things you can do when something like this happens. Be as creative as you can, and find a way in which your author can be positioned and pitched as an expert. For example, during the Gulf War, so many young women were terrified because their husbands and boyfriends went off to fight the enemy, and they didn't know if they would ever make it back home. One of my authors was a leading authority on separation anxiety. I got her on most of the major national television networks, offering advice to loved ones on how to cope with their fear and worry. After the TWA crash, the media started focusing on the loved ones of those who perished in the explosion. I was representing a grief counselor, who I was able to book on several radio shows, talking about surviving the mourning process.

If you're in the midst of a campaign and your author can't be presented as an expert, then you have to regroup. Last year, my firm was promoting a book on how to improve your sex life. The author was doing a twenty-five-city tour. While she was in her fifteenth city, three marines were kidnapped by Milosevich's regime, and suddenly, that was the only story in the news. There was no way I could position my author as an expert this time. We simply had to shift gears. I communicated with the publisher. We decided to take a wait-and-see approach. Within a month, the war in Yugoslavia was pushed to the media back burner, at which time we resumed our author tour. The publisher kept close touch with the bookstores to avoid returns. The ability to be flexible is important during a crisis. Had we kept trying to push the tour in the face of this huge news story, it would have been a waste of time and money. By being prudent and patient, and communicating with the retailers, we were able to avert any long-term consequences.

The bottom line is that sometimes a major breaking story in the news can be an opportunity for an author. Sometimes it's an obstacle. You have to think creatively, analyze all the elements, and make a judgment, then act on it with clarity, confidence, and flexibility.

Simple Steps to Crisis Management

No matter what the crisis, there are steps you can take to successfully come through it:

- *Breathe.* Often, when a crisis hits, your first instinct is to panic. Don't give in to that destructive impulse. Stop. Take a deep breath. Find a trusted colleague or friend whom you can talk things out with, and begin analyzing the specifics of your situation. *Don't assume anything.* If you're not sure of a particular fact, find the exact information first, *before* you weave any of that data into your analysis.
- *Don't React; Respond.* Think before you act and speak. Don't fly off the handle because you feel out of control. Do the opposite. Grab onto the handle with all your might and intelligence, and examine how and where you need to steer it. People who are out of control react. Leaders who know how to stay in control respond. Fear, anger, or confusion motivates a reaction. Intelligence, inner strength, and clear thinking inspire a response. Helpless people react. Empowered people respond.

- *Make a Decision and Don't Second-guess Yourself.* During a crisis, one of the most common mistakes publicists make is to make a sensible decision, then second-guess themselves out of taking action. You can't be wishy-washy when you-know-what hits the fan, or you'll get your face caught in the blade. After you've looked at all the elements top to bottom and discussed it with other professionals whose opinions you value, you've got to bite the bullet and implement your crisis management plan. This can be especially challenging for public-relations executives, because the media can spin a story in so many different ways; if the crisis is media-related, it's tough to know which end is up. The most important thing to remember is that consistency puts out a fire, and inconsistency spreads the flames. In other words, if you have an author who's embroiled in a scandal and you need to issue a statement to the press, make sure your author, the publisher, and anyone else who may be quoted is prepped and coached on the proper verbiage. There has to be a party line, and the message from everyone involved has to be consistent. If one person says one thing and another something else, the crisis will get bigger, not smaller.

Statements to the Press

Speaking of issuing statements to the press, there are several ways this can be done. Let's look at an example. Say you're publicizing an autobiography by a famous movie star whose ex-wife decides to go public with some dirty laundry from their marriage. She launches her little campaign the week the book comes out. You wake up one morning to find ugly stories about your author in virtually every newspaper in America. You can approach this in two ways. You could organize a press conference, in which you invite all the major media to one location to hear your author's response. Or you could handpick a few media outlets with whom you have a long and trusted relationship and offer them some form of exclusive on your author's response. I would opt for the latter for several reasons. Usually with book publicity, press conferences are less effective than one-on-one interview scenarios. In addition, your author has more control of how his response will be spun by the media if he does one-on-ones, as opposed to a press conference. With a press conference, he gives a lot of journalists a small amount of time, whereas with one-on-one interviews, he gives a chosen few a large amount of time.

In this case, I would give a major network newsmagazine show the television exclusive on his response to his ex-wife, and I'd offer one big national newspaper or weekly newsmagazine the print exclusive.

Bringing In the Law

Sometimes when you're faced with a publicity crisis, you have to call upon an attorney. This doesn't happen too often, but you need to know when it's time to bring legal minds into the picture. Here's the best advice I can give you: If someone has come forward and said something that could be perceived as slanderous, or someone is threatening to sue, then you must contact a lawyer. Never comment on a legal matter to the press. For example, let's say you're publicizing a biography of a well-known rock star, and one of the author's family members tells *USA Today* that they're suing because parts of the book are untrue. Should *USA Today* call you or your author for a comment, you should tell the reporter you'd be honored to get back to him shortly. Then, call an attorney, and either have her return the call to the reporter or provide you with a statement that you can communicate to the paper. In terms of knowing which attorney to contact, most publishers have in-house legal counsel. You could also ask the author if she has a lawyer she uses in matters such as these. Or you can use your own attorney. If you've never worked with a lawyer before and need to hire one, there are firms that specialize in publishing and media law. They would be my first recommendation. You can obtain lists of firms through the Internet. You can also call the bar association in your state for information.

Attorneys can be a publicist's greatest allies, especially during stressful times.

Another crisis that can occur that I want to touch upon briefly is the overzealous author. This is one of the areas where attorneys really come in handy. Whether you're the author or the publicist, please take what I'm saying here to heart. Remember in the last chapter we talked about dramatic rights? One of the worst mistakes authors make is to impulsively issue press releases about deals that aren't secured. You can't imagine how many times I've had to pull back the reins on authors.

Here's a typical scenario. An author has just launched her book, and it's doing well. Suddenly, a Hollywood studio calls and says they'd like to option the film rights to the book. The author and the studio talk and come to a verbal agreement on price and terms. The next thing you know, the author is chomping at the bit to issue a press release to *Publisher's Weekly* and *Variety* that a movie deal has just been struck. *Never, ever, ever* issue a press release about any deal until all parties involved have signed a contract. Nothing kills credibility faster or destroys trust more than someone who talks to the press about something that isn't *in stone*. Furthermore, even after all *t*s have been crossed on a contract, don't issue any press release to any media outlet until the attorney who negotiated the deal has reviewed it, and all the parties who've signed the contract have approved it. If you don't take these steps, you can end up jeopardizing the deal, not to mention looking like an arrogant fool. I know: Strong words, but they come from strong experience.

Next on our agenda—going outside for help. How to know it's time to hire an outside publicist.

When, Why, and How to Hire an Outside Publicist

B Y NOW, YOU SHOULD BE CONFIDENT OF YOUR UNDERSTANDING OF book publicity, public relations, and promotions. You know the nuts and bolts and can construct a campaign on your own. Sometimes, however, doing it yourself may not be enough. When, why, and how do you hire an outside publicist? In this chapter, we're going to explore this question and more.

There are a plethora of reasons why bringing in outside help can be profoundly beneficial. The most compelling are tied into manpower, expertise, and image. Let's look at each of those components one at a time, so you have a clear picture.

Manpower

Manpower is crucial to executing a successful campaign. You have to analyze realistically just how much you can do yourself. Being confident will empower you. Being cocky will undermine you. There are three basic elements to a standard book campaign that you must consider when assessing the manpower factor. First, how hard a sell is the book to the media? I normally base this judgment on a scale of one to ten. The higher the number, the more difficult the sell, and the stronger the likelihood that you'll need outside help. A hard sell takes significantly more time because it requires double or triple the media contact work you would have on an easier sell. That means more phone calls, mailings, production logistics, and coordination efforts. Second, manpower comes into play on the workload side.

Once again, be realistic. If you're doing a ten- or twenty-city tour with national print and broadcast placements, you'll probably need extra help implementing a promotion, or vice versa. Remember, publicity is a timing game. You have to make sure you have enough manpower to get what needs to be done completed before the newsworthiness diminishes. Third, if you're working on a campaign that explodes with sudden media interest, your manpower requirements can quadruple overnight, and if you don't respond immediately to all the media interest, you can lose those valuable opportunities in a blink. Monitor your progress daily. Don't overextend yourself, or something crucial can so easily fall through the cracks.

Expertise

Expertise is probably one of the most critical motivations for hiring an outside PR firm. It doesn't necessarily have to start at the marketing phase either. Frequently, an author will hire a publicist to help weave the publicizability factor into his book as he's writing it. Publicists can also edit manuscripts from the publicity perspective. Whether you're writing fiction or nonfiction, I can't encourage you enough to at least ask a qualified publicist to read the manuscript for any glaring potential publicity problems.

Outlined below is a partial list of what I normally look for when I'm assisting an author with manuscript development, as well as end-stage publicity edits.

Fiction

- Do any of the plotlines address an issue of specific current concern to the media? If so, how can the author make it edgier and even more pertinent? If not, how can we insert this ingredient into the story?

- Are there any minor characters in the book whose lives or circumstances relate to someone currently in the news? If so, how can that character or characters be fleshed out more?

- Does the author take an unusual position on a subject currently in the news, or a mainstream point of view on an underexposed but publicizable topic? If so, how can this be broadened or emphasized? If not, how can this be woven into the story line?

Nonfiction

- Are there any parts of the book that the media might consider too graphic or technical? If so, what can we do to adjust these sections without jeopardizing the integrity of the text?

- Does the book feature any personal stories or case histories? If so, are they compelling and newsworthy, and would any of these individuals be available for interview? If not, can we insert examples who would trigger print and broadcast interest?

- What is the controversy level of the book? Does it need to be edgier, or is it so controversial that the media might shy away from it? How can these elements be balanced so that the book is provocative, while still being keenly publicizable?

In addition to their expertise on the editorial side, it often pays to bring in an outside publicist for campaigns that demand a special point of view. For example, if you're new to the media game, and you're publicizing a book attached to a breaking or major national news story, a huge movie cross-promotion, major celebrity tie-in, potential legal complication, or a controversial spin, I would strongly advise you to seek outside public relations support.

Image

Another reason for farming out a book campaign is author image. It's usually one of two scenarios that are, ironically, the flip sides of the same coin. Sometimes a new author needs an established PR firm because she may not be able to access the necessary media contacts on her own to generate press coverage. Shy, less aggressive authors tend to fall into this category.

Writers who have achieved a certain level of success should also consider hiring a respected PR firm. There comes a point in every author's life when he has to communicate a message to the media that he's "arrived." Bringing a good, solid PR firm on board subtly gets the point across.

Freelance Publicist or PR Firm?

Outside PR assistance comes in all shapes and sizes. There are two primary categories: a freelance publicist or a public relations firm. A freelance publicist is someone who books media only and usually operates out of her own home, or the author's or publisher's office. Freelancers charge per hour, a flat rate per project, or a monthly fee plus expenses. Most freelancers work on a limited number of projects at a time, with each book campaign usually running three to four months.

A full-service PR firm is a company you hire to implement a comprehensive PR campaign. PR firms, or agencies, as they're sometimes called, can vary in size from a few employees to multiple departments. They generate media placements, facilitate promotions, consult on advertising, and offer a wider range of services than a freelance publicist. Firms normally charge a monthly fee plus expenses although, depending upon the client, they can also work on a per project basis.

How do you know whether to hire a freelancer or a firm? You have to analyze your own particular set of circumstances. If you have a more restricted budget and your primary goal is an interview blitz done in one shot, a freelancer may be a more cost-effective choice. If, on the other hand, you're seeking an integrated, aggressive strategy that combines publicity placements with promotions and marketing, you're probably better off contracting a PR firm. Though each individual situation is different, I recommend considering a freelancer as a good interim measure, if you're at a point where you need to go outside for PR support, but still don't think you're ready to make the leap to a PR firm.

What Are You Paying For?

One of the questions I'm most frequently asked by potential clients is, What exactly are they paying for in a monthly PR fee, and do I offer any guarantees? When you pay a freelancer or firm, you're not paying for results, *because no ethical publicist will guarantee publicity placements.* What you are paying for is their expertise, contacts, time, and best efforts. Sometimes this concept is difficult for new clients to accept, especially those who have been more exposed to advertising than public relations.

Another question I always get hit with is, instead of paying a monthly fee, can I pay you based on the sales your publicity generates? My answer is always "no." Why? Because publicity can't be measured the same way advertising can be tracked. For one thing, you can control the content of an advertising placement, because you pay for the space. With publicity, you can convince a reporter or editor to interview an author and cover their book, but you can't control how the article will read or what the spin will be.

The flip side, however, is that publicity is much more cost-effective than advertising. Think about it. If you send an author on a ten-city tour, you're looking at an expenditure of approximately $30,000. You could spend the same $30,000 on an ad in a national magazine, but that ad would only run once, whereas an author tour can generate hundreds of feature articles, as well as television and radio coverage. If you were to take all of the media placements from a ten-city author tour and estimate how much that coverage would cost if you paid for it like you would advertising, it would be in the tens of millions of dollars.

Once you've decided you want to hire a freelancer or firm, how much should you expect to pay? Every campaign varies. PR firms charge anywhere from $3,000 to $10,000 a month for a standard book campaign. The more publicity you want, the higher the fee. Freelancers are on the lower range of the same scale.

For a breakdown of estimated expenses, consult chapter 13.

Qualities to Look for in an Outside Hire

What should you look for in a freelancer or PR firm? Outlined below are qualities you should seek and questions you need to ask when you interview a potential publicist.

- A minimum of ten years' experience in book publicity, with a diverse client list that includes names of current and past clients you can call as a reference
- Detailed background information on past achievements, current client load, and staff experience (if PR firm)
- Creative, aggressive-thinking, a willingness to overcome obstacles no matter how formidable, a track record of having done so successfully
- An energetic and imaginative approach to marketing, with a proven knowledge of publicity, public relations, and promotions
- A track record of communicating honestly with clients
- Confident demeanor, without being arrogant

Questions You Should Ask Freelance Candidates
- How many books have you publicized in your career, and which genres do you enjoy the most?
- What authors and publishing houses have you worked with?
- What's the most difficult project you ever had, and how did you overcome the obstacles?
- May I see some of the press kits you've written?

- What was your most successful book campaign, and why?
- What are your strongest media contacts—print, television, radio, national, market-specific, or a combination?
- Where are you weak?
- What's your current workload, and are any of the other titles you're working on a competitive book with mine and a possible conflict of interest?
- Do you package shows for national television, such as gathering personal stories for talk shows and panel discussions?
- How do you charge?

Questions You Should Ask a PR Firm

- May I see a client list?
- How many publicists work at your firm, and what are their levels?
- Who would you assign to my account, and who would they answer to?
- May I see some of your press kits?
- What kind of accounts do you specialize in?
- What are your greatest strengths and weaknesses?
- Are you comfortable being aggressive on my behalf with the media?
- How many accounts does one publicist work on at a time at your company?
- What are your specific media objectives for my book?
- How do you charge?

When you negotiate a contract with a freelancer or firm, request a thirty-day out clause. Make sure the contract lists all expense categories that you will be charged each month. Travel and media entertainment expenses should include a clause indicating that they need to be approved in advance by the client. Verify that the contract has a section specifying that the client will receive regular verbal and written updates delineating campaign progress.

Don't expect any freelancer or PR firm to give you the media lists for your campaign, either during the course of your project, after it's completed, or should you and your publicist part ways. Media lists are proprietary information. What you should expect, however, are interview schedules with contact names, addresses, phone numbers, and interview logistics upon all confirmed placements.

A few personal notes on working with outside PR people. Pay attention to the nuances of communication between you and your publicist. Demand honesty in all matters, and listen to what your publicist says to you and not what your ego wants to hear. Be realistic in your expectations, yet at the same time, push your publicist to be as aggressive and creative on your behalf as possible. If you're new to the media game, make a concerted effort to learn how the media works. A good publicist who's worth her weight in gold will be thrilled that you want to learn about the media and will be happy to offer her knowledge. Informed clients are so much easier to work with because they understand the challenges, are patient for results, and appreciate on a richer level the shared triumphs.

Give Credit Where Credit Is Due

As you've probably ascertained from reading this book, being a publicist is a hard job. It takes a lot of courage, grit, and creative acumen. Rejection is part and parcel of the publicist's daily grind. We're dealing with producers and reporters who are taxed and overworked themselves, and who sometimes just don't have the luxury of listening to a pitch. Remember, your publicist is human. Communicate your complaints with kindness and respect, and make it a point to listen to their responses.

For too many PR people, their most formidable hurdles are their clients' egos. Keep in mind that when a television show or magazine chooses not to interview an author, even after the publicist has gone to them with countless new pitches, it isn't the author that the media contact is rejecting. It's the timing or the subject matter. It's not personal. Along the same lines, when that incredible interview does come through, realize who was responsible. Take the time to say thanks and give credit where credit is due. *Authors who forget run the risk of being forgotten.*

Using the Internet as a Publicity Tool

Your PRESENCE ON THE INTERNET IS IMPERATIVE BECAUSE IT SERVES two important publicity purposes. First, you have the ability to provide your readers universal access to your book and the media constant access to your press material. Second, it allows consumers and the press to find you through a variety of ways—search engines, viral marketing, a forwarded e-newsletter, or from an initiative that you create, such as a direct mailing.

With value-driven content, a design concept that is consistent in promoting your book's "brand," and a good Internet publicity strategy, it is possible for your Web site to draw the attention of readers worldwide. It's estimated that there are now 50 million consumers online. Think of the impact that a good Web site could have on your book sales—retail and online, bulk sales to schools and libraries, state and local governments, profit and nonprofit organizations, and corporations. It may also serve as a catalyst for e-books or audio rights. You may draw the attention of foreign publishers' willing to purchase the rights to your work.

Since all books begin with an equal shot at getting attention online, let's begin with a thorough discussion of what should be included on your Web site that will both attract publicity and be newsworthy since many journalists now admit to getting story ideas from the Web.

Your Book's Web site

It is important to have the Web site complete, or as complete as possible *before* your book launch and you begin your media and consumer blitz. To capitalize on the media attention that you generate, remember to have your Web address chyroned (scrolled on-screen when you're being interviewed) during your television appearances. Television outlets often will post a link to your site. This keeps your interview alive long after you have left town. During radio interviews, you can either give out your URL (Web site address) or have the interviewer do it for you. Radio stations often provide links as well.

The importance of having your site complete is dramatically demonstrated by the following real-life experience: A well-respected businesswoman and speaker released a book that unexpectedly jumped onto the *New York Times* expanded best-seller list immediately. The subject was timely and compelling, and publicity was astounding—over 100 television and radio interviews, and dozens of print articles, including front page features, book signings that drew hundreds, and a dozen speaking engagements. Unfortunately, she was caught unprepared without a Web site. Rather than rushing to get just anything online and displaying several pages of "under construction," the author chose to wait until all of the content was complete before going live with it. It took several months before everything came together. During that time, countless leads were lost. It took tenacity for anyone to find her online, even to simply contact her. A reporter from a large metropolitan newspaper made it as far as her site's homepage. All that was "live" was the link to her e-mail. The reporter was on deadline, so she e-mailed a last-minute interview request. The author did not receive the e-mail until after the deadline. Yes, it was unprofessional of the reporter; however, if the site had been live, the reporter could have downloaded the entire press kit, complete with photos, a JPEG of the book cover, and quotes on the book's subject. Consider yourself forewarned—lost interviews, leads, book sales, and seminar bookings are difficult to regain.

Objective and Design

What is the objective of your site? Is it simply to sell books? Think this through clearly. Do you want to have an e-commerce site? If the answer is yes, a few things to think about are state sales tax, shipping options, and setting up credit card accounts. Another way to create your site is to link to one or more of the online booksellers. This route is cost-effective and a huge timesaver for a single title Web site. This leaves you the time to focus on what you do best.

The name (URL) of your site is one of your prime marketing and publicity tools. Would surfers be more likely to look for your site by your name or the book title, or both? Decide which one serves your primary objective, and go with that one. You can have more than one and funnel them all into one homepage. Choose only one as your branding tool, then use it everywhere—on all printed materials, as your e-mail signature, on shirts—wherever your book is seen in print do your best to be sure that your URL is right behind it.

The design of your site is critical. Who will design your Web site? I would recommend that you hire a professional. Perception is everything, so I would not advise you to have your child or neighbor design this critical component of your overall marketing effort. Cheap design is going to look like cheap design. Have a budget in mind. Remember, you can always add on to your site as your Internet presence and your budget grows. A different option is to go to a reputable college or design school. For example, in an effort to save funds, the creators of a bestselling book series approached the local college to design their first Web site. This worked out well for them until the series grew, and they had the need and could afford to hire a Webmaster full-time.

It is important to think through and communicate to the designer the overall look and feel of how you want your information to be presented. Keep in mind that your site design should be consistent from page to page. If you have some examples of other sites that you like, show him those as a starting point. Remember to allow the designer to be creative in doing his job. If you dictate every little thing to him, you are not reaping the benefits of his experience.

So, you have your URL and you've secured a designer. Where do you go from here? Content! Valuable content! Remember our discussion on positioning, especially mainstream and special interest positioning? Think of those points as you create content for your site. You're already well on your way because you've already created your perfect press kit! All you need to do is have the designer make them Internet friendly.

Let's examine a sample outline of the content that could be included in your site and presented to the Web designer in a way that will avoid any miscommunications.

1.0   Home page
    1.1   Navigation tabs or buttons
        1.1.1   Home
        1.1.2   The Book
        1.1.3   Seminars
        1.1.4   Media Room
        1.1.5   Contact Information
        1.1.6   Newsletter
        1.1.7   Resources
    1.2   Brief overview of the author and why you wrote the book.
    1.3   JPEG photo of the book.
2.0   The Book
    2.1   Table of Contents
    2.2   Excerpt of the book
    2.3   Testimonials

Keeping In Touch—Creating Your Database

As your designer creates a form for feedback, be thinking about the ways that you are going to store that information. You will need to create a database. If you are trying to create a database for sending out an e-newsletter, or simply sending out an occasional message, handling the process by yourself can eat up a lot of valuable time. As you launch, this may be possible, but as your list grows and the management tasks involved keep multiplying, your time demands will increase also. There is software available, but if you choose to create your database in Excel or Access, talk to your Web designer about building into your site the basis of a database for future use. There are also mailing list services widely available as well. Again I would remind you to keep in mind your skill set and the demands of your time versus your budget.

Using Internet Publicity Tools to Bring 'Em In

Remember that famous movie line, "If you build it, they will come?" Well, not necessarily. The good news is that you can build targeted traffic and sales with Internet directories, search engines, online chats, newsletters, links, and Web excerpts. Using readily available tools on the Web you can dramatically increase visibility and exposure both for yourself as an author, and your book title. Think of all of the special interest groups that are represented on the Internet—they're everywhere—personal groups, professional groups, students, the list is endless. Each of these groups is hungry for relevant information pertaining to their own interest. Keep in mind that promotion on related Web sites is important for getting media attention also. All of the ways to reach out and touch these people we're about to explore can be done for you at a reasonable cost by professionals, saving you time, and allowing you to focus on the things that you do best.

Search Engine Optimization (SEO)

Now that you're in a position to launch your Web site, you need to build a strong "foundation" of targeted traffic to become aware of your book. Search Engine Optimization is the most critical part of your online strategy. It's purpose is to increase your number of Web site visitors by ranking very high in the results of searches using the most appropriate keywords that describe the content of your site. Choose your key search words carefully. If you search on those words, you will see the leading site in the rankings.

Since approximately 87 percent of Internet users find Web sites with search engines and the Internet directories, assuring that your site is on the first page of these sites is critical. For that reason, and the amount of search engines with their ever-changing requirements, I would recommend that you hire a professional.

The top-rated and most prestigious SEO is a service called *submitawebsite.com.* They will analyze and optimize your site for the search engines, and guarantee premium placement. Joe Griffin, president and CEO of the organization, offers this advice to authors, "Good search engine design can help your Web pages draw better results which will bring you a steady stream of long-term traffic. Bad search engine design can cause you to be ranked poorly or not to be listed at all—resulting in little or no traffic or book sales." He continues, "Search engines do not automatically know your Web site. It is necessary to register a Web site with a search engine before the search engine can find it. If a site has not been properly registered with search engines, it cannot be found with search engines. Once the search engines know that your site exists, they can find it, but there is no guarantee that it won't be the last site on the list, if someone searches for your book or its subject. If a site is not listed in the top forty of a search it is unlikely it will be seen. Be sure to have your site built using meta tags, keywords, and other tricks of the trade, to get it listed higher on search engines."

Internet Directories

Be sure that you also submit your Web site to the "Top 100" Internet Directories—this is one of the best investments that you will make in your book. Among the benefits of being listed you can be sure that you have an inexpensive source of targeted traffic (the average cost per visitor is less than one cent), you gain link popularity for search engine optimization, you increase your search engine traffic, and the long-term benefits are strategic—submit once and you receive traffic for as long as your Web site is online.

Links

Link building today is more important than ever, but it must be done right. This is the targeted, professional way to announce your book and build awareness for your site within your niche market online. A high percentage of sites in a link popularity campaign will be glad to link to your site IF you offer the content of value as we discussed before. Therefore, it is always in your best interest to include a liberal amount of relevant content on your site to generate the highest percentage of links back to you. This is a time-consuming process that must be done by hand, one at a time. There are no shortcuts. The goal is to establish a professional and mutually fruitful relationship with the right link partners for your business.

As with SEO, in the interest of time, you may want to seek out the services of a professional to do this for you, but you can also do it on your own. You want to establish or add to your network of incoming links in order to increase the quality and quantity of your traffic directly AND to improve your "link popularity," which is now a key factor in achieving your best possible positioning on today's major search engines and directories.

How do you establish links with the best Web sites for your on-line objectives? Surf the Web and research the top sites that are the most relevant to your target audience. Then contact and request links from each of them individually. Now, I don't mean to play favorites, but because it is the largest search engine, and most everyone is familiar with it, I will use Google as an example. Begin by looking for the best link partners for your book on Google (it should always be an objective to improve your PageRank on Google). Identify link partner sites with a minimum Google PageRank of 3 so that you are sure Google is properly indexing them. Today anything less than PR 3 is irrelevant.

You won't see results overnight. The effect of these efforts can take up to eight to ten weeks (or longer, depending on the particular search engine). Also be aware that search engines must find your incoming links on their own as they spider the sites linking back to yours. These search engines will also continue to consider other key elements in the ranking of your site for a given search phrase, including your site content as well as the use and placement of your keywords. If you're not linked online to your target audience, they cannot know you are there and will not find you. If you have no traffic, you have no book sales.

Chats, Author Forums, and Discussion Forums

Find the time to position yourself as an expert when you visit chatrooms, or offer yourself as a chat guest in your niche market to increase the exposure for your book. Many bookstores sponsor online chats. Traditionally, chats do not draw an enormous amount of participants, but don't write them off. The transcript of the chat (even if it's only between you and the host) can be found online and take on a life of its own. Be sure that the chat host has copies of your online press kit, including the suggested questions, so that he can prepare the announcements, and to help get the chat started.

Ongoing discussions can breath life into your book as it takes off, and fresh life into it as it slows down. It is important that you monitor the discussion for a few days to see the feedback it's generating. Regulars to discussions are sensitive to the hit and run operators and they don't appreciate being used like that. Post your reviews and comments, and have back-up material ready to e-mail when requested. Being an active participant in these forums earns you a great deal of respect among your target audience. The easiest way to start looking for the forums that pertain to your subject are Yahoo!Groups and Topica. Participate as much as possible, but be respectful as you "pitch" your book. Try not to be a commercial for yourself; offer your URL as a source for further information. Remember, the Internet in many ways is similar to the media. Position yourself as an expert and promote your book subtly and with dignity. Just like you wouldn't say on a *Today Show* interview "in my book, in my book," you need to observe the same decorum doing Internet interviews, chats, etc.

E-Newsletters

E-newsletters are everywhere—heck, I even get e-newsletters about e-newsletters! Your newsletter is a key part of your online publicity effort. Begin each newsletter with the thought that you are going to create and present something of value to your reader every single time. If you begin with your message, then allow your marketing message to tag along for the ride at the end you will gain the respect and generate loyalty from your readers.

Creatively, the newsletter should look and feel the same every time, so that your readers begin to recognize it. Choose the "subject" line of your newsletter just as carefully as you chose your book title. Keep in mind that readers and journalists use e-mail filters to lock senders out of their mailboxes. You want to avoid sending a subject heading and serving up content that is not useful, banishing you forever from mailboxes. If you are going to ask for a reader's time, they expect relevant and timely information about the subject. Besides the fact that you could be a possible interview, a journalist may be looking for artwork, background materials, documents or other information. By now you get the point—everything you do online should be of use to your targeted audience and the media.

Web Excerpts

Keep writing! Write articles, and send excerpts from your book to Web magazines. They need good content on a steady basis to hold on to their readers and to support their advertising rates. Here are three reputable online sources to send your information to:

www.e-zinez.com/articles/index.html
www.ideamarketers.com
www.ezinearticles.com

Post these articles on your own Web site as well. Remember, you need to keep your content fresh—it's the only way to bring 'em back!

I'd like to address one last item before closing out this chapter. As mentioned above, I absolutely recommend you allocate the time and money to launch a Web site if you're serious about book publicity. Mainstream print and broadcast media use Web sites and e-mail more now than ever to locate experts and resources for stories. However, if you don't have the budget to do a Web site, that doesn't mean you can't take advantage of the Internet. There are e-mail campaigns, banner promotions, on-line chats, Web sites that post book reviews, among many other publicity opportunities online. The best way to discover these opportunities is to simply to surf the Internet, seeking out Web sites, forums and chats that could benefit from your story or expertise. Once you locate these sites, you can usually e-mail the Webmaster. Sometimes, phone numbers are even provided. The more familiar you become with surfing, the more adroit you'll be at communicating with these sites and utilizing them for publicity exposure.

I'd like to share a secret with you, too. It took me a long time to warm up to the Internet. I've always been a meat and potatoes publicist. When the Internet became dominant, I knew it was time for me to "get with the program." Hence, I had a Web site designed, learned how to do Internet research, pitch Web sites for chat opportunities—the whole nine yards. Yet I knew I'd never be as Internet savvy as the twenty-some-things just now entering the workforce. One of the best skills a good publicist—or anyone for that matter—can have is to know your limitations. If you're immersed in the day-to-day mainstream publicity campaign demands as I was and don't have time to do all the Internet stuff too, find a college student who's looking for extra money and ask him to do the surfing for you. It will save time, won't be expensive, and you'll be providing a young person with valuable work experience and something wonderful on his resume. How many students get to say they worked on a bestselling book? And if you play your cards right, that's exactly what can happen to your book—best-selling status!

Happy cyber-trails!

Publicity, public relations, and promotions are the wind beneath a book's wings. My hope is that the time we've shared together, dear reader, has empowered you to soar to unexpected heights. I would wish you luck, but with your talent and determination, I know you won't need it. Fly fast and far, straight to the bestseller lists!

Appendix

Resources

BULLDOG AND LIFESTYLE
5900 Hollis Street
Suite R2
Emeryville, CA 94608
Sales Rep: Janie
(510) 596-9300

CONTACTS
500 Executive Boulevard
Ossining, NY 10562
(914) 923-9400

PARTYLINE
1040 First Avenue
Suite 340
New York, NY 10022
(212) 755-3487

EMILY LAISY
Promotion Network
P.O. Box 388
Fallston, MD 21047
(410) 877-3524

THE CENTER FOR PUBLISHING
New York University
11 West 42nd Street
New York, NY 10036
(212) 790-3232

BACON'S MEDIA GUIDE
332 South Michigan Avenue
Chicago, IL 60604
(312) 922-2400
Account Rep: Rachel Hughes

Index

Books from Allworth Press

Allworth Press is an imprint of Allworth Communications, Inc. Selected titles are listed below.

The Author's Toolkit: A Step-by-Step Guide to Writing and Publishing Your Book, Revised Edition
by Mary Embree (paperback, 5½ × 8½, 192 pages, $16.95)

Starting Your Career as a Freelance Writer
by Moira Anderson Allen (paperback, 6 × 9, 256 pages, $19.95)

writing.com: Creative Internet Strategies to Advance Your Writing Career, Revised Edition
by Moira Anderson Allen (paperback, 6 × 9, 288 pages, $19.95)

The Complete Guide to Book Marketing, Revised Edition
by David Cole (paperback, 6 × 9, 256 pages, $19.95)

Business and Legal Forms for Authors and Self-Publishers, Revised Edition
by Tad Crawford (paperback with CD-ROM, 8½ × 11, 192 pages, $22.95)

The Writer's Legal Guide: An Author's Guild Desk Reference, Third Edition
by Tad Crawford and Kay Murray (paperback, 6 × 9, 320 pages, $19.95)

Marketing Strategies for Writers
by Michael Sedge (paperback, 6 × 9, 256 pages, $16.95)

How to Write Books That Sell, Revised Edition
by L. Perry Wilbur and Jon Samsel (hardcover, 6 × 9, 224 pages, $19.95)

How to Write Articles That Sell, Revised Edition
by L. Perry Wilbur and Jon Samsel (hardcover, 6 × 9, 224 pages, $19.95)

The Writer's Guide to Corporate Communications
by Mary Moreno (paperback, 6 × 9, 192 pages, $19.95)

Writing for Interactive Media: The Complete Guide
by Jon Samsel and Darryl Wimberley (hardcover, 6 × 9, 320 pages, $19.95)

Please write to request our free catalog. To order by credit card, call 1-800-491-2808 or send a check or money order to Allworth Press, 10 East 23rd Street, Suite 510, New York, NY 10010. Include $5 for shipping and handling for the first book ordered and $1 for each additional book. Ten dollars plus $1 for each additional book if ordering from Canada. New York State residents must add sales tax.

To see our complete catalog on the World Wide Web, or to order online, you can find us at
www.allworth.com.

CPSIA information can be obtained
at www.ICGtesting.com
Printed in the USA
LVOW04s1139020216

473319LV00010B/24/P

9 781581 153491